Designing Boundaries in Ea

Ancient Chinese walls, such as the Great Wall of China, were not sovereign border lines. Instead, sovereign space was zonally exerted with monarchical powers expressed gradually over an area, based on possibilities for administrative action. The dynamically shifting, ritualized articulation of early Chinese sovereignty affects the interpretation of the spatial application of state force, including its cartographic representations. In *Designing Boundaries in Early China*, Garret Pagenstecher Olberding draws on a wide array of source materials concerning the territorialization of space to make a compelling case for how sovereign spaces were defined and regulated in this part of the ancient world. By considering the ways sovereignty extended itself across vast expanses in early China, Olberding informs our understanding of the ancient world and the nature of modern nation-states.

Garret Pagenstecher Olberding is Associate Professor of History at the University of Oklahoma. He is the author of *Dubious Facts: The Evidence of Early Chinese Historiography* (2012).

Designing Boundaries in Early China

The Composition of Sovereign Space

Garret Pagenstecher Olberding

University of Oklahoma

CAMBRIDGE
UNIVERSITY PRESS

Shaftesbury Road, Cambridge CB2 8EA, United Kingdom

One Liberty Plaza, 20th Floor, New York, NY 10006, USA

477 Williamstown Road, Port Melbourne, VIC 3207, Australia

314–321, 3rd Floor, Plot 3, Splendor Forum, Jasola District Centre, New Delhi – 110025, India

103 Penang Road, #05–06/07, Visioncrest Commercial, Singapore 238467

Cambridge University Press is part of Cambridge University Press & Assessment, a department of the University of Cambridge.

We share the University's mission to contribute to society through the pursuit of education, learning and research at the highest international levels of excellence.

www.cambridge.org
Information on this title: www.cambridge.org/9781009074667

DOI: 10.1017/9781009075862

First published 2022
First paperback edition 2022

A catalogue record for this publication is available from the British Library

Library of Congress Cataloging-in-Publication data
Names: Olberding, Garret P. S., author.
Title: Designing boundaries in early China : the composition of sovereign space / Garret Pagenstecher Olberding, University of Oklahoma.
Description: Cambridge ; New York : Cambridge University Press, 2022. | Includes bibliographical references and index.
Identifiers: LCCN 2021025347 (print) | LCCN 2021025348 (ebook) | ISBN 9781316513699 (hardback) | ISBN 9781009074667 (paperback) | ISBN 9781009075862 (ebook)
Subjects: LCSH: China – Boundaries – History. | China – Historical geography. | China – Territorial expansion – History. | China – Politics and government. | BISAC: HISTORY / Asia / General
Classification: LCC DS706.5 .O43 2022 (print) | LCC DS706.5 (ebook) | DDC 911/.5109–dc23
LC record available at https://lccn.loc.gov/2021025347
LC ebook record available at https://lccn.loc.gov/2021025348

ISBN   978-1-316-51369-9   Hardback
ISBN   978-1-009-07466-7   Paperback

To my beloved wife and daughter, by whose light I labor

Contents

Maps

Acknowledgments

Sections of this work were supported in part by grants from a 2012 University of Oklahoma Faculty Investment Program Grant (2012), a University of Oklahoma Faculty Enrichment Grant (2012), a University of Oklahoma US–China Institute Grant (2015), an Arts and Humanities Faculty Fellowship from the Arts and Humanities Working Group through funding from the University of Oklahoma Office of the Vice President for Research (VPR) (2016) and a munificent Scholar Grant from the Chiang Ching-Kuo Foundation for International Scholarly Exchange (2016), as well as a sabbatical through the University of Oklahoma College of Arts and Sciences (2019). Myriad colleagues assisted me in thinking through or offering useful research suggestions for various portions of the project: Robin Yates, Yuri Pines, Vera Dorofeeva-Lichtmann, Damien Chaussende, Romain Graziani, Albert Galvany, Robert Rundstrom, Amy Olberding, Linda Rui Feng, Michael Nylan, Daniel Morgan, Kathy Linduff, Vincent Leung, Tamara Chin, Paul Vieth, Peter Gries, Kyle Harper, Daniel Snell, Newell Ann van Auken, Armin Selbitschka, Clifford Ando, Patrick Crowley, Michelle Wang, Agnes Hsu-Tang, and Ping Foong, among others. I would also like to thank the anonymous readers who evaluated this manuscript and to Lucy Rhymer and Rachel Blaifeder for being such generous, patient, and considerate editors, particularly as the world suffered through the pandemic. Exceptional gratitude is also due to the University of Oklahoma Library and its wonderful librarians, especially Karen Rupp-Serano, Laurie Scrivener, Starla Doerscher, and Lawrence T. Austin, for procuring for me all of the materials I need, in spite of dire economic circumstances and lack of broad political support for humanities education.

Permission to use sections of my article, "Movement and Strategic Mapping in Early Imperial China," published in *Monumenta Serica: Journal of Oriental Studies* 64, no. 1 (2016), copyright © Monumenta Serica Institute reprinted by permission of Taylor & Francis Ltd, http://www.tandfonline.com on behalf of Monumenta Serica Institute, was graciously granted by *Monumenta Serica*/Taylor and Francis.

Chronology

Shang dynasty	ca. 1600–1050 BCE
Western Zhou period	ca. 1050–771 BCE
Eastern Zhou period	770–256 BCE
Warring States period	ca. 481–221 BCE
Qin dynasty	221–207 BCE
Han dynasty	207 BCE–220 CE
Jin dynasty	266–420 CE
Sui dynasty	589–618 CE
Tang dynasty	618–907 CE
Song dynasty	960–1276 CE
Yuan dynasty	1276–1368 CE
Ming dynasty	1368–1644 CE
Qing dynasty	1644–1911 CE

Preamble

In this work, I explore the complexities attached to interpreting the geographically mapped visual in early China, particularly with how geographical representations of space originated, what purposes they might have served, and what symbolic meanings they may have contained and communicated. Visually representing space is a way of understanding it, but the meanings of visual geographic representations – whether maps or landscape paintings – are not obvious. Perhaps because of the modern state's emphasis on precise borders, with a correspondingly precise exercise of privileges and sanctions, there is a retrogressive application of this sensibility onto premodern civilizations, which, as James C. Scott has discussed in his *Seeing Like a State: How Certain Schemes to Improve the Human Condition Have Failed*, had no such precise notions.

And yet we can nevertheless assert that there was a notion of sovereignty in early China that applied to territorial expanses. The powers of the monarch, essential to any definition of early Chinese sovereignty, was exercised in a number of territorially expressive capacities – military, of course, but also legal, political, cultural, and ritual. Discussions of territorially expressive sovereign powers are not confined to, or defined by, the use of any one word or set of words in early China. This monograph focuses on how monarchial power was expressed territorially from various vantage points. My investigations pursue the designing of sovereign boundaries when borders were more zonal than linear definitions, when sovereignties would overlap, when the demands of a monarchial center competed with demands of other sovereign entities.

Though my analyses will draw upon and highlight salient structural patterns and observations from eras up to the Tang–Song, my temporal focus will be on the ancient historical epoch, from the Western Zhou to the Qin–Han era. Much of this early period is defined – as is common in studies of the ancient world – by the pockmarked availability of historical materials, as well as the uncertainty in their provenance and their political or rhetorical agenda. While I must acknowledge there are shortcomings of such an approach (one that many early China studies have), this investigation attempts to work around the uncertainties endemic to the ancient Chinese world by underscoring how a variety of its structural patterns are shared across ancient civilizations. Indeed, it is my hope that the shared similarities will facilitate a richer dialog that will more regularly include early China.

If borders in early China were more zonal than lineal, a concern central to the designation of boundaries would be how to square the use of lineal marks – such as walls or lines on a map – with such a conception. This problem is the focus of the initial sections of this study. I scrutinize how terrestrial space was conceptualized and represented in the ancient world, in its mensurative and, quite relatedly, aesthetic aspects. I commence with an analysis of the term *tu* 圖, most basically meaning "diagram" but commonly translated as "map." Analysis of the term reveals its spatial function but does not conclusively determine its mensurative functionality. Indeed, it is not clear to what degree we can distinguish early "maps" from landscape art.

The discussion of early Chinese maps is naturally limited by the current scarcity of possible exemplars. Most scholarly evaluations of them focus on the several from Fangmatan and Mawangdui that seem to mark a relatively broad expanse of terrestrial space. It will be to these that much of my discussion of map exemplars will turn, though I will also refer to a few other examples from the early and middle imperial periods to expand on argumentative points. After a discussion of the level of mensurative accuracy likely for early Chinese maps, I proceed to discuss the aesthetic similarities between landscapes and early maps. To conclude the examination of the visual modeling of space, I pursue the question, parsing a lengthy anecdote in the Han historical record highlighting abusive terrestrial mapping, what it might have been for a premodern map to have been legible and thus functional, to whatever degree.

Unfortunately, as the Han example reveals, like other political documents, all early maps were highly vulnerable to distortion and misappropriation. Because of this, I then argue, a deeper sense of how sovereign terrestrial space was appropriated and defined better serves to explain the "mapping" of political sovereignty. The permission or denial of movement through space was a definitive marker of sovereignty. Symbolic markers of this phenomenon were those activities that asserted such permissions or denials. The remaining sections of this study then analyze symbolic markings of permission or denial from three perspectives – the internal marking of space through ritual activity and concepts; the regulation and prohibition of external intrusions through a sense of bounded terrestrial space, the separation of inner from outer, and the characterization of uninvited penetration of sovereign space; and finally, the ritual regulation of the transgression of sovereign space, in the figure of the diplomat.

Although conceptualizations of terrestrial space and the designing of ancient borders have received significant attention in past work across a variety of languages, especially work focused on the classical Mediterranean world, we have yet to rectify the misapplication of modern lineal, scientistic thinking to the early Chinese context. Scholars have frequently been very interested in determining exact locations drawn from texts and graphics. A few, such as Mark E. Lewis, have examined conceptions of space more broadly, but this study is the first, to my knowledge, that broaches the denotation of sovereign space head-on, from the internal, external and transgressive angles. A further fundamental aspect of this study is the contention that ritual permissions are a key indication of the extent of sovereignty. Contesting other more insistently secular readings of Chinese border negotiations, my contention is that ritual distinctions carried politico-legal weight. Indeed, I would hazard that to study ritual is to engage to some extent with law. It is in the application of legal – and thus, I argue, ritual – force that sovereignty is most clearly in evidence. To rename a ritual boundary, to insist on a supervenient spiritual organization, to prohibit or permit ritual activities is an essence in the claiming of sovereign power – the assertion of this power is not found in the simple placement of lineal marks, militarily reinforced or not. It is the aim of this study to show how carefully we must attend to more diurnal, even mundane activity, rather than explosive violent confrontation and its lines of engagement, to determine the limits of the sovereign realm.

1   The Basis of Ancient Borders

The marking of borders is primordial, defining the limits of habitat and control. Economic and political force finds its root in the divide, the fencing off of one area of control from another. Indeed, any sovereign border is most basically that which should not be transgressed without express permission, and thus is always a site of potential confrontation. A marked boundary may awaken a desire to conquer what lies beyond it, to expand the dominion one would claim, or tempt those outside to transgress, to challenge a dominion so explicitly asserted. Marking a border thus can generate concrete effects, even as it is an exercise in abstraction – an effort to conceptualize and create divisions in a physical landscape that are neither natural nor given. Dividing and bounding landscapes is now ubiquitous, but abstracting boundaries to mark possession and dominion occurred only gradually, with cultural sophistication and complexity, evolving with time and circumstance. Prior to the development of agriculture, settlement, and, more importantly, taxation, there would presumably be little need to carefully mark the edges of fields, to distinguish that which would be taxed from that which wouldn't. Analogously, prior to the rise of suzerainty there would be no need to precisely identify sovereign borders, or international borders prior to the rise of the nation-state. What I am trying to emphasize here is this: defining limits is requisite of the animal condition; how humans conceptualize and problematize a limit is complicated by the various circumstances in which we live.[1] What laying a boundary means and does, either materially or symbolically, will depend on complex contingent meanings present in a historical circumstance. Early Chinese conceptualizations of space, landscape, and boundaries had their own distinctive material and symbolic logic, a logic I here hope to articulate.

To understand what bounded terrestrial divisions signify requires probing into the very fundaments of sociopolitical organization, of what

---

[1] Julian Reid, "Foucault on Clausewitz: Conceptualizing the Relationship Between War and Power," *Alternatives* 28 (2003), 5.

4

territorially associable power networks denotate. Contemporary discussions of territorially associable networks are commonly tied to a notion of the "state." According to the most common notions, the state is, as Carl Schmitt explained, "the political status of an organized people in an enclosed territorial unit," with its borders being militarily, and at least somewhat precisely, delineated.[2] John Baines, writing about the early Chinese polities centered around Anyang and Erligang from an ancient Egyptian perspective, composed a somewhat similar definition, designating the state as that "in which a single culture predominates and fills its territory, defining itself to a great extent by its boundaries."[3] Yet critics charge that the very assertion of the state – and any substate networks – as a coherent object of historical analysis is debatable. According to Philip Abrams, the state "represents a fetishization of twentieth-century political ideology as deep metahistorical structure: 'The state is at most a message of domination.'"[4] In detailing the early Chinese state's territorially associated apparatuses, we need to trace the structural *effects* "of detailed processes of spatial organization, temporal arrangement, functional specification, and supervision and surveillance."[5] When tracing these effects, we should ask how territorially penetrative were the state's power structures?

In many respects, it seems, the penetration was inconsistent and vulnerable to local contestations, subversions, and rejections. According to James C. Scott, likely generalizing about non-Chinese state structures, the premodern state was "in many crucial respects, partially blind; it knew precious little about its subjects, their wealth, their landholdings and yields, their location, their very identity. It lacked anything like a detailed 'map' of its terrain and its people. It lacked, for the most part,

---

[2] Carl Schmitt, *The Concept of the Political*, trans. George Schwab (Chicago: University of Chicago Press, 2007), 1.

[3] John Baines, "Civilizations and Empires: A Perspective on Erligang from Early Egypt," in *Art and Archaeology of the Erligang Civilization*, ed. Kyle Steinke (Princeton, NJ: Princeton University Press, 2014), 100. Cited in Haicheng Wang, "Western Zhou Despotism," in *Ancient States and Infrastructural Power: Europe, Asia, and America*, ed. Clifford Ando and Seth Richardson (Philadelphia: University of Pennsylvania Press, 2017), 110n37. Baines, writing about Erligang from the ancient Egyptian perspective, does not consider the earliest Chinese polities centered on Erlitou and Anyang to fit "easily with the concept of a territorial state." At a later stage, the Anyang period, for instance, "offers a case of significant diversity in the culture of elites in a number of societies located within essentially the same region: although a single center may have predominated, it did not exercise exclusive political power or cultural hegemony."

[4] Cited in Adam T. Smith, *The Political Landscape: Constellations of Authority in Early Complex Polities* (Berkeley: University of California Press, 2003), 97.

[5] Timothy Mitchell, "The Limits of the State: Beyond Statist Approaches and Their Critics," *American Political Science Review* 85, no. 1 (1991), 95; cited in A. Smith, *Political Landscape*, 97.

a measure, a metric, that would allow it to 'translate' what it knew into a common standard necessary for a synoptic view."[6] Our current expectations about what the boundaries of a state *bound* – a unitary culture, a known people, a unit of coherent power or purpose – simply fail to account for how ancient bounded regions could and did operate.

Without anachronistic assumptions about how boundaries may work, it seems clear that territorial demarcations in political texts or visual images are assertions of possessive interest, whether aspirational or active. Thus when discussing and analyzing the measures of early Chinese territorial maps or textual descriptions of territory, it is important to keep firmly in mind that the basic definition of a politically sovereign administration or interest is not the line but the possibility of enforcement of politico-legal, or military, force. Territories are defined with reference to where sovereign authority structures can extend or reach, not by boundary marking itself. Employing Adam T. Smith's condensed formulation, "Sovereignty refers to the establishment of a governmental apparatus as the final authority within a polity and therefore entails both the definition of a territorial extent beyond which commands go unenforced and unheeded and the integration of discrete locales into a singular political community."[7] Naomi Standen makes similar remarks in her study of tenth-century Chinese frontier life: "Tenth-century people seem not to have thought so much in terms of borderlines but rather organized themselves according to administrative centers and allegiances." What counted at various levels of administration was not "where the borderlines lay (although these could always be calculated, and officials reported incursions across them), but where the official in charge placed his allegiance." She continues

If the official in his county, prefectural, or provincial seat decided to change his allegiance – say, by surrendering his city to a military attacker – his action affected the whole of his district by virtue of the taxation records and administrative machinery housed in the city's government offices. When an official did this, the borderline around the district at the next level up moved to place the surrendered district on its other side.

Thus, again, what most defines ancient boundaries is not a ruler's asserting a crisp and militarized line but his success in securing the far more fungible acceptance of administrative force, or even an overlapping medley of forces.[8]

---

[6] James C. Scott, *Seeing Like a State: How Certain Schemes to Improve the Human Condition Have Failed* (New Haven, CT: Yale University Press, 1998), 2.

[7] A. Smith, *Political Landscape*, 155.

[8] Naomi Standen, *Unbounded Loyalty: Frontier Crossings in Liao China* (Honolulu: University of Hawai'i Press, 2007), 23. Previously, Standen also explained that, in Five Dynasties and early Song maps, although the same area of "China proper" is marked in

Visualizing a space so bounded, principally through the use of maps, is itself an exercise of power and assignment of meaning.

Distinguished from the associations to state-enforced power, the visual horizon at its most epistemically basic provides a limit to what can be perceived and known. The horizon provided by a map is a limit of visually displayed knowledge.[9] The relation between viewer and map is, in an abstract sense, bidirectional: the viewer looks at the map, but the map also "looks back" at the viewer, in that its fields of meaning, and their articulation, borrow from the viewer's preconceptions of what a map can and should show. The reader of the map can actualize its content, the possibilities of travel and use, within the map.[10] According to James Corner, in an active sense, "mappings are not transparent, neutral or passive devices of spatial measurement and description. They are instead extremely opaque, imaginative, operational instruments."[11] The map is a spatial text embedded in a discursive process with its viewer, a text in the process of performance and creation, a process closer to an oral dialog than that of an active reader encountering a static textual product.[12] Furthermore, the reader's distant viewership, not infrequently from above, allows for a type of panopticon effect, a viewership from both nowhere and everywhere, an anonymous assertion of force.

In an interview, Michel Foucault emphasized the military origins of a sovereign map, noting that Western spatial metaphors applied to the map are "equally geographic and strategic ... The *region* of the geographers is the military region (from *regere*, to command), a *province* is a conquered territory (from *vincere*). *Field* evokes the battlefield."[13] For state purposes, a map is, in sum, a power discourse, but its use, as

part by the Wall, were a district within the Wall administered by a non-Chinese power, this, too, was clearly marked. "Hence although the Wall is there, it seems to function more as a point of reference than as a line to be held. It defines the limit of the empire as the Song cartographers wished the empire to be; *it did not have to reflect the limit as it actually was.*" Standen, *Unbounded Loyalty,* 22. Italics mine.

[9] Michel Foucault, "Questions on Geography," in *Power/Knowledge: Selected Interviews and Other Writings, 1972–1977,* ed. Colin Gordon (New York: Pantheon Books, 1980), 68.

[10] "The eye can travel haphazardly over the surface of the map or follow plotted itineraries corresponding to particular destinations, seeking a piece of information or locating a place." Christian Jacob, *The Sovereign Map: Theoretical Approaches to Cartography Throughout History,* trans. Tom Conley (Chicago: University of Chicago Press, 2006), 256.

[11] James Corner, "The Agency of Mapping: Speculation, Critique and Invention," in *Mappings,* ed. Denis E. Cosgrove (London: Reaktion Books, 1999), 250.

[12] "During the sixth and fifth centuries BC [in the ancient Mediterranean world], one can see the origins of both a distinction and interaction between map and discourse. The map helped to gather, organize and unify a heterogeneous knowledge about places and tribes, but its purpose was also more abstract and theoretical." Christian Jacob, "Mapping in the Mind," in *Mappings,* ed. Denis E. Cosgrove (London: Reaktion Books, 1999), 29.

[13] Foucault, "Questions on Geography," 69.

Foucault acknowledges, extends far beyond the martial; indeed, its origins are just as rooted in economic, or even ritual, concerns as military. However, no matter what its use, the map requires the notion of a border, a boundary, the separation of one space from another, the marking of one point in relation to another, and their separate identity. If there are no such definitions, the map blanches.

A provisional definition of a map is an encoded graphic image that can be explained to some extent by text and is representative of functional relationships.[14] But these functional relationships may not always, or even most powerfully, be secular. In the premodern world, the relationships portrayed on maps could have ritual or religious significances that impacted, or even were definitive of, governmental power structures. The ritual acknowledgment of dominance was not simply symbolic theater. In the case of Siam, for instance,

the notion that the realm was conceived as a sacred topography is evident in the terms denoting a kingdom or a sovereign territory. Literally, the term *anachak* means the sphere over which the king's *chak* – a sunlike disk representing sovereignty – could orbit. Another term, *khopkhanthasima*, literally means the sphere bounded by sanctuary stones. *Sima* or *sema* is the stone boundary marker of consecrated space, normally in a temple, within which an ordination can be performed. It also refers to stones of similar shape on the top of a city's wall. Thus a realm was said to be a sacred domain under the power of the king's wheel or a consecrated territory as within a sanctuary's *sima*.[15]

For Thongchai Winichakul, the sovereign map thus cannot be secularized. Neither its symbols nor even its bounding lines can be treated simply as indicating discrete, nonporous, nonoverlapping spaces of political hegemony. Indeed, as Winichakul makes abundantly clear in the arbitrations between British and Siamese over sovereign boundaries, Siamese officials could not accept the totalizing, fixed lines insisted upon by the British.[16] Sovereignty, in the Siamese conception could not only overlap, it could be shared "not in terms of a divided sovereignty but rather a sovereignty of hierarchical layers."[17]

Sensibilities similar to those Winichakul asserts for the Siamese polity also existed in ancient China. Sovereignty in early China was neither wholly secular nor was it unmixed. The ritually instantiated aspect of early Chinese sovereign boundaries was substantial and active, reinforced by the actions of inhabitants who, by acknowledging fealty to a sovereign

---

[14] Jacques Bertin, *Semiology of Graphics*, trans. William J. Berg (Madison: University of Wisconsin Press, 1983), 11.

[15] Thongchai Winichakul, *Siam Mapped: A History of the Geo-Body of a Nation* (Honolulu: University of Hawai'i Press, 1994), 24.

[16] Winichakul, *Siam Mapped*, 35, 55, 63–80.   [17] Winichakul, *Siam Mapped*, 88.

are acknowledging his legal–administrative oversight, as well as his moral force. A sovereign boundary was not defined by the inhabitants' ethnicity – not whether one was Chinese or not – but by whether the sovereign figure was ritually, fiscally, and legally *a* lord over the territory – not necessarily the exclusive lord but at least a regular and substantial one. As proprietary enclosures for permitted activities and movements, boundaries were not ultimately or absolutely defined by concrete, static markers but by the activities of those counted as members of the realm. These "legalized" activities – to occupy, use, move through, contest, pray at, and so forth – were what mark boundaries. This ritually instantiated aspect is perceivable not only in the politically unstable hegemonic order between a dominant parent state and a subservient client state (*shuguo* 屬國) but also in the assertion and contestation over ritual structures within state boundaries and in those areas over which a state is newly asserting hegemonic status.

Conceptual Mapping in Imperial Rome

The notion of a bright line fixing the ancient border not only infiltrates current scholarship on the early Chinese cartographic consciousness, it also infects scholarship on a similarly potent ancient Western civilization, the Roman Empire. While I will not linger extensively on Rome, I will employ pertinent insights taken from various studies on it, and other ancient Mediterranean and Near Eastern civilizations. My interest, as with my references to Siam, is to highlight structural patterns that have not yet been stressed sufficiently, or even observed, in early China scholarship.

According to Bradley Parker, contemporary scholars depict Roman borders, like their modern cousins, with solid lines or color contrasts. But the idea that Roman frontiers – with or without walls – functioned as clearly demarcated lines is vehemently contested.[18] Another contested premise is that of the "natural" boundary, the expectation that the limits of ancient states and empires were set by geographic constraints "such as rivers or mountain ranges."[19] Strabo of Amaseia (63 BCE – ca. 21 CE) notes that sections of Parthian territory were held by Romans and phylarchs of the Arabs, "making a revealing comment about the role of the Euphrates river as the frontier between the Roman and Parthian empires": "The boundary of Parthian power with the country opposite

---

[18] Bradley J. Parker, "At the Edge of Empire: Conceptualizing Assyria's Anatolian Frontier ca. 700 BC," *Journal of Anthropological Archaeology* 21 (2002), 372.
[19] Parker, "At the Edge of Empire," 373.

(i.e., the Roman Empire) is the Euphrates river. But parts within [Parthian territory] are held by the Romans and the phylarchs of the Arabs as far as Babylonia; some of them adhere more to the Parthians and others more to the Romans who are their neighbors."[20] This passage from Strabo, Parker notes, is one of the "many oft-quoted examples from the Roman period used to illustrate that rivers served not as 'natural' boundaries but as corridors of transportation and communication," and thus, I would add, potential upheaval.[21]

Not only is it doubtful that secular lines authoritatively served in making state borders, it is not even clear how truly three-dimensional early Roman cartographic thinking functionally was. A story in Suetonius's *Lives of the Caesars* recounts Julius Caesar losing his way while on a trip in an area with which he was very familiar, a misapprehension that troubles scholars. Suetonius records that Caesar strangely lost his way in an area where, had he possessed any kind of conceptual map of the area, he should have been able to find his way: "It was not until after sunset that he set out very privily with a small company, taking the mules from a bakeshop hard by and harnessing them to a carriage; and when his lights went out and he lost his way, he was astray for some time, but at last found a guide at dawn and got back to the road on foot by narrow bypaths."[22] For Caesar, as perhaps for other early Romans, the "only limit is the mental image of where the road ended, since the road brought order to the unknown ... Beyond the end of the route all was 'deserted and *nameless*,' says Arrian."[23] The only names, the only markings that truly mattered, it seems, were those that the Romans themselves had instituted. The importance of names, and how they were devised and imposed, will be examined in a later chapter.

It appears that the road, and thus perhaps two-dimensional, directional thinking, was the means by which exploration was taken, both physically and conceptually. According to C. R. Whittaker, in the early Roman world, one of the rare recorded cases of conceptual exploration – that is, a pre-expedition conceptual mapping of an area to be entered, pursued

---

[20] Strabo 16.1.28, cited in Parker, "At the Edge of Empire," 373.

[21] Parker, "At the Edge of Empire," 373.

[22] Suetonius *Caes.* 31. See Suetonius, "The Deified Julius," in *Lives of the Caesars*, vol. 1, *Julius. Augustus. Tiberius. Gaius. Caligula,* trans. J. C. Rolfe (Cambridge, MA: Harvard University Press, 1914), 77. Christian Jacob, in his "Mapping in the Mind," states that: "As a matter of fact, Roman itineraries, in the areas familiar to the Romans, appeared as very exact." This however renders the question of how Julius Caesar got lost even more perplexing. Jacob, "Mapping in the Mind," 37.

[23] C. R. Whittaker, "Mental Maps: Seeing Like a Roman," in *Thinking Like a Lawyer: Essays on Legal History and General History for John Crook on His Eightieth Birthday,* ed. Paul McKechnie (Leiden: Brill, 2002), 107. Italics mine.

with intelligence about the area acquired before the event – was Gaius
Caesar's invasion of Parthia, an incursion "planned on the base of the
road to Kandahar described by Dionysius of Charax."[24] Pretravel conceptual organizations and explorations of physical space were rare enough
that they never appear in Frontinus's *Strategemata*, a text devoted to
military strategems. Frontinus "never once mentions a map of any
sort – not even where you might expect it; for example, when he discusses
how to choose a site for battle, or how to select a rendezvous in retreat."[25]
From this, Whittaker concludes that there was no evidence of
a government office or officer in control of gathering and organizing
general mapping intelligence in the later empire, which would suggest
none also in the early empire. The most frequently cited exemplars of an
early Roman mapping sensibility, the Antonine Itinerary and the
Peutinger map "are thought to be unofficial initiatives." There is "little
to show that mental mapping played any part in the planning of individual
campaigns, the same is true *a fortiori* of the Grand Strategy of frontiers –
that is, assuming we can even begin to talk of such a concept."[26] In short,
we seem to have an organizational sensibility that depended more
heavily on vectors of movement than on geometries of sight. It was
these vectors of movement that territorialized – that made, and unmade –
territories.[27]

If early cartographic thinking was not reliably three-dimensional, then
a variable, moving perspective might have influenced not only the creation of maps but the whole conceptualization of lived space. This would
pertain to a sense of direction, the composition of relative position, and
the formation of strategies for the acquisition and possession of new
space. The hackneyed regularities and imprecision in relative placement
and directionality, as are common in early maps, in fact may have been
indications of a limited development of three-dimensional organizational
skills in early mapmaking technology. As Svetlana Alpers cautioned, in
mapmaking, "it is not the differences between things but their resemblance that is most problematic," because it shows the use of formulaic
criteria by which the mapmaker captures complex details.[28] For John
Pickles, the lines that so entrance and guide our sense of formal borders
are nothing more than the interpretive representations of lived space – the
line cannot be separated from the sense of what the bounded space

[24] Whittaker, "Mental Maps," 108.   [25] Ibid., 109.   [26] Ibid., 109.
[27] Gilles Deleuze and Félix Guattari, *A Thousand Plateaus: Capitalism and Schizophrenia*
(Minneapolis: University of Minnesota Press, 1987), 202ff.
[28] Svetlana Alpers, *The Art of Describing: Dutch Art in the Seventeenth Century* (Chicago:
University of Chicago Press, 1983), 77.

represents, and how what it represents is distorted to capture politicized preference.[29]

The celebrated Peutinger map illuminates this problem. Created around 1200 CE, the map is the most complete specimen depicting the world known to Roman antiquity, extending from the eastern coast of Britain to India and Sri Lanka, with the city of Rome placed basically in the center of the map.[30] Whether the map is derived from an ancient precursor or is a Carolingian map drawing from archived Roman knowledge, as Emily Albu has argued,[31] is somewhat irrelevant. The knowledge basis on which the map was made appears to have been largely, if not completely, Roman, and thus many of the choices regarding what was depicted or emphasized would likely have been informed by such knowledge. In accord with the Roman concern with geographic expansion and political control of settled lands, the map underscores some features, such as travel routes (though its presentation has too many shortcomings to be practically useful), and deemphasizing others, like bodies of open water.[32] Only by reducing the representation of open waters could the mapmaker ensure "adequate coverage of landmasses for his representation of routes there."[33] The stated lengths of the routes themselves were unconnected to their depiction.[34] Population markings in the map, as Richard Talbert notes, were also uneven, with many more peoples "marked to the north and east of the Roman world than to its south in Africa."[35] Certain insignificant places are "given prominence of a symbol at all, when some notable cities have none, and others have a very modest

---

[29] John Pickles, *A History of Spaces: Cartographic Reason, Mapping, and the Geo-Coded World* (New York: Routledge, 2004), 3.

[30] Richard Talbert, "Peutinger's Roman Map: The Physical Landscape Framework," in *Wahrnehmung und Erfassung geographischer Räume in der Antike*, ed. Michael Rathmann (Mainz: Philipp von Zabern, 2007), 225.

[31] Emily Albu, "Imperial Geography and the Medieval Peutinger Map," *Imago Mundi* 57, no. 2 (2005).

[32] Richard Talbert, "Cartography and Taste in Peutinger's Roman Map," in *Space in the Roman World: Its Perception and Presentation*, ed. Richard J. A. Talbert and Kai Brodersen (Münster: LIT Verlag, 2004), 122–123.

[33] Talbert continues, "As a result, the Bay of Biscay, the Mediterranean, the Adriatic, the Black Sea, the Red Sea, the Indian Ocean and the Caspian Sea are all reduced to relatively narrow channels; the Aegean Sea is compressed, and the Hellespont and Propontis are effectively eliminated. By contrast, the Bosporus between Europe and Asia is made broader than necessary, and thereby emphasized." Though the graphic representations were reduced or removed, the names for the parts of open waters were not necessarily. Talbert, "Peutinger's Roman Map," 225.

[34] "The length of the corresponding stretch of route as shown on the map bears no relation to the mileage given for it; the briefest stretch on the map can represent a great distance, a really elongated stretch [or] a very modest one." Talbert, "Cartography and Taste in Peutinger's Roman Map," 125.

[35] Talbert, "Cartography and Taste in Peutinger's Roman Map," 123.

one in relation to their importance."[36] Yet it is difficult, if not impossible, "to distinguish between those which are fundamental components of the physical landscape base, and those more likely to have been added later after the placement of other features."[37] For Talbert, the mapmaker's main purpose appears to be to "boost . . . pride in the range and greatness of Rome's sway historically" – thus are Mila, Carthage, and Alexandria "all deliberately denied prominence."[38] If Roman knowledge indeed underlay the composition of the Peutinger map, then it is fair to say that the bounding of the area in the ancient Roman world often represented much less than a precise, formal, "objective" delineation.[39] In spite of the possibility for careful surveys in the Roman world, metric accuracy of boundary delineations appears to have been in no way a guiding principle. If this is so, we should revisit whether metric accuracy, a notion lent credibility by the apparent precision of the line, is one that applies to any of the cartographic regimes of the ancient world, and specifically, of early China.

In the Roman world, ritual was highly significant for spatial sovereignty, if invoking the gods during military campaigns is evidence. As with the early Chinese (among other early civilizations), Romans saw their "barbarian" neighbors and subjects as lacking in cultural sophistication, and passing the borders beyond their "civilized" realms was fraught with ritual significance. Whittaker expounds:

Rivers, ploughed lines and walls to demarcate a magico-religious boundary figure prominently in Roman foundation myths, and they remained intensely real to the Romans on the frontiers of the Empire . . . So the Roman imperial edict in AD 17/18 ordering the erection of triumphal arches and statues on the borders of the empire was not a statement of the termination of empire, but defined a sacred threshold that assumed a transition to the world beyond. The same argument can be applied to rivers and bridges, which in Roman imagination were ritual boundaries to be crossed, not defensive frontiers.[40]

---

[36] Talbert, "Cartography and Taste in Peutinger's Roman Map," 124, 127.
[37] Talbert, "Peutinger's Roman Map," 230.
[38] Talbert, "Cartography and Taste in Peutinger's Roman Map," 128.
[39] Indeed, according to Whittaker, "notwithstanding the importance of land surveys in the law and life of Rome, when it came to wider spatial perceptions Romans did not think like land surveyors." He continues, "when it came to topography, it is very doubtful whether all those land cadasters that were recorded on *varias formas* of wood, bronze or parchment and kept as copies in a central records office in Rome were ever consolidated into anything like master Ordinance Survey maps, not even in the case of Italy. A recent commentary on the *agrimensores*, for example, suggests that the *forma* for the settlements at Lucus Feroniae in Latium would have been difficult to locate on a map of Italy." C. R. Whittaker, *Rome and Its Frontiers: The Dynamics of Empire* (New York: Routledge, 2004), 69.
[40] Whittaker, *Rome and Its Frontiers*, 4.

Despite their significance, these religiously instantiated frontiers did not impose a totalitarian religious possession. Instead, as appears to be the case in early imperial China, the Romans moderated any imposition of their gods with a tolerance of local worship, establishing their gods alongside local deities. However, this tolerance did not undermine the pressure on provincial peoples to give a prominent theological role to the deified Roman emperor. According to Clifford Ando, local denizens "could accommodate" the deified Roman emperor "as a worldly representative of whatever local or personal deity they worshiped." Rome "exported to the provinces the 'god of the Romans,' the deity of 'Roman religion,' namely the emperor."[41] But there was one potentially significant difference with early imperial China: the Romans did not attempt to eradicate or supervene the religious associations of the indigenous names of locales.[42] Such a permission in the marking – and thus conceptualization – of areas of sovereign space would have manifold effects pertaining to the function of boundaries and their transgression, when a ritualized possession was important for sovereignty.

Conceptual Mapping in Early China

The origin of ancient maps is plainly rooted in both secular and sacred concerns, in the economic and military but also the ritual and religious, as is evident in the premodern topography of Siam. Nonetheless, at least in early Chinese maps or official spatial descriptions in the early Chinese histories, religious and ritual space does not appear to effect a greater impact than in the Roman maps. Indeed, religious and ritual markings are often so obscured or fused with other salient administrative divisions that their surface presence is inconspicuous, almost imperceptible. The interpretive possibilities then would appear to be: (1) unlike in premodern Siam, religious and ritual considerations did not affect efficacious administrative divisions; (2) such considerations did affect efficacious administrative divisions, but only nominally and unsubstantially; (3) these considerations were involved in administrative divisions but were identifiable with or subsumed under other administrative considerations, at least in name; or (4) the aspirations of early Chinese official spatial descriptions and extant maps were circumscribed to more discrete tasks and functions, that they were not meant to capture the realm in which religious considerations would have had some bearing and through which broader sovereignty would have been defined.

---

[41] Clifford Ando, *Imperial Ideology and Provincial Loyalty in the Roman Empire* (Berkeley: University of California Press, 2000), 392.
[42] Clifford Ando, personal communication, 10/27/19.

It would seem unusual that any ritual markings of sovereignty should be absent, even from such circumscribed descriptions of space. It would, in brief, be odd to find that ritual sensibilities, so prevalent in early China, fail to feature in or influence cartographic processes. In point of fact, in the Shang and Zhou periods, evidence of increasing Chinese ritual influence and authority were apparent in the design and type of ritual vessels on the inner Asian frontier. Excavated evidence points to the insinuation of Chinese ritual power in various border areas. For Wei Cao and Yuanqing Liu, "These combinations of local and dynastic features of ritual paraphernalia and burial kits perhaps underlay an effort [by inner Asian cultures] to hold on to local identity while at the same time aggrandize themselves by recognizing the authority of or by displaying affiliation with the dynastic power."[43] There appears to be sufficient evidence that ritual or religious considerations pertaining to territorial issues were also present in the early imperial period, in both pictorial representations and in official descriptions, and even more importantly, in the historically described function of boundaries and borders. Indeed, as Martin Kern has observed in other administrative texts, sacred and religious aspects of various official actions are frequently omitted or obscured, even as we know they are exercising influence.[44]

If the description of the office of the Supervisor of Strategic Obstructions (*sixian* 司險) in the *Zhouli* 周禮 or the essay on *ditu* 地圖 in the *Guanzi* 管子 are any indication, there was a concerted effort to understand strategic obstructions in early China. But how these strategic considerations figured into an overarching conceptualization of sovereign space is not exactly clear. One hint at the considerations of sovereign possession might be seen in a map, or terrestrial diagram, from an early Han-era tomb at Mawangdui (see Map 1).

As Haicheng Wang details, the diagram includes a number of symbols and textual remarks that appear to indicate its possible employment for demographic or military purposes, "showing the kind of detailed information about settlement locations and populations that the state needed in order to carry out large-scale relocations."[45] For Wang, the diagram was, as with other early terrestrial diagrams, a "token" of "territory

---

[43] Wei Cao et al., "The Rise of States and the Formation of Group Identities in the Western Regions of the Inner Asian Frontier (c. 1500 to the Eighth Century BCE)," in *Ancient China and Its Eurasian Neighbors*, ed. Katheryn M. Linduff et al. (New York: Cambridge University Press, 2018), 161, 163. Such combinations of local and dynastic features might also point to possible signs of resistance against dynastic incursions.

[44] Martin Kern, "Early Chinese Divination and Its Rhetoric," in *Coping with the Future: Theories and Practices of Divination in East Asia*, ed. Michael Lackner (Leiden: Brill, 2018).

[45] Haicheng Wang, *Writing and the Ancient State: Early China in Comparative Perspective* (New York: Cambridge University Press, 2014), 204.

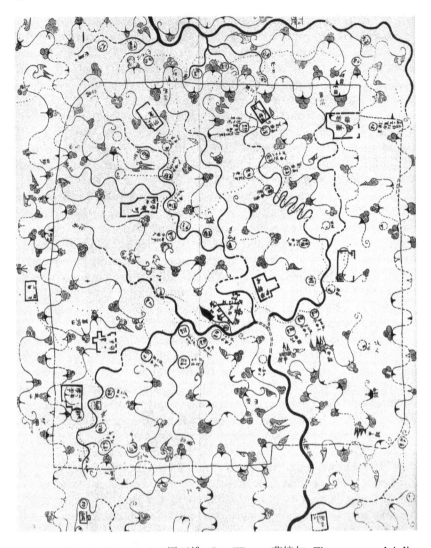

Map 1 Mawangdui 馬王堆. Cao Wanru 曹婉如, Zhongguo gudai ditu ji: Zhanguo – Yuan 中國古代地圖集，戰國—元 (Beijing: Wenwu chubanshe, 1990), image 26

ruled," with the diagrams reflective of the extent, the boundaries of sovereign space. Wang suggests that the previous Qin empire's territorial expansion was also mirrored in terrestrial maps: "As the expanding Qin state acquired territory, the map collection of the future First Emperor must have grown apace, and the curators of his collection may well have been constantly updating and enlarging a comprehensive map of his possessions."[46] For Wang (among many others), the terrestrial diagrams metrically approximate the physical extent of sovereignty, with their secularized diagramming of natural and constructed features an accurate locating of the sovereign's domain. Though much investigative work has been done on these early Chinese exemplars, we may still ask: In what way are they maps? How exactly are their definitional lines rendering them recognizably such?[47] More generally, on what basis, metric or otherwise, can we treat the lines as reliable indicators of accurate divisions, both metrically and relative to other delineations on the diagram? Unfortunately, from all indications, it appears that we cannot. As my earlier work demonstrates, in the political arena, accuracy was not paramount. What was primarily at issue was what bore upon the good of the state, however that was defined.[48]

Despite repeated attempts to demonstrate the metric accuracy of early Chinese maps, definitions and textual explications in various sources indicate that they were more likely constituted by the active use of space, as space-in-time, not as a static, surveyed space.[49] In the next chapter I examine the etymology of the Chinese term *tu* 圖, commonly translated as "map," and canvass early textual descriptions of geographic space, descriptions influenced or even defined by strategic concerns. I maintain that, even when mathematical surveying techniques were available, for much of the imperial period maps captured personal travel more than accurate geographic measurement and served the purpose of facilitating further movements and laying strategic placements. Thus, early mapmakers did not in the main, to quote Michel de Certeau, "remove [themselves] from the obscure interlacings of everyday behavior and make [themselves strangers]

---

[46] Wang, *Writing and the Ancient State*, 204.

[47] For example, Wang, among others, contends without justification that the regularly undulating lines with clover-leaf shaped designs on their apexes that cover much of the space of the diagram are mountains. I am not arguing that they are not, but if they are, their regularity and unvarying size render them physically "illegible," less than useful as physical signage and thus the diagram less identifiable as a "map." Just as Alpers warned, the resemblances between the representations of different objects are problematic. See Wang, *Writing and the Ancient State*, 206.

[48] Garret Olberding, *Dubious Facts: The Evidence of Early Chinese Historiography* (Albany: State University of New York Press, 2012), 74.

[49] The presumption that early Chinese space, even as far back as in the early Zhou period, was surveyed in some way, and that quasi-accurate maps, as opposed to rough sketches or diagrams, were produced from such surveys, continues to pervade current scholarship. See for instance, Wang, "Western Zhou Despotism," 98–99.

to it."[50] Rather, their sketches graphically simplified and reduced everyday behavior, rendering the journeys of those who reported on the areas to be mapped into abstract and general form. Maps joined, collated, and combined multiple such renderings, the resulting product effectively a ghostly assembly of collected footsteps, delivering to the map user the essentials of what, in a given land space, would hinder or assist movement. In contrast to the "functionalist totalitarianism" of modern metrically accurate statist maps, with their aspirationally totalizing and immobile reflections of a static geography,[51] early Chinese maps (and we might generalize to say ancient maps as a whole) are somewhat haphazard, incomplete legends of the memorable and noteworthy. Appreciation of this difference should inform both analysis of early Chinese maps and how their signs should be read. If what early Chinese maps primarily record are their informers' traversing and inhabiting of space, we must carefully rethink how the markings of lived experience pervade and distort the static representations of the sketch or map.

Walls and Boundaries

For many scholars, sovereign borders are primarily, if not solely, fixed by their martial function. According to the prevailing view, the celebrated "Great Wall" (better translated as "long wall" or "long walls") was built to limit migration and defection, and to defend against attack.[52] Demarcation of Chinese territory by the wall defined Chinese sovereignty, both in the contours of its space and the response of those excluded from it. For Owen Lattimore, "This Chinese-initiated process of demarcation in turn created nomadic hostility ... hostilities with the nomads are not so much their cause as their consequence."[53] Yet, as Arthur Waldron acknowledges, sovereign borders were not so defined as the construction of walls might suggest: "the idea of clear boundaries is not, in the earliest period of history, a particularly strong one in the Chinese tradition. Early texts were rather vague about China's borders:

---

[50] Michel De Certeau, "Practices of Space," in On Signs, ed. Marshall Blonsky (Baltimore, MD: Johns Hopkins University Press, 1985), 124.

[51] De Certeau, "Practices of Space," 141.

[52] The view of the Great Wall as being primarily a defensive structure, serving functionally as a national border, is shared by many, whether explicitly or implicitly. See, for instance, Luo Zewen et al., The Great Wall (New York: McGraw Hill, 1981), and Édouard Chavannes, "Les deux plus anciens spécimens de la cartographie chinoise," Bulletin de l'École Française de l'Extrême-Orient 3 (1903), 221.

[53] Arthur Waldron, The Great Wall of China: From History to Myth (New York: Cambridge University Press, 1990), 30–31.

they described not a single frontier, but rather a series of zones."[54] This accords with the discussion of a famous early Han minister Jia Yi 賈誼 (ca. 200–168 BCE) about the method by which the Chinese could control a northern non-Chinese population, the Xiongnu.[55] In his discussion, Jia Yi does not even mention walls. Instead, he suggests the Xiongnu should be brought to heel with governance. Though we cannot deny that the walls served a military function, whether that was their only function or even their primary function is contestable.

An answer to this question is crucial, for military boundaries have often been conflated with the boundaries of the sovereign state.[56] Arguments about the direction and extent of their construction impact the calculation of the ambitions of the central government and its supposed negotiations with or campaigns against antagonistic peoples. For Waldron, the location of the northern stretches of the Qin walls are associated with the northern defense "lines" of the state. However, this conception of boundary "lines" is anachronistic, a notion more appropriate to the modern nation-state than to any premodern polity. In his *Ancient China and Its Enemies*, Nicola

---

[54] Waldron, *Great Wall of China*, 42. To draw from a comparative context, Charles S. Maier notes, "The Turkish historian Suraiya Faroqui reports that the Ottomans during their heyday in southeastern Europe negotiated linear borders really as temporarily acceptable halting points . . . It is not that empires do not have walls; indeed, they do, but the walls tend to emerge as structures of defensive consolidation when the energy of expansion flags, or when prudence prevails over ambition as the peoples encountered in the intermediate trading zone become threatening, whether as ethnic immigrants or hostile soldiers. Frontiers as the edge of an expanding empire were thus *zonal, not linear – more regions of cultural and ethnic osmosis than firm barriers.*" Charles S. Maier, *Once Within Borders: Territories of Power, Wealth, and Belonging since 1500* (Cambridge, MA: Harvard University Press, 2016), 20. Italics mine.

[55] Jia Yi 賈誼, "Xiongnu" 匈奴; in *Xinshu jiaozhu* 新書校注 (Beijing: Zhonghua shuju, 2000), 4.135.

[56] This conflation is still widely pervasive, continuing even in current studies, including those not directly related to borders, such as Robin Yates' and Anthony Barbieri-Low's translation and commentary on the Zhangjiashan legal manuscripts. In their introduction to the Zhangjiashan text "Ordinances on Fords and Passes" (*jinguan ling* 津關令), which details the military fortifications at certain areas and the measures taken to protect them, they state: "Historians of borderland regions often characterize premodern boundaries between major polities as porous zones of contact, where diverse people interacted and contested ownership and identity, without the hard, fixed borderlines of modern nation-states. These ordinances suggest, however, that the early-imperial Chinese government expended great effort to create as hard and definite a borderline as was logistically possible. Walls, trenches, palisades, and fences were all employed to make it quite unambiguous on which side of the border one was located." Anthony J. Barbieri-Low and Robin D. S. Yates, *Law, State and Society in Early Imperial China: A Study with Critical Edition and Translation of the Legal Texts from Zhangjiashan Tomb no. 247* (Leiden: Brill, 2015), 1115. Standen, admittedly writing about the much later Liao period, also averred broadly that "Borders are primarily the demarcations – more or less accurate and open to dispute – agreed in peace treaties." However, she also acknowledges that the administration of these borders is much messier than any line might suggest. Standen, *Unbounded Loyalty*, 19.

Di Cosmo addresses concerns with conflating walls with sovereign military borders and reevaluates the ultimate purpose of the northern walls.[57] Why the earliest walls were constructed and what function they served are, as Di Cosmo notes, open to question. The assumed primacy of their defensive function, of keeping non-Chinese peoples out of Chinese sovereign space, is called into doubt by data from recent excavations. Studies by Chinese archaeologists on the northern walls and the surrounding cultural remains in the northeastern state of Yan in the late Warring States period have confirmed that "*both* 'outside' *and* 'inside' this line of fortifications the *only* cultural remains are 'non-Chinese'."[58] The major ramification of this is that the Yan walls did not separate "steppe and sown, nomad and farmer." In Di Cosmo's view, the walls were not simply, or even most basically, to repel invaders so much as to control the movement of populations more generally, "be they nomads, moving across plains, hills, or mountain passes; peddling merchants; transhuman populations; or hostile armies." Di Cosmo concedes that the walls also served a defensive (if not also offensive) purpose, "but that purpose," he acknowledges, "must be seen in light of what they were actually defending." The walls of the northern border states were located at great distance from farming settlements and constructed in nonarable territory; thus, "we can safely exclude that the protection of Central States' agriculture was a strategic goal."[59]

[57] A recent example of this conflation can be seen in Haicheng Wang's *Writing and the Ancient State*: "Walls mark boundaries both physically and psychologically. The Warring States defensive walls became the de facto political boundaries between competing states ... The state as a political entity enclosed by walls could not be comprehended in its entirety until it was abstracted onto a flat map." For his extended discussion, see Wang, *Writing and the Ancient State*, 198–199.

[58] Nicola Di Cosmo, *Ancient China and Its Enemies* (New York: Cambridge University Press, 2002), 149. Italics mine. Indeed, as Paul Goldin has noted in a recent paper, the *Zuozhuan* "depicts non-Chinese groups living uneventfully in the proximity of major Chinese settlements ... Thus, it makes more sense to imagine the Western Zhou kingdom not as a continuous territory with fixed borders but as a royal ritual center surrounded by satellite ritual centers in all directions." Goldin hazards that these regional lords probably never surveyed their lands or the occupying tribes systematically. Paul R. Goldin, "Representations of Regional Diversity During the Eastern Zhou Dynasty," in *Ideology of Power and Power of Ideology in Early China*, ed. Yuri Pines, Paul R. Goldin, and Martin Kern (Leiden: Brill, 2015), 36, 42. Even early Chinese writers, such as Cai Yong 蔡邕 (132–192 CE) averred that the Wall acted as a cultural boundary: "Heaven set mountains and riverways, Qin constructed the Great Wall, Han erected barriers and ramparts in order to segregate inner from outer, and set apart the various customs" 天設山河，秦築長城，漢起塞垣，所以別內外，異殊俗也. Fan Ye 汜曄, *Houhanshu* 後漢書 (Beijing: Zhonghua shuju, 1965), 90.2992. Hereafter cited as "*HHS*."

[59] Di Cosmo, *Ancient China and Its Enemies*, 149. Gideon Shelach-Lavi makes a similar point when he notes that, again according to archaeological excavations, the northern Qin walls constructed under Qin Shihuangdi "were located to the north of the walls constructed by the states of the Warring States period." It is thus "reasonable to assume that it was built in territories taken from Qin's enemies." Gideon Shelach-Lavi, *The*

The equation of walls with discrete, "hard" sovereign borders appears to be bound up in part in the unthinking foisting of present onto past. Anthony Giddens, in his *The Nation-State and Violence*, asserts that pre-modern polities were not as formidable a presence, and their borders not nearly as formalized, as is considered more common in modern states. The focused surveillance of precisely delineated boundaries is a phenomenon of the modern state, not the premodern: "All states have a territorial aspect to them but, prior to the advent of the nation-state, it is unusual for the administrative power of the state apparatus to coincide with defined territorial boundaries."[60] Giddens helpfully differentiates between primary settlement frontiers, those created by an expansionist agenda into territory previously either uninhabited or populated by those politically unaffiliated, and secondary settlement frontiers, "those within the territory of a state only sparsely inhabited for one reason or another – usually because of the infertile nature of the land or because of the general inhospitality of the terrain." "In all cases," Giddens concludes,

'frontier' refers to an area on the peripheral regions of a state (not necessarily adjoining another state) in which the political authority of the centre is diffuse or thinly spread. A 'border', on the other hand, is a known and geographically drawn line separating and joining two or more states. While there may be, and often are, 'mixed' social and political traits displayed by groups living in border areas, those groups are *distinguishably subject to the administrative dominion of one state or the other*. Borders, in my view, are only found with the emergence of nation-states.[61]

Walls, like other artificial partitions (such as fences, ditches, or moats), are generally constructed only when natural boundaries are not sufficiently assertive of an administrative area and hostile actions by competitive peoples are not adequately remediated with any consistency by economic or political means (such as advantageous arranged marriages, trade agreements, or punitive sanctions). The Romans, Giddens observes, "tended to treat their walls as primary settlement frontiers, establishing farmers in the adjoining areas, *agri limitanei*." Referring to Lattimore's work, Giddens asserts that the Great Wall was both meant as a defensive measure against "foraging nomads" and a limit on the mobility of "peripheral" interior groups. In neither Rome nor China, he contends, "did the walls correspond to the

---

Archaeology of Early China: From Prehistory to the Han Dynasty (New York: Cambridge University Press, 2015), 316.

[60] Anthony Giddens, *The Nation-State and Violence*, vol. 2 of *A Contemporary Critique of Historical Materialism* (Cambridge: Polity Press, 1985), 49.

[61] Giddens, *Nation-State and Violence*, 50. Italics mine. One might wish to amend this categorical statement about the administrative purview of a sovereign party with the following qualification: dominion could be limited to a certain time or for a specific purpose.

limits of 'national sovereignty' in the sense in which that term is applied today. Rather, they formed the outer extension of an 'in-depth' defensive system." By contrast, for modern states borders are "nothing other than lines drawn to demarcate states' sovereignty."[62]

In Rome, walls and natural boundaries, such as rivers, were not immediately identifiable with defensive boundaries. Political networks on the other side of constructed or natural obstacles were also employed. Though his wall in Britain is celebrated as a frontier marker, as Whittaker notes, "Hadrian and his successors did not abandon the use of friendly kings beyond the frontiers, as is so often asserted by those who imagine the empire isolated in a sort of protective cocoon."[63] Whittaker further adds that Hadrian's wall had an offensive function: "If Hadrian's Wall in Britain had originally been designed as a closed, defensive barrier, careful detection reveals that it was necessary, even before it was finished, to improve its 'offensive capability' and its control of the North ... The presence of officers' wives at High Rochester and Risingham, posts well in advance of Hadrian's Wall, make it an unlikely defensive war zone."[64] In the Balkans and the Alps, Roman walls and barriers "were either not frontier lines, or, in the case of the Alpine constructions, were probably intended to impede rivals in the civil wars of the later Empire rather than to repel invaders."[65] In eastern Europe, settlements north of the Danube "show 'intensive contact' with the province of Pannonia lasting into the third century."[66] Other Roman wall systems in North Africa and Germany also show a defense system that was not identifiable with any wall. The German Antonine wall and fort system beyond the Upper Rhine, Whittaker observes, must have been "'negotiated', since it runs dead-straight in parts, with no attempt to follow a strategic line."[67] Judging from all these examples, boundaries in Rome – whether walls, rivers, or lines of forts – did not demarcate definitively any division between external and internal peoples. Hostile parties could live within these boundaries, administered parties outside them. As observed by Di Cosmo, this arrangement was also the case in early China.[68] With this being the case, we need to look elsewhere for the bounds of sovereignty.

---

[62] Giddens, *Nation-State and Violence*, 51.   [63] Whittaker, *Rome and Its Frontiers*, 9.
[64] Ibid., 9–10.   [65] Ibid., 11.   [66] Ibid., 10.   [67] Ibid., 10.
[68] Even as far back as the *Zuozhuan*, the intrinsic weakness of any wall was recognized, that the true source of any robust defense was with those who lent their loyal support to a sovereign area: "As long as it cannot be defended, a wall does no good. In ancient times, the defensive line of the Heaven-appointed king lay among the outlying Yi in all four directions. When the Heaven-appointed king was brought low, his defensive line lay among the princes. The defensive lines of the princes lay among their neighbors in all four directions. When the princes were brought low, their defensive lines lay on their own [frontiers] in all four directions. In their caution over these [frontiers] in all four

Liminal Edges of the State

The economic foundation of an agricultural state is in the extraction of revenue from agricultural production. In order to do this efficiently, responsibilities for the produce of the land must be assigned. Likewise, the calculation by which revenue is extracted and regulations governing its extraction must be carefully formulated to obviate unnecessary loss, fraudulent or otherwise, or disputes over its extraction. One of the most basic devices for this extraction is the establishment of bounded plots, and thus cultivated field borders (*jie* 界),[69] proposed by governing powers. Indeed, according to Sima Qian, after the floods, Yu 禹 demarcated the traditional nine provinces and stipulated tribute amounts from each.[70] These territorial demarcations were also attributed to the roving Xiongnu, even in their early pre-state periods. According to the *Shiji*, though the Xiongnu have "no walled cities, no fixed lodgings, and no agricultural occupations … they each have divisions of land."[71] Agricultural activity thus was not the definiens of early land divisions; instead, the definiens was the intrinsic prohibition against transgression and unsanctioned use. The definition of a discrete, hard border is just that which is framed by this prohibition. The border is definable as the site of a potential confrontation, the marking of a terrain that should not be transgressed – politically, militarily, economically, or even culturally.[72]

directions, they formed alliances with supporters in all four directions. The people were at ease in the countryside, and their duties in the three agricultural seasons bore fruit. The people suffered neither from disturbances within the domain nor from alarms originating outside. What use did they have for walls? … Long ago, the Liege of Liang dug a moat around his lord's palace and the people scattered. As the people had abandoned their superiors, what did the superiors expect, if not a loss?" 苟不能衛，城無益也，古者天子守在四夷，天子卑，守在諸侯，諸侯守在四鄰，諸侯卑，守在四竟，慎其四竟，結其四援，民狎其野，三務成功，民無內憂，而又無外懼，國焉用城？⋯昔梁伯溝其公宮而民潰，民棄其上，不亡，何待？ *Zuozhuan*, Zhao 23.9; Yang Bojun 楊伯峻, ed., *Chunqiu zuozhuan zhu* 春秋左傳注 (Beijing: Zhonghua shuju, 1981), 4:1448; *Zuo Tradition (Zuozhuan): Commentary on the Spring and Autumn Annals*, trans. Stephen Durrant, Wai-yee Li, and David Schaberg (Seattle: University of Washington Press, 2016), 2:1625, translation modified.

[69] From its use in the *Mengzi*, *jie* seems almost technically aligned with the precise linear borders of settled fields, and, by extension, administrative districts. This usage is found in both received texts, such as the *Shuijing zhu*, and excavated texts, such as in the Juyan documents, where it refers to the northern edge of a district supervised by a military garrison. See Paola Calanca and François Wildt, "Les frontières: Quelques termes-clés," *Extrême-Orient-Extrême-Occident* 28 (2006), 21–22.

[70] 唯禹之功為大，披九山，通九澤，決九河，定九州，各以其職來貢，不失厥宜. Sima Qian 司馬遷, *Shiji* 史記 (Beijing: Zhonghua shuju, 1959), 1.43. Hereafter cited as "*SJ*."

[71] 毋城郭常處耕田之業，然亦各有分地. *SJ* 110.2879.

[72] Whittaker offers similar observations: "Both the Chinese state and the Roman state made an enormous effort to post several hundred thousand men on the periphery of their empires. But each frontier remained 'far more zonal than linear, despite the illusion of

Construction activities in the state's periphery are describable as "episodes of conquest advancing a claim to political legitimacy based on the power of the king to subdue the 'wilderness' and call forth an ordered landscape."[73] The sovereign power of construction lay in the "tectonic" charisma of the monarch. There is also in early China, similar to Adam T. Smith's description of the Urartian regimes in ancient Turkey, an emphasis on disorder before the arrival of a sovereign power, exemplified in the ordering efforts of the sage king Yu. "By defining a preexisting locale as a tabula rasa, rival understandings of place that might compete with, undermine, or question those advanced by the royal regime were excluded."[74] As will be expounded later, local people, and local memory, were intentionally eliminated or reordered, whether through physical deportation or the assertion of a supervenient memorialization of territorial possession, instantiated through devices such as the imperial stele inscriptions. Early Chinese regimes were, like the Urartian, intent on "more profoundly transforming the political subject through a brutal reordering of the cartography of memory achieved in both the destruction of place and the production of forgetting."[75] In addition to marking places, identifying resources, or delineating territorial possession, locations on a map would have served to record the intentionally enforced reorderings of memory. Through mapping, one can reorder or obliterate old lived memories under more current concerns, associations, and priorities. Places on the map can be the results of contestations over the loci of memory – their fixing, their relation to other memories, and, very importantly, their (re)naming.[76]

Generally, as with other instances of confirmation bias, people explore, they "decipher" terrestrial organizations in order to prove preconceived notions of the world, notions that are modified only with difficulty. Observations that would disconfirm or challenge preconceived expectations may be dismissed as deceptions that can be ignored.[77] (Of course,

---

walls that emphasized it.' Rivers, says a recent study of ancient north Britain, 'make poor boundaries and the distribution of late prehistoric settlements . . . is such as to suggest that river valleys acted as foci rather than boundaries for tribal groups.'" Those tribespeople who had contractual or subsidiary arrangements with the Romans were still "*membra partesque imperii* – integral parts of the body of the empire, beckoning Rome onward . . . They were not a defensive cordon sanitaire." Furthermore, Whittaker notes, forts, or even walls, may not only serve to prevent enemy movement across a region; they may also be lines of communication. C. R. Whittaker, *Frontiers of the Roman Empire: A Social and Economic Study* (Baltimore, MD: Johns Hopkins University Press, 1994), 84.

[73] A. Smith, *Political Landscape*, 160–161. Smith applies this claim to Urartian monarchial regimes (ca. 850–643 BCE).

[74] A. Smith, *Political Landscape*, 162–163.   [75] Ibid., 168–169.

[76] See Jacob, *Sovereign Map*, 254.

[77] Such a sentiment is akin to the one Foucault ascribes to Don Quixote, who "reads the world in order to prove his books." Each of Don Quixote's adventures is an attempt "to

without memory or conception, territory is an unknown blank, endlessly offering the peril of being lost, until one establishes memory, and the territory becomes "found.") These cognitive operations – the searching for a preconceived notion of the world – affect how we read and understand maps. To read a map carefully against any preconceived notions of its ordering, one must expect that some of its organization may be distorting, obliterating, or incorporating under a new name, previous organizations – including, and perhaps especially, previous ritual organizations. The current selection and organization may also very well be designative and prescriptive, not descriptive.

The inaugural use of terms for "borders" and the first disputes over their placement in Chinese bronze inscriptions pertain to their assignment – where or whether they were marked, or whether marked correctly. The *Sanshi pan* 散氏盤 is, to date, the earliest inscription concerning a case surrounding the demarcation of territory resulting from a conflict between two competing Western Zhou families.[78] Its inscription describes its boundaries through an active or imagined walking off of the territory in the various cardinal directions and an establishment of raised earthen mounds or walls, *feng* 封, at certain landmarks – a lake, a riverway, a willow tree, a mountain, a tamped earthen wall, and so forth.[79] No numerical measurements of distance are utilized. In its lengthy inscription, a dispute over the setting of agricultural boundaries is recorded, with the limits of the terrain denoted by the planting of trees on the *feng*.[80] As Yang

---

transform reality into a sign," to transform his perceptions into mapping legends. As with Foucault's analysis of the pre-Renaissance era, Chinese mapping appears to be more of resemblance than of post-Cartesian identity and measurement. See Michel Foucault, *The Order of Things: An Archaeology of the Human Sciences* (New York: Pantheon Books, 1970), 46–52.

[78] For a translation of a relevant passage from the *Sanshi pan*, see Wang, *Writing and the Ancient State*, 197.

[79] For a complete interpretation of the inscription, see Na Zhiliang 那志良, *Liangjian zhuming de guobao* 兩件著名的國寶 (Taipei: Guangwen shuju, 1964), 50–69, or Wang Jing 王晶, "Sanshipan mingwen jishi ji Xi Zhou shiqi tudi peichang anjian shenli chengdu kuitan" 散氏盤銘文集釋及西周时期土地赔偿案件审理程度窥探, *Changchun gongye daxue xuebao* 長春工业大学学报 24, no. 1 (2012). Robin Yates argues the *feng* constructed under Lord Shang Yang dividing the agricultural fields "were miniature replicas of the walls that divided the contending states from each other and that established their separate identities," though on what basis he argues this is not stated. Robin D. S. Yates, "Cosmos, Central Authority, and Communities in the Early Chinese Empire," in *Empires: Perspectives from Archaeology and History*, ed. Susan Alcock et al. (New York: Cambridge University Press, 2001), 361. The *Zuozhuan* also makes reference to these boundary ridges: In Zheng, Zichan (anno 543 BCE) partitioned off agricultural fields marked with *feng* and irrigation ditches (田有封洫). See Yang Bojun, *Chunqiu zuozhuan zhu*, 3:30.1181.

[80] Indeed, the inscription repeatedly and crucially depends on the term *feng* 奉, "to offer up," the Zhou form of the graph an apparent semantograph of two hands pointing

Shuda 楊樹達 remarks, the use of trees in the *Zhouli* to make *feng* boundaries, while not necessarily limited to agricultural purposes, are frequently for such. Yang contends that, because when describing agricultural boundaries the early Chinese often used trees, it seems likely that the *Sanshi pan* case also involved the marking of agricultural boundaries.[81] Further evidence for Yang's supposition about the earliest marking of boundaries being for agricultural purposes can be found in texts such as the *Zuozhuan* 左轉, *Mengzi* 孟子, and *Hanshu* 漢書. In the *Mengzi*, for instance, to "land" (*yu* 域) commoners – that is, to settle them and claim them as part of one's sovereign territory – is implicitly defined as being within those marked by the limits of taxable agricultural fields – in other words, by the commoners' economic employment.[82] The *Zuozhuan*, in various instances, speaks of the boundaries of fiscally profitable territories – fundamentally, agricultural

upwards, above which the graph of a tree is located, suggesting that the hands are "offering up" a tree. In the context of its use on the inscription, transliterators and paleographers such as Guo Moruo and Li Xueqin have substituted *feng* 奉 with *feng* 封. However, some interpreters suggest that *feng* 封 should simply signify an earthen road, symbolizing a discrete line. Sun Yirang 孫詒讓 interprets the process of *feng* as the creation of earthen boundaries, quoting Cui Shi 崔氏 as stating that "to *feng* a boundary or frontier march (*jiang* 疆境) and draw a border (*jie* 界), one mounds up earth to create a terrace by which one marks the boundary. Drawing a border, one erects a low wall between two *feng* terraces." Li notes that in the Qin legal document "Laws Pertaining to Agricultural Fields," there is a rule stating that "the *feng* should be four-*chi* 尺 ("feet") tall, should be as large as it is tall, the wall a *chi* tall and two-*chi* thick below" 崔氏, 《古今注》：「封疆畫界者，封土为台，以表识疆境也。画界者，于二封之间又为墙埒，以画分界域也」《为田律》：「封高四尺，大称其高；埒高尺，下厚二尺」 Li Xueqin 李學勤, "Xi Zhou jinwen zhong de tudi zhuanrang" 西周金文中的土地转让, in *Xin chu qingtongqi yanjiu* 新出青铜器研究 (Beijing: Wenwu chubanshe, 1990), 108. See also Wang Jing, "Sanshipan mingwen jishi ji Xi Zhou shiqi tudi peichang anjian shenli chengdu kuitan," 48; Na Zhiliang, *Liangjian zhuming de guobao*, 54.

[81] Yang Shuda 楊樹達, *Ji wei ju jin wen shuo* 積微居金文說 (Beijing: Kexue chubanshe, 1959), 33–34. See also *Zhouli zhushu* 周禮注疏 (Beijing: Beijing daxue chubanshe, 1999), 1:311–312: Li Xueqin interprets *feng* 封 as denoting the *process* of creating place-marks at the boundaries, whereon trees were planted. In the *Zhouli*, Li maintains, a statement descriptive of the activity of the "feng ren" 封人 supports this view (though no planting of trees is explicitly mentioned): "In general, in the enfeoffing of a state, one puts in place the earthen walls of its altars of soil and grain, modeling the four boundaries [of the state]. The creation of the enfeoffed territory of large and small towns is also [done] like this" 凡封國設其社稷之壇，封其四疆，造都邑之封域者亦如之.

[82] 域民不以封疆之界，固國不以山谿之險. *Mengzi* 2B, "Gongsun chou xia" 公孫丑下; *Mengzi zhengyi* 孟子正義 (Beijing: Zhonghua shuju, 2009), 1:253–254. Similarly, the *Mengzi* states, the securing of a state is not with impenetrable mountains and valleys. What protects a state and keeps people to remain in one's territory is good governance. It should be noted that in the earliest texts, such as the ode entitled "Siwen" 思文 in the *Shijing* 詩經, *jie* 界 is frequently used to describe the limits of agricultural fields. See also *Mengzi*, "Teng wen gong shang" 滕文公上 3A3, *Mengzi zhengyi*, 1:348: 經界不正，并地不鈞，穀祿不平. In Bryan Van Norden's translation: "If the field boundaries are not straightly set, the well-fields will not be equal, and the grain income will not be even." *Mengzi, with Selections from Traditional Commentaries*, trans. Bryan W. Van Norden (Indianapolis, IN: Hackett Publishing, 2008), 68.

fields – being redrawn or set.[83] And the *Hanshu* records a conflict over the extent of agricultural territory "mistakenly" marked in a commandery map, the rectification of which led to a reimbursement to a family of a large amount of grain.[84] Thus the description of carefully delineated, exacting boundaries in early texts often had to do with those that pertain to the extraction of revenue and the agricultural resources, not more abstract sovereign state borders.

In sum, the operations of *feng* – as well as any major early Chinese method of determining sovereign space – can be tied intimately to the settled occupation of a space, to the number of occupants committed to its agricultural employment. For Feng Li, "While *feng* signifies the action of 'planting' trees to define borders, the component *yi* 邑 (settlement) in *bang* suggests that it refers to the area of residence defined by such trees, resulting from the action of *feng*."[85] In a Han-era Dunhuang manuscript, the creation of a hamlet (*yi* 邑) for a "feudal lord" (*liehou* 列侯) is, at least partially, defined in demographic terms. In the Shuihudi manuscripts, *feng* is defined very explicitly in terms of agricultural land area, but this again is truly meaningful not in terms of the land itself but in terms of the income from that area of land.[86] All these are settled *places* that can be set up, dissolved, attacked, separated off in physical terms.

The question is, are these areas lineally defined? More precisely, are they – abstractly or not – separable by walls, at the local level, or at the grander political level? And if these "lines" are present, do they signify the precise end of a sovereign space? Or are the edges of sovereignty fuzzy, defined more accurately by the activity than by the actual ground space? Perhaps the question can be decided with reference to the precision by which the lineally defined boundaries of a terrestrial space could be marked, and the reasons for their marking. With relatively small

[83] See for example, Ding 4.1e: "Borders were set for his territory [more appropriately, agricultural lands], stretching from Wufu in the south as far as the northern frontier [march] of Putian" 封畛土略，自武父以南，及圃田之北竟. Wen 1.6: "In autumn, the Prince of Jin redrew the [boundaries] of the Qi territory" 秋，晉侯疆戚田. ("Territory" here is simply "agricultural fields," redrawn for fiscal reasons, presumably.) *Zuo Tradition* (*Zuozhuan*), 1:463, 1749. Other examples of administrative, fiscal areas being defined by *feng* can be seen in the "Wangzhi" 王制 chapter of the *Liji*. For instances, see *Liji jijie* 禮記集解 (Beijing: Zhonghua shuju, 2010), 1:315–316.

[84] *Hanshu* 漢書 (Beijing: Zhonghua shuju, 1962), 81.3346. *Hanshu* hereafter cited as "*HS*."

[85] Feng Li, *Bureaucracy and the State in Early China: Governing the Western Zhou* (New York: Cambridge University Press, 2008), 48n10.

[86] I say only "partially" because the passage is fragmentary: "☑者眾八千人以上，封列侯邑。" See 《甘肅敦煌酥油土漢簡》. See www.chant.org, 簡帛書1 database, accessed 9/18/19. See also 《睡虎地·封診式》"封有鞫者某里士五（伍）甲家室、妻、子、臣妾、衣器、畜產。" *Shuihudi Qinmu zhujian* 睡虎地秦墓竹簡 (Beijing: Wenwu chubanshe, 1978), 249; 《睡虎地·法律答問》： "如為「封」？「封」即田千佰。頃半（畔）「封」殹（也）" *Shuihudi Qinmu zhujian*, 178.

agricultural fields, one might suppose lineal boundary marking could be achieved with relative ease – especially when the sight lines are clear, the land is somewhat flat, and the forming of earthen boundaries manually feasible, as in the case when fields are small. But is this the scope of sovereign territory defined by *feng*? Such does not seem to be the case, for the scope of sovereign territory is much larger, the size of a politically significant unit, which was, judging from the excavated records, a hamlet (*yi*) or larger, and thus as a settlement area potentially spatially unstable. The borders of a settlement may have had surveyable parameters, but, depending on the sight lines, perhaps may not. Certainly there is no documented evidence that measured, mathematically precise state surveys were regularly performed and recorded in the pre-imperial or early imperial period. Indeed, even on the smallest scope of the field, quantification and number do not inevitably figure into their sizing.

In short, it is the unquantified (or not completely quantified) marking of – and instantiation of means against the transgression of – an economically valuable, revenue-producing area that is the found of the state border. Crucially and quite significantly, the earthen walls or mounds, the *feng*, also had ritually instantiated meaning. Grander borders, such as city or state walls, likewise carried significant ritual meaning. Walls on the micro- or macroscale were to be treated as religio-moral boundaries as well, boundaries that expressed real, active political effects. Indeed, as stated in the Warring States-era "Rongchengshi" 容成氏 manuscript, one of the ancient sage Yu's first acts after dispelling the floodwaters was to establish "walled settlements" for people to occupy.[87] This active religio-moral effect did not depend on the existence of a constructed wall but was efficacious in the very notion of the border, again in both its preservation and its transgression.[88] The concepts that applied to field boundaries, captured in words such as *jie* 界, *jiang* 疆, and *jing* 境,[89] would be applied to larger sovereign state borders, as *feng* was to larger areas of property.

[87] 禹乃因山陵平隰之可封邑者而繁實之. "Rongchengshi 容成氏," in *Shanghai bowuguan cang Zhanguo Chu zhushu* 上海博物館藏戰國楚竹書, ed. Ma Chengyuan 馬承源 (Shanghai: Shanghai guji chubanshe, 2001), 263–264, slip 18.

[88] Standen expounds on the walled reification of a conceptual border thus: "The most striking method of attempting to assert authority on the basis of borderlines is the attempt to reify a line on a map or a conceptual boundary by creating a physical demarcation. Examples include the Berlin Wall … In historical terms the Great Wall of China is a classic example of this reifying endeavor, illustrating the multiple uses for such demarcation." Standen, *Unbounded Loyalty*, 22.

[89] In the *Shuowen jiezi*, *jing* 境 is not only defined by referring to another concept, *jiang* 疆, definitive of a type of agricultural boundary, but is itself a definiens of other words, such as *jie* 界 and *gang* 阬, also applicable to agriculture.

With relation to city walls, Yinong Xu contends, they were designed "to awe and affirm, only secondarily to defend."[90] Conceived more generally, walls were knowledge platforms, boundaries of cultural discourse, effecting the division – however porous – of cultures, separating the mannered from the ill-mannered, the civilized from the uncouth. They were, quite literally, cultural edifices, platforms of knowledge, through which the unknown, the formless is formed, or comes to be formed. Walls were concrete metonyms for sovereign borders, on whatever scale, small or large.[91] To close their openings was to shut off the violent propensities of the external wilds; city gates symbolically represent the political concentration of civilization against the influence of the violent, vital forces of the external world.[92] Those who were reputed to have no walls or forts, like the northern non-Chinese Xiongnu or the southern Yue 越, were by definition wild, uncultured.[93] Broken walls required repair to maintain the symbolic integrity of the state, and to raze walls was to literally raze the perimeters of civilization.[94] Indeed, the Qin emperor, at the beginning of his imperial reign, intentionally razed walls, demolished borders and

---

[90] Yinong Xu, *The Chinese City in Space and Time: The Development of Urban Form in Suzhou* (Honolulu: University of Hawai'i Press, 2000), 87. They were, naturally, not merely forceful symbols, yet their defensive function, as this quote from the *Guanzi* demonstrates, could not suffice without proper governance: "Four things determine whether a state is to know safety or danger. To defend it with city and suburban walls and guarded passes alone is not enough" 國之所以安危者四，城郭險阻，不足守也. See *Guanzi jiaozhu* 管子校注, Li Xiangfeng 黎翔鳳 comp. (Beijing: Zhonghua shuju, 2004), 1:59; *Guanzi*, trans. W. Allyn Rickett (Boston, MA: Cheng and Tsui, 2001), 101.

[91] See *Guanzi* 管子, "Ba guan" 八觀; *Guanzi jiaozhu*, 1:256; *Guanzi*, 228.

[92] According to Whittaker, Romans also gave their walls ritual, symbolic significance: "The sacredness of the walls of the city, epitomized in the story of Remus, who was killed for the sacrilege of leaping over the unfinished walls of Romulus, was equally significant for the wall or the entrenchment of the military camp, where death was the penalty for anyone who tried to climb over them and avoid the gates. Doubtless that was true also of the artificial barriers around the Empire, although the sources do not say so specifically." Whittaker, *Rome and Its Frontiers*, 127.

[93] See Zhufu Yan's 主父偃 and Liu An's 劉安 addresses to Emperor Wu of Han, *SJ* 112.2954–2957 and *HS* 64.2778.

[94] The *Huainanzi* 淮南子 speaks repeatedly of broken walls, of the need to repair them. (修城郭, in "Tian wen," "Shi ze xun"; 築修城 in "Ren jian xun") The *Huainanzi* furthermore emphasizes the moral–cultural significance of walls in condemning their transgression: "To clamber over city walls;/ to sneak around precipices and barriers,/ to feign tallies of authority,/ to rob offices of their gold,/ or to commit regicide and usurpation and [presume to] carry out punishments in the ruler's name; such actions are not in the nature of human beings" 越城郭，逾險塞，奸符節，盜管金，簒弒矯誣，非人之性也. *Huainanzi*, "Fanlun xun" 范論訓; Liu An, *The Huainanzi*, trans. John S. Major et al. (New York: Columbia University Press, 2010), 520. And Han Anguo 韓安國 (?–127 BCE), an early Han minister, declared, "Waging battle against a state razes city walls" 伐國墮城, razing the symbols of the state. See Olberding, *Dubious Facts*, 122; *HHS* 52.2402.

created his own, as an act of self-definition, of the definition of his new state.[95]

In spite of revenue-producing areas serving as the monetized centers of sovereign power, in many texts, it is the natural boundaries, such as mountains and riverways, that are often treated as the abiding, vital borders of the sovereign state. In the same *Mengzi* passage mentioned above, Mengzi implicitly asserts this by denying the equation of the securing of the state with the "strengths" of its mountains and rivers.[96] But like frontier walls such as the Great Wall, these natural boundaries functioned, as was also the case in later eras, "more as a point of reference than as a line to be held."[97] Both mountains and rivers, as will be discussed in more depth, were prominent sites of sacrifice to local or regional spiritual entities, but they were also sites of communication and transformation, places in which knowledge about unvisited areas, areas within the visual horizon, could be garnered. Mountaintops in particular gave access to the limits of the known, taking "the viewer above the here-and-now, offering a grand vista of the natural and the human world, of the past and the present."[98] The power of the mountain can thus be said to be in some relation to the power afforded by the surveying gaze, the power of elevation. Both mountains and rivers, as natural boundaries, act as the "walls" of civilization. It is not by accident that the most important imperial sacrifices were frequently conducted on mountaintops and that all save one of the Qin stele inscriptions by the First Emperor were placed on mountains.[99] Mountains and rivers

[95] 墮壞城郭，決通川防，夷去險阻。地勢既定，黎庶無繇，天下咸撫 ... 事各有序 (*SJ* 6.252). According to the *Shiji*, this passage was from an inscription carved on the gate of Jieshi 碣石門. In Burton Watson's translation, modified here, the text is rendered as follows: "[The emperor] demolished walls and fortifications, opened up waterways, cut through embankments, and leveled the steep declivities. When the [propensities] of the land had been fixed, the masses were freed from corvée labour, and all the empire was comforted ... each affair [was] ranged in proper order." Sima Qian, *Records of the Grand Historian: Qin Dynasty*, trans. Burton Watson (New York: Columbia University Press, 1993), 52. Translation modified.

[96] *Mengzi*, "Gongsun chou xia" 公孫丑下: 固國不以山谿之險. *Mengzi zhengyi*, 1:254.

[97] Standen makes this claim for the earliest printed maps of China, from the Southern Song: "it is worthy noting that the maps for each of the Five Dynasties, and for the expansion under the first two Song emperors, show the borders of the states concerned. While the same area – China Proper – is shown on each map, there is no fudging of reality: where districts within the Wall were administered by other powers, this situation is clearly marked. Hence although the Wall is there, it seems to function more as a point of reference than as a line to be held. It defines the limit of the empire as the Song cartographers wished the empire to be; it did not have to reflect the limit as it actually was." Standen, *Unbounded Loyalty*, 22.

[98] Hans Frankel, *The Flowering Plum and the Palace Lady: Interpretations of Chinese Poetry* (New Haven, CT: Yale University Press, 1976), 113.

[99] Indeed, the inscription on the First Emperor's stele on Mount Tai declares that he has ascended to survey "encompassingly" the eastern extent of his sovereign space 周覽東極, the limits of his sovereignty bounded only by the sea. (For a complete translation of the

are fundamental signifiers of the liminal, of the edges of the known and the knowable, and of access to the unknowable, their political import both secular and sacred. Mountains and waterways were contrastive of solidity and movement, power and breaches of power, the executive and his advisers, the empire and its challengers. They are not infrequently emphasized as strategic points of blockage and entry.[100]

Similar to walls, mountains offered a visual panorama that bore into both the territorialized, culturally commanded sovereign area and the nonterritorialized, culturally noncommanded area. For an illustrative instance of the power of the visual panorama afforded by elevated position, in the Tang-era capital of Chang'an, Linda Feng writes,

[a]ccess to vertical space complicates the spatial division designed to maintain hierarchies. If one's gaze could rise high enough, distinctions between the inside and outside of a walled space would disappear; if one's body could transcend walls, then distinctions between public and private would be challenged … From the higher elevations, rulers could survey their subjects and in turn be safeguarded from the commoner's gaze. As Mark Edward Lewis points out, urban architecture that manifests sovereign power through verticality arose in the Warring States period. Just as towers augmented the breadth and extent of a ruler's gaze, so did high walls shield him from the prying eyes of his subjects.[101]

---

inscription, see Martin Kern, *The Stele Inscriptions of Ch'in Shih-huang: Text and Ritual in Early Chinese Imperial Representation* (New Haven, CT: American Oriental Society, 2000), 17–23.) His interest was also, as with any sovereign tour, to gain a sense of the goings-on in his realm. He wished to personally tour and inspect "the distant realms and [their] common peoples" 親巡遠方黎民, to understand how and where his sovereign control was being compromised, where those who had come to pay respects at court (*binfu* 賓服) were not truly governing as he would wish them to. (*SJ* 6.243) The legendary emperor Shun 舜 also conducted sacrifices on mountaintops during the tour of the empire he completed every five years on which he would inspect the five celebrated mountains, beginning with Mount Tai, performing sacrifices to Heaven, the *wang* 望 sacrifice to the mountains and rivers, and hold meetings with the feudal lords. See *SJ* 28.1355–56. These inspections, sacrifices, and meetings were tied to imperial assertions of sovereignty.

[100] As Liu An states to Emperor Wu, "Being blocked by tall mountains – where the traces of men disappear and carriage roads do not pass through – this is the means by which outside and inside are separated in the natural world. Were they to enter into the Central States, they would necessarily have to go down tributary mountain rivers" 限以高山，人迹所絕，車道不通，天地所以隔外內也。其入中國必下領水。Ban Gu 班固， *HS* 64.2781; Olberding, *Dubious Facts*, 195.

[101] Linda Rui Feng, "Negotiating Vertical Space, Vistas, and the Topographical Imagination," *T'ang Studies* 29 (2011), 28. Legal prescriptions pertaining to the management of the elevated gaze are manifest in the *Tang Code*, whether related to the looking into the imperial palace from a high place, as in article 66, or to the guarding of lookouts, as with article 89: "Not aware of refers to the road on which Chinese or foreign villains leave or enter. These are the responsibility of lookouts. The areas that can be seen define responsibility. This means areas that can be seen by the lookouts" 不覺謂內外姦人出入之路關於候望者，目所堪見為關，謂在候望之內。*The T'ang Code*, vol. 2,

Indeed, one could go so far as to say that walls are as fundamentally about the gaze, and thus the knowledge, afforded by vertical elevation, as about physical direction, acting as structures directing movement.[102]

We can find evidence for the power of gazing into the distance in literary descriptions, in a writer's poetic act of climbing or ascending heights to liberate himself from the pedestrian grime and toil and literally gain a wider perspective on his world. Feng catalogues numerous literary episodes from Tang China in which denizens overcame visual impediments, whether by privately building tall structures, like pavilions, or climbing to public lookouts, as is evident in the Tang "climbing heights" *deng gao* 登高 poetry subgenre.[103] This liberating act of ascension is also a central feature in the early Han elegy, the "Lisao" 離騷. In Vincent Leung's analysis, the freedom afforded by the ascent to soaring heights is contrasted with the ideologically homogenous, unelevated space desired by imperial regimes such as the Qin, and by implication, the Han. Grounded upon a calculated "making and remaking of landscapes,"[104] imperial power aspires to a geographic totalitarianism, a totalizing spatial order, of which the "Lisao," and the *Songs of the Chu* (*Chuci* 楚辭) in general, are an inversion.[105] The Qin vision extends ritualistic and strategic sovereignty to impose a "grand, perfect order," expressed in the comprehensive mapping of the known world on the floor of the First Emperor's tomb. In their placement on mountains, the Qin steles also emphasize the encompassing, "mapping" power of the sovereign gaze over his domain.[106] For the Qin, the cosmos is perfectly ordered – "everything is exactly where [it belongs] and all can be 'at rest in his home' (*ge an qi yu* 各安其宇)."[107]

By contrast, the *Chuci* depicts a world where "all things are displaced, and home is where one wants to be but cannot remain":[108] "I [surveyed] all around over the earth's four quarters,/Circling the heavens till at last I alighted./ I gazed on a jade tower's glittering splendor/And spied the lovely daughter of the Lord of Song."[109] In the narrator's vertiginal wandering, there is, Leung notes, a sense of dislocation and visual

---

Specific Articles, trans. Wallace Johnson (Princeton, NJ: Princeton University Press, 1997), 28–29, 57.

[102] The *Mozi* indirectly acknowledges the access to knowledge afforded by walls: 廧外之利害未可知也. Mo Di 墨翟, *Mozi xiangu* 墨子閒詁 (Beijing: Zhonghua shuju, 2001), 347.

[103] Feng, "Negotiating Vertical Space," 32–35.   [104] A. Smith, *Political Landscape*, 5.

[105] Vincent Leung, "On the *Chuci* as a Literary Artifact of the Spatial Politics of the Han Empire," unpublished manuscript, 22. Cited with permission of the author.

[106] See, for instance, Kern, *Stele Inscriptions of Ch'in Shih-huang*, 19, 30, 35, 38, 44, 45.

[107] Leung, "On the *Chuci*," 21.   [108] Leung, "On the *Chuci*," 22.

[109] 覽相觀於四極兮，周流乎天余乃下。望瑤臺之偃蹇兮，見有娀之佚女. Leung, "On the *Chuci*," 14. Translation modified.

distortion, but also one, as the "Lisao" states, "exalted with a reckless sense of freedom."[110] In all this, the extension of sight lines is crucial for the liberation of the self. Verbs expressing these aspirations for broad optical compass, such as *guan* 觀, "surveying," or *wang* 望 "gazing afar," are repeatedly employed in the poem. Virtually all of the sages listed in the "Lisao" poem, Lewis observes, "have towers associated with their world-ordering world."[111] Perhaps not coincidentally, as shall be discussed later, *wang* also is employed for certain state sacrifices performed on mountaintops.[112]

In spite of the monarchial occupation and ritual possession of visual geographic space, the visualization of geographic space was not proprietary, nor was its mapping. Anyone who acquired sufficient informational sources could sketch a plausibly representative geographic diagram. The problem was merely of collecting sources across a broad domain without suspicion or intervention by officials. Methodically touring a landscape was an official prerogative, one that the monarch, or his representatives, undertook repeatedly and purposively. For such touring, the primary means to geographic location was the direction. In many tours and monarchial portrayals of spatial possession, there is thus an emphasis on physical orientation.

On the far side of these liminal edges of knowledge, that which lay beyond walls or mountains would be difficult or impossible to see and know. To stand atop walls and look abroad or to ascend mountains and gaze afar would afford strategically beneficial expanses of intelligence. This monitoring, surveilling gaze was crucial to the preservation and extension of sovereignty. Likewise, circumscribing the gaze of others was necessary to securing exclusive authority and bar transgression. Various passages in early texts highlight the prohibitions of the edifice on the gaze and the possible transgression in attempting to peer over a wall. According to Feng, "There were longstanding associations between political authority and the power of observation through 'overlooking' (*fushi* 俯視)."[113]

---

[110] 意恣睢以担撟. Leung, "On the *Chuci*," 15, 17.

[111] Mark E. Lewis, *The Construction of Space in Early China* (Albany: State University of New York Press, 2006), 300.

[112] See p. 113.

[113] Feng, "Negotiating Vertical Space," 28. A comparable observation is made in an essay by Jie Shi: "During the visit to the ancestral temple on the first day of the first month of the year ... Emperor Shun, one of the legendary sage rulers, opened the four gates and four windows of the building to conveniently peer into all four directions 'and allowed no corner under heaven to be concealed.' The political metaphor is unmistakable: commanding a panoramic view over surrounding areas represents an exemplary ruler's thorough and brilliant control over his country. Perhaps following this example, emperors of the Han dynasty ritually scaled high buildings to stare into the distance."

Lewis makes a similar point with respect to towers in Han dynasty marketplaces. In a depiction of a Chengdu market on a Han tomb tile, a two-story tower lies at the center. These marketplace towers were "the most visible manifestation of government control," serving "as the base of operations for the officials in charge ... The tower had a flag on top and a drum in the upper chamber that were used to signal the opening and closing of the market ... they were the highest structure in the market, both to manifest state power and to guarantee that signals were clearly visible to people in the most distant corners."[114] Any commoner standing at a height in the marketplace would be ostensibly arrogating undeserved visual powers to himself, as a critique in the *Mengzi* of men who constantly sought to obtain a higher vantage point in the marketplace illustrates.[115] The Weiyang Palace 未央宮 built under Han Gaozu 漢高祖 itself loomed over Chang'an.[116] Accessing its walled interiors, if Tang dynasty codes are any indication, would likely have brought severe punishment. Crossing over the walls of the imperial palace in the Tang capital, Feng notes, was punishable in the *Tang Codes* "by exile at a distance of 3000 *li*. The most severe punishment, strangulation, is reserved for climbing over the wall of an imperial audience hall."[117]

Boundary walls, like roads, acted as elevated walkways, as transmitters or facilitators of goods and knowledge, as venues of economic and informational contact, both along and across. Around both city and border wall gates, marketplaces would often form, taking advantage of entering and egressing traffic. The importance of walls as knowledge platforms can

---

See Jie Shi, "The Overseeing Mother: Revisiting the Frontal-Pose Lady in the Wu Family Shrines in Second-Century China," *Monumenta Serica* 63, no. 2 (2015), 281. I am grateful to an anonymous reader for this reference.

[114] Lewis, *Construction of Space in Early China*, 160. "Passages collected in the Song encyclopedia *Tai ping yu lan* contain references to terraces ... Anecdotes emphasize their great height, in one case saying that the tower was about 160 yards high and reached the clouds. This great height allowed a ruler to survey his own domain and even spy into neighboring states. Other stories show that the terraces were used to intimidate foreign visitors and gain their submission through demonstrating the wealth of the builder and the extent of his gaze." Lewis, *Construction of Space in Early China*, 154.

[115] "When the ancients had markets, they were for exchanging what they had for what they lacked. The officials merely kept order. But there were some base fellows there who would seek for a 'vantage point' and climb up on it. They would gaze left and right, monopolizing the profit from the market. Everyone thought they were base, so they followed up by fining them" 古之為市也，以其所有易其所無者，有司者治之耳。有賤丈夫焉，必求龍斷而登之，以左右望而罔市利。人皆以為賤，故從而征之。 *Mengzi*, "Gong sun chou xia" 公孫丑下; *Mengzi zhengyi*, 1:301–302; *Mengzi, with Selections from Traditional Commentaries*, 2B11.3, 59.

[116] Wu Hung, *Monumentality in Early Chinese Art and Architecture* (Stanford, CA: Stanford University Press, 1995), 152.

[117] Feng, "Negotiating Vertical Space," 29.

also be seen in the prohibition of the *Liji* 禮記 (*The Book of Rites*) against pointing or calling out when one has climbed a city wall, for to do so could cause alarm.[118] At the top of walls would often be a platform broad enough to allow quick movement of men and supplies. According to the Han-era *Jiuzhang suanshu* 九章算術, the upper width of a city wall was two *zhang* 丈, or 4.62 meters.[119] This accords closely with the upper width prescribed in the Mohist texts of 17 to 24 *chi*, or 3.93 to 5.52 meters wide, amply sufficient for movement of men, draft animals, and supplies. The upper widths were of import to military strategists who, as Needham and Yates remark, were concerned with the positioning of men and defensive engines.[120] Information gathering was further architecturally facilitated by the construction of lookout towers from which one could survey the external landscape.[121] Permission to access physical heights, a disposition allowing for more expansive survey, was the mark of social elevation, and its loss, a demotion.

Sensibilities about the transgressions of visually or physically surmounting walls are readily apparent in early Chinese texts, facilely traceable through the use of *kui* 窺, "to steal sight of" or "to surreptitiously peer at," used to describe when one intentionally transgresses visual boundaries, whether constructed or natural. Often the transgression is portrayed as violation, but sometimes, such as when committed by a ruler, "stealing

[118] *Liji*, "Quli" 曲禮: "When one has ascended the wall of a city, he should not point, nor call out" 登城不指，城上不呼. James Legge explains in a footnote that such conduct would cause the person to be made "an object of general observation." *Li Chi: Book of Rites*, trans. James Legge (New York: Oxford University Press, 1885), 1:70 and note 5. Yet according to Zheng Xuan 鄭玄, it is because such distracts and confuses people (*wei huo ren* 為惑人), which, given the general reason for pointing and shouting at the top of a wall, would suggest it could cause alarm. *Liji jijie*, 1.25.

[119] *Jiuzhang suanshu*, "Shang gong" 商功, j. 5, Zhang Cang 張蒼 (漢), *Jiuzhang suanshu* 九章算數 (Chongqing: Chongqing daxue chubanshe, 2006), 120. Joseph Needham and Robin D. S. Yates, *Science and Civilisation in China*, vol. 5, *Chemistry and Chemical Technology*, pt. 6, *Military Technology: Missiles and Sieges* (New York: Cambridge University Press, 1994), 302.

[120] *Yinque shan Han mu zhu jian* 銀雀山漢墓竹簡 (Beijing: Wenwu chubanshe, 1985), 128, slip 796; Needham and Yates, *Science and Civilisation in China*, vol. 5, pt. 6, 307.

[121] Emperor Guangwu 光武帝 of the Latter Han once ascended to a wall tower to corroborate with his general, Deng Yu, what was portrayed on a map, castigating him for its inaccurate representation: 光武舍城樓上，披輿地圖，指示禹曰：「天下郡國如是，今始乃得其一。子前言以 吾慮天下不足定，何也？」 See *HHS* 16.600 and Joseph Needham and Ling Wang, *Science and Civilisation in China*, vol. 3, *Mathematics and the Sciences of the Heavens and the Earth* (New York: Cambridge University Press, 1959), 537. For details on the construction of towers in the premodern period, see Needham and Yates, *Science and Civilisation in China*, vol. 5, pt. 6, 373–398. The ancient Greek strategist Aineias the Tactician also recommended that cities under siege post daytime scouts "in front of the city, at an elevated point visible from as great a distance as possible." Aineias the Tactician, *How to Survive Under Siege*, trans. David Whitehead (New York: Oxford University Press, 1990), 50.

sight" is implicitly sanctioned. In the *Xunzi*, a ruler's limited comprehension of the problems of his realm is analogized with the limitations of his senses. These limitations would naturally affect his accurate perception of any spatial representations, because of which the ruler would need to depend on substitutes – bluntly, on spies – to act as his eyes and ears: "The ruler's favorites and members of his immediate circle are the gates and windows by which he [steals sight of] what is far away and receives the masses."[122] Nevertheless, the monarch's sanctioned prerogative of "stealing sight" is a rare exception to the rule, in the service of an accepted dominance. More commonly, as with the *Mengzi*'s disapproving description of men and women boring holes through walls to visually evaluate each other's physical attributes before marriage, peering through walls was in violation of established norms and was to be punished.[123] A passage from the *Analects* also admits that the vision gained into a private compound could reveal secrets of both religious and political significance, insinuating the comprehensibility, even the advantage, of their protection and selective dissemination.[124]

Visual prohibitions against surreptitious gazing also blocked the ocular entrance of enemies, such as the Xiongnu, contributing stoutly to the establishment of sovereign boundaries. As Yang Xiong 揚雄 states in his remonstrance to Emperor Jing 景 of Han, "Because of the power of the First August Emperor of Qin and the fearsomeness of [his general,] Meng Tian, with his more than forty thousand armored infantry, [the Xiongnu]

---

[122] *Xunzi*, "Jun dao" 君道: 便嬖左右者，人主之所以窺遠收眾之門戶牖鄉也. Wang Xianqian 王先謙, ed. *Xunzi jijie* 荀子集解 (Beijing: Zhonghua shuju, 1997), 1:244; *Xunzi: The Complete Text*, trans. Eric L. Hutton (Princeton, NJ: Princeton University Press, 2014), 130.

[123] "But those who do not wait for the command of their parents or the words of a matchmaker and instead bore holes through walls to peep at one another and jump over fences to run off together are despised by parents and everyone else in their state" 不待父母之命、媒妁之言，鑽穴隙相窺，踰牆相從，則父母國人皆賤之. "Teng wen gong xia" 滕文公下; *Mengzi zhengyi*, 1:426; *Mengzi, with Selections from Traditional Commentaries*, 3B4.3, 79.

[124] *Lunyu*, "Zi zhang" 子張, 19.23: "Zigong replied, 'Let us take a perimeter wall as an analogy. My wall is shoulder high, so one can [steal sight] of the charm of the buildings inside. The Master's wall, on the other hand, is massive, rising some twenty or thirty feet in the air. Without gaining entry through the gate, one cannot see the magnificence of the ancestral temple or the lavishness of the estate inside" 子貢曰：「譬之宮牆，賜之牆也及肩，窺見室家之好。夫子之牆數仞，不得其門而入，不見宗廟之美，百官之富。」 *Lunyu jijie* 論語集解 (Beijing: Zhonghua shuju, 2010), 1:1337; *The Analects of Confucius: A Philosophical Translation*, trans. Roger T. Ames and Henry Rosemont Jr. (New York: Ballantine Books, 1998), 223–224. Translation modified. For a brief discussion of the wall as a trope as an obstruction to knowledge, see A. C. Graham, *Later Mohist Logic, Ethics and Science* (Hong Kong: Chinese University of Hong Kong, 2003), 223–224.

did not dare peer (*kui* 窺) across the western section of the [Yellow River] and thus [Meng Tian] built the Great Wall to delineate a border (*jie zhi* 界之)."[125] If this remark is any indication, the Wall's importance was not simply as a defensive (or offensive) physical obstacle but also as obstruction to the forbidden gaze, and thus to unsanctioned knowledge. Providing a remarkably reduced representation of physical space, the transgressive potency of the gaze is most abstractly and broadly at issue in the use of the map.

Chapter Summary

With the territorial markings of the ancient Chinese state more zonal than lineal, discussions of sovereign borders must rely upon an analysis of the breadth of applied politico-legal or military force. But the representation of such is not inevitably secular; indeed, it requires a keen appreciation of ritualized markers and activities that effectively claim an area as part of a sovereign domain. The topography of the ancient state was no disenchanted breadth; sovereign possession was sanctified. Ritualized actions of its inhabitants were that which reinforced, or weakened, the sovereign's claims.

Abstract representations of borders and boundaries, maps were assertions of interest in the area. However, given the zonal conceptualization of early Chinese space, their lines are somewhat deceptive. Indeed, if work on early Roman cartographic thinking is any indication, it is not clear how consistently three-dimensional exploratory visualizations were. Rather, the maps seem more driven by two-dimensional, directional frameworks. A variable, moving perspective appeared to have influenced the whole conceptualization of lived, and thus possessed, space. Passing beyond any sovereign boundary had ritualized signifiers. These boundaries, however, should not be conflated with militarized structures, such as walls. From both literary and excavated evidence, it is still very unclear exactly how definitive of any possessive boundary early Chinese walls were. The sovereign asserted a supervenient ritualized memorialization, using *feng*-type markers, perhaps inclusive of walls. Boundary walls or markers not

---

[125] 以秦始皇之彊，蒙恬之威，帶甲四十餘萬，然不敢窺西河，乃築長城以界之 (*HS* 94B. 3813). A similar visual threat is recorded in the *Zhanguoce*: "Ch'in greatly desires to attack Han in order to move east and be able to [peer] into the palaces of Chou" 秦之欲伐韓，以東窺周室. *Zhanguoce*, "Huo wei Han wang" 或謂韓王; He Jianzhang 何建章, ed., *Zhanguoce zhushi* 戰國策注釋 (Beijing: Zhonghua shuju, 1990), 1:1050; *Chan-Kuo Ts'e*, trans. James I. Crump (New York: Oxford University Press, 1970), 493, translation modified.

only affirmed sovereign power, they were vital knowledge platforms, as well as prominent sites of sacrifice to indigenous local or regional entities, through which such entities were incorporated into the over-arching sovereign space. Their elevation brought with them the power of the surveying gaze, crucial to any sense of mapping.

2 The Visual Modeling of Space in Text and Map

Map as a Diagram of Shadows

In the ancient world, there is a definitional ambiguity behind any notion of map. Many ancient languages had no single word for what we now call a map. The word "map" itself derives from the Late Latin *mappa*, meaning "a cloth." In many European languages, the word for "map" derives from the Late Latin *carta*, a formal document. Further etymological obscurities in words translatable as "map" come from the various nuances attributed to each. In the medieval and Renaissance periods, "it was common to use words such as 'picture' or 'description' for what we would today call a map."[1] The word for "map" in Indian languages, according to J. B. Harley and David Woodward, derives from the Arabic *napshah*, "but other meanings attached to it include picture, general description, and even official report." Harley and Woodward also correctly note that, in Chinese, *tu* can mean "a drawing or diagram of any kind."[2]

It is unclear what exactly the difference between a terrestrial map and a landscape was in the ancient world. For Harley and Woodward, maps can be defined as "graphic representations that facilitate a spatial understanding of things, concepts, conditions, processes, or events in the human world."[3] But this definition in itself does not pose any sure criterion by which we could distinguish landscapes from maps in the ancient world. As Denis Cosgrove maintains, "a sharp distinction between chorographic mapping [i.e., of discrete places] and landscape painting is historically impossible to make. Yet there are compositional and technical features of chorographic maps that direct vision beyond the accidental and specific towards spatial harmonies and order, whether intrinsic or adventitious."[4]

---

[1] J. B. Harley and David Woodward, eds., *The History of Cartography*, vol. 1, *Cartography in Prehistoric, Ancient, and Medieval Europe and the Mediterranean* (Chicago: University of Chicago Press, 1987), xvi.
[2] Harley and Woodward, *History of Cartography*, 1:xvi, n7.   [3] Ibid., 1:xvi.
[4] Denis Cosgrove, *Geography and Vision: Seeing, Imagining and Representing the World* (New York: I. B. Tauris, 2008), 24.

A crucial question will be: "how far was the resemblance with the visible world to be pursued by [early mappers], and by what means?"[5] We can further ask: How much concern with accuracy is there with mapmaking? What does this say about the divide between the mechanical/functional and the aesthetic *tu*, or diagram? Do the aesthetic norms of *hua* 劃, of "painting" broadly speaking, apply to *tu*? What can be made accurate? What *is* made accurate? What is preserved and what is left out? Do these norms and decisions apply to all representational *tu*? Do early mappers worry about realism in every form of representational *tu*, equally? Were *tu*/maps conceived in the pre-Han and Han periods as providing access to a composite, secret knowledge, to a type of reason, or merely to a mode of political action? Could we contend that early maps were, in part, symbolic reenactments of previous actions, whether ritual or physical? How was the power of the *tu*/map conceived? Could mapping have been conceived as a secretive, potentially transgressive activity?

As discussed in Chapter 1, vertical elevation, provided by walls, and more abstractly, maps, affords transgressions of protected space, of defended, defensible space, an invasive terrestrial gaze (akin to an invasive personal one),[6] requiring the bird's-eye view; it has everything to do with control and access to movement. Without a privileged height, captured in the surveying mapped viewing, one cannot take full advantage of what lies within a protected area. And the more valuable the interior of a protected zone, the more likely it will be defended against visual probing. With early Chinese maps, we can ask how much do we feel, as Svetlana Alpers felt with Goltzius's panoramic landscapes, "that we are situated apart from the land, but with a privileged view ... the curious mixture of distance preserved and access gained"?[7]

Thongchai Winichakul writes of the precedence of the conceptual arbitration of space over its physical description in the construction of historical maps of Siam. In the history of Siam, the map was "a model *for* rather than a model *of*, what it purported to represent."[8] To comprehend the function of the map, we thus must first attempt to divine what it

---

[5] Lucia Nuti, "Mapping Places: Chorography and Vision in the Renaissance," in *Mappings*, ed. Denis E. Cosgrove (London: Reaktion Books, 1999), 91. A similar question could be posed as the one Christian Jacob posed in reference to Robert Louis Stevenson's map of Treasure Island, first published in *Treasure Island* in 1884, is – how does one create a world ... and make it credible? What features of the map are necessary to map it credibly? Jacob, *Sovereign Map*, figure 41.

[6] See Michael Nylan, "Beliefs about Social Seeing: Hiddenness (wei 微) and Visibility in Classical-era China," in *The Rhetoric of Hiddenness in Traditional Chinese Culture*, ed. Paula Varsano (Albany: State University of New York Press, 2016), nn14–15.

[7] Alpers, *Art of Describing*, 141–142.

[8] Winichakul, *Siam Mapped*, 130. Italics mine. Winichakul continues: "A map was not a transparent medium between human beings and space. It was an active mediator ... all

attempts to model, and how that model was meant to be used, how it was meant to be read. A perfectly effective map, the ideal map, is "transparent because it is a signified without a signifier. It vanishes in the visual and intellectual operation that unfolds its content . . . The map is not an object but a function."[9] But this, of course, is merely an ideal. All constructed maps reveal and blind simultaneously; their construction is naturally driven by preferential choices. Many current evaluations of historical maps by historians of Chinese cartography aim to excavate their material grist – the location of the objects in the maps, and thereby their truth value, their ostensible "reality." Yet these analyses inevitably impose how maps are currently read and constructed, a construction aspiring to a static, unmoving organization with the greatest merit placed on accuracy, onto maps that were constructed and read under extremely different auspices. Christian Jacob outlines the genesis of this hermeneutic error:

a toponymic and geographical knowledge is mobilized before any attention is drawn to an abstract disposition of lines, forms, colors, and inscriptions. And yet, paradoxically, what defines the map is the mediation of representation, a mediation that is a signifier with its own codes and conventions (symbolization, schematization, miniaturization, colors, nomenclature, vertical overview, etc.). Such representation is a patient labor of construction, technical gestures, graphic conventions, and different kinds of visual artifice. The map generates an illusion of which it is itself the first victim, an illusion whose nature Franco Farinelli has so tersely defined: "The history of geography is the history of the confusion between the model and the reality."[10]

Fundamental to any analysis of the visual modeling of physical space is the recognition that maps are embedded in their cultural and historical confines. To understand how the map was to have been used, it is important to articulate as far as possible the conventions underlying its construction.

In early China, the notion of a map was linked to the material inscription of a visual image, which was, in some regard, reflective of an abstract delineative overview of a physical space. However, this overview was not thereby equatable with a static, comprehensive overview, but was affected, as will be discussed later, by the dynamic use and appropriation of space. The aim of early Chinese maps, as is generally the case with most maps, was not so much to make the geophysical objects – such as mountains, rivers, and towns – pictorially visible. Rather, maps were keyed to the organization and use behind them, and they rendered legible

---

the requisites of the map of a nation had not been given in premodern Siam and thus had to be created to meet the demands of a map."
[9] Jacob, *Sovereign Map*, 11.   [10] Ibid., 12.

functional truths difficult or impossible to perceive without the pictorial organization of a map. As Jacob observes, "A map is defined less by its object than by the organization and the new visibility it imposes on this object: reticulation, spatial divisions, and complex structures resulting from the juxtaposition of its constituent parts or from their imbrication."[11] The inscribed pictorialization represented the incomplete, sometimes intentionally distorted "shadows," the images, of the things themselves. Thus, the map was really a useful fiction, a "noble lie," assisting the reader to see what useful function lay behind their situation or arrangement.[12] Mapping images, akin to Plato's notion of modeling shadows, "directly express principles of action that flow from [reasoned] beliefs."[13] The shadows, the images of the map assist in rendering its concepts visible. However, it must be stressed that the diagrammatic techniques of the map are, like mathematical diagrams, for "conveying, *not finding*, abstract concepts."[14] By reading the map, abstract possibilities of future action become manifest.

The shadows that lie behind the composition of an ancient map are those of memory. While memory may, in the form of faulty recollection, be passively deceptive, it can more actively deceive. Memory can be misleadingly rendered or reordered, distorted to suit the purposes of the map's composer or its end user. Indeed, the cartographic endeavor itself recursively contributes to an enforced reordering or even the erasure of memory. Through the act of mapping, old lived memories can be reordered or entirely crushed under the needs of current strategic concerns. Describing memory is not simply an objective, passive activity but involves prescriptive, active agendas. Referenced denotation of objects, the relative placements and sizes of objects signify their salience and insinuate distortion. No map is thus truly lived or experienced as

---

[11] Jacob, "Mapping in the Mind," 12.

[12] In these abstract concerns about the connection of a mapped representation to its functional reality, the study of Plato could be of assistance. As Danielle Allen relates, "useful fictions" or "serviceable lies" were defined by the Socrates of Plato's *Republic* as "lies that are assimilated to the truth as much as possible ... and, through proximity to the truth, foster in hearers and readers an assimilation of correct principles and rules for action ... The consequences of believing the serviceable lie should look very nearly identical to the consequences of knowing the truth." Danielle Allen, *Why Plato Wrote* (Chichester, UK: Wiley-Blackwell, 2013), 66.

[13] Allen, *Why Plato Wrote*, 58.

[14] Ibid., 52. Italics mine. Indeed, maps share some similarity with abstract conceptual art. Though early Chinese maps are not iconographic works – not works surfeit with symbolism – and not surreal signages, they are abstractions, albeit realist. Yet we must ask: What do they represent? Do they represent merely the surface, the physical phenomenon, uncluttered and readily accessible? Can scientific diagrams be treatable as art? Are they composed only with an eye toward their utility without any aesthetic considerations at all impacting their design?

represented. As in personal memory, some facets are conspicuous, others are not.

That which features on the map is therefore connected with not only the memorials, physical and written, of contemporary travelers but also the memorialized ordering of past travels, whether of local commoners or sovereign officials, among others. This often ritualized ordering of geography, of movement and action, is not necessarily just human; it could be additionally informed by location and the spatial efficacies of spiritual powers. These movements carried both a moral force and, in the assertion of the connection between human and spiritual powers, a politico-legal one. Travel, mapped or not, could become lines of sovereign efficacy, with private and public memory being fused together in the map. Even ethnographic sight, seeing the tribal relationships that influenced a sense of sovereignty was a seeing in memory, with memorialized associations.

Yet for a map to have been functional, it could not have simply been an imitation of any reality. It had to be both metaphysically, logically sound, reasonable in its arrangement, and practically efficacious. Indeed, maps are only as sound as they are efficacious, that is, as the user *needs* them to be. The mapped image is one that captures past and present action to mold future action. In sum, maps not only illustrate abstract truths through the representation of concrete particulars but recommend possibilities of future action. These definientia are at the root of the distinction between landscapes and maps. Landscapes need neither to be reasonable in their arrangement nor to be pragmatically efficacious. Their functionality is not necessarily in their use or application to questions pertaining to the use and manipulation of physical space. Their art, like that of maps, may have associations with the bodily use of space, but theirs is not necessarily put to any larger strategic purpose, as maps generally are. Both, however, are usually inscribed or painted representations; thus any analysis of maps can derive some measure of benefit, as Jacob insisted, from an examination of their aesthetic conventions. But before we evaluate the aesthetic conventions of early Chinese maps, we need to better grasp the conceptual employment of the early Chinese notion of *tu* and to what extent accuracy might have influenced the composition and functionality of a map.

Conceptual Definition of *Tu*

The most basic conceptual operations that characterize the use of land are those that divide or combine segments of it, employing sight to construct visualized geometry of defined space or using mental arithmetic to measure out numerically articulated area. In the early legends of Yu, China's primeval civil engineer,[15] he is described as "spreading the earth," dividing the earth, separating the lands and defining the nine provinces. Moving along the mountains, he cut down trees, and, with a possible spiritually sovereign reclaiming of these territories from ancient indigenous natural powers – the removal of trees from mountains reminiscent of the connection between trees and the establishment of the mounded *feng* borders – created channels to redirect floodwaters and set the arrangement of the prominent mountains and major rivers. With this physical, ritualized reorganization of spiritually potent natural boundaries, Yu defined the borders between the provinces.[16] In the *Shanhaijing* 山海經 (*The Classic of Mountains and Seas*), Yu orders his assistants Da Zhang 大章 and Shu Hai 豎亥 to "pace out the size of the world," with Shu Hai holding the counting-rods in his right hand and pointing to the north of Green Mound with his left.[17] This pacing out, peripatetically mapping out the land, mirrored a corresponding pacing or mapping out of the celestial sphere.[18] As Richard Smith notes, in the early imperial period, more common than

---

[15] According to certain texts, Yu was assigned the office of the *sikong* 司空, the civil engineer, "Minister of Works," by Shun. See *SJ* 1.38: 舜謂四嶽曰：「有能奮庸美堯之事者，使居官相事？」皆曰：「伯禹為司空，可美帝功。」舜曰：「嗟，然！禹，汝平水土，維是勉哉。」

[16] 禹敷土，隨山刊木，奠高山大川. See "Yugong" 禹貢 ("The levies of Yu"), *Shangshu*; in Li Xueqin 李學勤, ed., *Shangshu zhengyi* 尚書正義 (Beijing: Beijing daxue chubanshe, 1999), 133–134. Similar statements can also be seen in the "Rongchengshi" 容成氏 manuscript. Following Sarah Allan's translation: "Yu then established regions and walled settlements in accordance with the (topography) of the mountain ranges and flat marshes, and caused them to be populated and flourish" 禹乃因山陵平隰之可邦邑 (slip 18). Sarah Allan, *Buried Ideas: Legends of Abdication and Ideal Government in Early Chinese Bamboo-Slip Manuscripts* (Albany: State University of New York Press, 2015), 207–208. In early Greek mythology, mountains and rivers often are the locations of the monstrous, the wild and untamed. In Babylonian and early Greek myths, "a young warrior-god who represents harmony and order as well as nationhood goes forth to battle a 'chaos-monster' that threatens the world order." Debbie Felton, "Rejecting and Embracing the Monstrous in Ancient Greece and Rome," in *The Ashgate Research Companion to Monsters and the Monstrous*, ed. Asa Simon Mittman and Peter Dendle (Burlington, VT: Ashgate, 2012), 107. With the very natural forces unleashed in the mountains and rivers themselves untamed and "monstrous," it would be not unreasonable to argue that Yu is playing a somewhat similar role to the early Greek and Babylonian warrior-gods.

[17] *Shanhaijing*, j.9: 帝命豎亥步，自東極至于西極，五億十選[萬]九千八百步。豎亥右手把算，左手指青丘北。一曰禹令豎亥。一曰五億十萬九千八百步. *Shanhaijing* 山海经, comp. Fang Tao 方韜 (Beijing: Zhonghua shuju, 2011), 250. In Anne Birrell's translation: "The great god commanded Youth Dozen [Shu Hai] to pace out [*bu* 步] the distance from the East Pole to the West Pole. It came to 5,109,800 paces. Youth Dozen held a calculating device in his right hand and pointed with his left hand to the north of Green Mound. One author says that it was Yü who ordered Youth Dozen to do this, and that the figure came to 5,109,800 paces." *The Classic of Mountains and Seas*, trans. Anne Birrell (London: Penguin Books, 1999), 128.

[18] In his article on the Han cosmic boards, Donald Harper mentions a shamanistic dance, "Pacing the Mainstay" (*bu gang* 步綱), which was "a tantric onestep along the Big

religiously grounded and externally inspired maps were indigenous depictions of the cosmological relationship perceived by the Chinese between earthly forms and heavenly images. This pervasive idea of physical and metaphysical correlations, derived from the hallowed *Yijing* ..., had many manifestations in traditional China. One of the most widespread was the theory of *fenye* 分野 (field allocation). According to this tenaciously held world-view, each major geographical area of China had a corresponding celestial "field" in which astronomical events served as portents for earthly administrators. As the Han scholar Zhang Heng put the matter: "[Heavenly bodies] are scattered in confused arrangement, but every one of them has its own distant connections ...."[19]

Dipper," a dance that had been assimilated with the older Pace of Yu, a shamanistic dance preserved in Zhou literature. In essence, the sky was "mapped" through dance for meditative and magical purposes. See Donald J. Harper, "The Han Cosmic Board (*Shih*)," *Early China* 4 (1978), 5. Filippo Marsili also makes mention that, in the "Book of Astronomy" in Sima Qian's *Records*, the Northern Dipper is "associated with the emperor's chariot and patrolling expeditions (*xunshou* 巡狩)." Filippo Marsili, *Heaven Is Empty: A Cross-Cultural Approach to "Religion" and Empire in Ancient China* (Albany: State University of New York Press, 2018), 197. Both terrestrial and celestial maps were magical objects possessed of extraordinary potency. As Michael Lackner states about *tu* more generally, "Durch die Vorstellung, der Erhalt von *t'u* sei identisch mit der Zuweisung des himmlischen Mandats sowie durch die gesamte in den mythischen Bereich verlegte Offenbarungsgeschichte der *t'u*, schließlich noch durch das große Gewicht divinatorischer Anteile, besitzen diese zusätzlich eine magische Qualität." Michael Lackner, "Zur 'Verplanung' des Denkens am Beispiel der t'u," in *Lebenswelt und Weltanschauung im frühneuzeitlichen China*, ed. Helwig Schmidt-Glintzer (Stuttgart: Steiner Verlag, 1990), 139. Physically "measuring" or "pacing out" a map's schema appears to have been a means to access its powers. The correspondence between the celestial and terrestrial spheres was, both mathematically and symbolically, also the basis for Ptolemy's geographic calculations: "In geography one must contemplate the shape and extent of the whole earth, and also its position under the heavens, in order rightly to state what are the size and nature of the known part, and under what parallels of the celestial sphere the individual places are located, for so one will be able to discuss the length of its days and nights, the fixed stars which are overhead, the stars which always move above the horizon, and those which never rise above the horizon; in short all information included in an account of our habitations." Georgia L. Irby-Massie and Paul T. Keyser, *Greek Science of the Hellenistic Era* (New York: Routledge, 2002), 145. The regularities of geography were just those involving the patterns of the heavens, as reflected in the human intelligence's "highest and most exquisite contemplation (*theôria*), mathematics." These statements of Ptolemy suggest intimations of the almost mystical Pythagorean fascination with the movements of the celestial sphere. As Irby-Massie and Keyser note, Pilolaus of Kroton, a follower of Pythagorean teachings, around 420 BCE "either introduced or popularized the notion that the earth and the *kosmos* were shaped as and harmonized by the sphere." Clearly the idea that the celestial sphere's regularities could reveal the form of the terrestrial sphere was enduringly influential. See Irby-Massie and Keyser, *Greek Science of the Hellenistic Era*, 49. For the Pythagorean notions on the intimate connection between the structures of mathematics and the patterns of the heavenly spheres, see "Metaphysics," in *The Complete Works of Aristotle*, vol. 2, ed. Jonathan Barnes (Princeton, NJ: Princeton University Press, 1984), 985b23–986a12.

[19] Richard J. Smith, *Chinese Maps: Images of "All Under Heaven"* (New York: Oxford University Press, 1996), 36–37. According to Donald Harper's article about two diagrams in Mawangdui tomb three, their mapping function was both physical and metaphysical. See Donald J. Harper, "Communication by Design: Two Silk Manuscripts of

Though pacing is, in this ambitious cosmological context, connected with shamanistic activities or quasi-mystical associations, in many other texts, it is clear that an actual quotidian "pacing out" of physical space was the standard means by which geographical features were measured and recorded.[20] Indeed, as I have underscored, the variable perspective so common in imperial Chinese maps serves as an analogue to the viewpoint of the traveler, connecting it to the lived experience on different areas and strata of the map. Such would be in keeping with the frequently observed commonality of well-traveled or structurally important areas being more accurately depicted than more distant areas.[21] But this "pacing out" involved in the creation of a map or diagram also signals a personal or ritual investiture, as insinuated by Confucius's famous bemoaning the lack of appearance of a diagram (*tu*) from the Yellow River, which, under traditional interpretations, was a sign that a sage king had not yet appeared.[22]

In the *Shiming* 釋名 (*Explicating Names*, ca. 200 CE), Wolfgang Behr points out, *tu*, which relates to mapping or designing a plan, is glossed by

Diagrams (*tu*) from Mawangdui Tomb Three," in *Graphics and Texts in the Production of Textual Knowledge in China: The Warp and the Weft*, ed. Francesca Bray and Vera Dorofeeva-Lichtmann (Leiden: Brill, 2007), 125.

[20] As Dorofeeva-Lichtmann argues, the schematic representations of the Nine Provinces, as well as their representation as topographical maps "show their relative dispositions in space and how their arrangement constitutes the general framework of the civilized world," which "in turn highlights the sequence of their foundation by Yu." The "pace" of Yu, his stepwise process of marking out of territory is indicative of the importance of the movement of a sovereign, or his representatives, through space and that this movement marks out what is civilized, separable from the uncivilized, the internal sovereign from the external wilds. See Vera V. Dorofeeva-Lichtmann, "Ritual Practices for Constructing Terrestrial Space (Warring States–Early Han)," in *Early Chinese Religion, Part One: Shang Through Han (1250 BC–220 AD)*, ed. John Lagerway and Marc Kalinowski (Leiden: Brill, 2009), 622. Hilde De Weerdt also points out, "'maps of "The Tribute of Yu"' and 'maps tracing the tracks of Yu' became generic names for maps of the empire." See Hilde De Weerdt, "Maps and Memory: Readings of Cartography in Twelfth- and Thirteenth-Century Song China," *Imago Mundi* 61, no. 2 (2009), 150. In the thirteenth-century encyclopedia by Zhang Ruyu 章如愚, *Qunshu kaosuo* 群書考索 [Investigations into multitudes of books], Zhang correlated jurisdictions to the constellations. See Hilde De Weerdt, "The Cultural Logics of Map Reading: Text, Time, and Space in the Printed Maps of the Song Empire," in *Knowledge and Text Production in an Age of Print: China, 900–1400*, ed. Lucille Chia and Hilde De Weerdt (Leiden: Brill, 2011), 264–265; *Qunshu kaosuo*, qianji, 59.1a.

[21] This is the case with not only secular maps but also those with religious aims. Hong Key Yoon, for instance, observes in geomantic maps that "the expression of landform patterns and scales are more accurate near [auspicious places] and the accuracy diminishes quickly in places distant from a geomancy cave on the map." Hong Key Yoon, "The Expression of Landforms in Chinese Geomantic Maps," *Cartographic Journal* 29 (1992), 13.

[22] 子曰：「鳳鳥不至，河不出圖，吾已矣夫！」 See *Lunyu*, "Zi Han" 子罕; in *Lunyu jijie*, 2:588–590.

du 度, **daas*, a measure of length, limit or bounds. The lemma head character for *tu* 圖, *tu* 土, meaning "to measure, to lay out," is attested in the *Zhouli*, in the commentaries of which it is usually analyzed as a loan for *duo* 度<*dak<*ddak, "to measure."[23] Behr further elaborates that, judging against its word family background, *tu* 圖 emerges "as an abstract concept 'position', which had a material counterpart, 'chart, map' (a 'positioner', so to speak) in early investiture inscriptions, and served as root for a various [*sic*] verbal activities involving the manipulation and ordering of objects in space."[24] In essence, defined by the *Shiming*, *tu* is a medium of calculation and prediction. In the *Shuowen jiezi* 說文解字 (*Explaining Graphs and Analyzing Characters*, ca. 100 CE, hereafter "*Shuowen*"), however, the character is analyzed into an "enclosure" component and the character *bi* 啚, which is extrapolated to suggest that the process of creating a plan, and any diagrammatic expression of it, is difficult and must be handled with care, in full anticipation of unforeseen complications.[25] Indeed, the enclosure around *bi*, together forming the character *tu*, "coreferential with the top part of *yi* 邑," iconically signifies a walled city, "according to a widespread paleographic consensus."[26]

Among more modern archaeologically rooted explanations, Bernhard Karlgren interprets *tu* as a noun, to refer to a physical drawing or map, or a verb with its root in planning or calculating. Nevertheless, as Karlgren denotes with two Zhou inscriptional forms of the graph, at least some of its early forms are pictographs, indicating the location of a field.[27] The eminent paleographer Qiu Xigui classifies *tu* as a "syssemantograph," meaning a graph "combining two or more semantic symbols in order to express a meaning independent of these semantic symbols."[28] According to Qiu, *tu* was originally written simply as *bi* 啚, in both its bone and seal script forms, meaning not so much a field as the "area around a city." *Bi* 啚 is the protoform of *bi* 鄙, which, Qiu notes, are incorrectly separated in the *Shuowen*. In early China, "the area on all sides of a city was called *bi* 鄙; the people living in this area were mainly engaged in agricultural

---

[23] Wolfgang Behr, "Placed into the Right Position: Etymological Notes on '*tú*' and Congeners," in *Graphics and Text in the Production of Technical Knowledge in China*, ed. Francesca Bray, Vera Dorofeeva-Lichtmann, and Georges Métailié (Leiden: Brill, 2007), 122–123.

[24] Behr, "Placed into the Right Position," 125.

[25] Florian C. Reiter, "Some Remarks on the Chinese Word *t'u* 'Chart, Plan, Design,'" *Oriens* 32 (1990), 315–316; *Shuowen jiezi*, 6B.277a (hereafter cited as "*Shuowen*").

[26] Behr, "Placed into the Right Position," 115.

[27] Reiter, "Some Remarks on the Chinese Word *t'u*," 316; Bernhard Karlgren, *Grammata Serica Recensa* (Stockholm: Museum of Far Eastern Antiquities, 1957), 36–37; Axel Schuessler, *A Dictionary of Early Zhou Chinese* (Honolulu: University of Hawaii Press, 1987), 616.

[28] Xigui Qiu, *Chinese Writing* (Berkeley, CA: Institute of East Asian Studies, 2000), 185.

production."[29] The graph, he asserts, consists of two elements, the top part of which is the graph denoting an area of land, the bottom of which is a protoform of *lin* 廩, a grain repository. Thus the *bi*, as Qiu analyzes it, should not be rendered as meaning something to do with the difficulty of creating a plan but with the plotting out of fields around a city.

In some regard, the original meaning of *tu*, as Qiu posits it, is closer to the *Shuowen*'s explication of *bi* 啚 and its cognate, *bi* 鄙, than of its explication of *tu*.[30] In the *Shuowen*, the simple form, *bi* 啚, is explicated as *se* 嗇, graphically derived, in part, from *lin* 㐭, defined as "receiving" or "taking in" (*shou* 受). *Se* 嗇 is definable as *se* 穡, "stored grain." The more complex form of *bi*, 鄙, is explicated in the *Shuowen* as five *zan* 酇, a *zan* being a unit of local government outside the royal domain, or, in Charles Hucker's translation, a "precinct."[31] Clearly, if its cognate relationships are any indication, *tu* is concerned with preparation and planning of definite spatial consequence. Maps were in some respect magical objects, endued with the power of foresight. Yet their spatial planning principle may not have had simply a secularly technical aspect, but also a ritual or cosmological one.[32]

From the historical record, there appears to be a keen interest among certain rulers in *tu*. Indeed, as Fan Lin underscores, map production and use were closely monitored by rulers and their officials because of the politically and militarily valuable territorial logic they revealed.[33] What *tu* in fact denote has much to do with how we can assess their functionality. For some scholars, such historical references to *tu* still very simply are what we would now deem "maps," with equivalent functionality and purpose: "The grandeur, expansionism, and cosmopolitan spirit of the Han period encouraged an interest in maps of both the Chinese empire and the larger world. Thus, for example, when Zhang Qian returned from his famous journeys to Central Asia in 126 BC, Emperor Wu consulted 'ancient maps and books'."[34] The function of textual travelogues and

[29] Qiu, *Chinese Writing*, 203.

[30] See Xu Shen 許慎, *Shuowen jiezi zhu* 說文解字注 (Shanghai: Shanghai guji chubanshe, 1988), 5.230, 6.277.

[31] Charles O. Hucker, *A Dictionary of Official Titles in Imperial China* (Stanford, CA: Stanford University Press, 1985), 516.

[32] "It is very likely that the object designated by *tú* had a ritual or cosmological, rather than a merely technical function in the Zhōu bronzes." Behr, "Placed into the Right Position," 116.

[33] Fan Lin, "Cartographic Empire: Production and Circulation of Maps and Mapmaking Knowledge in the Song Dynasty (960–1279)" (PhD diss., McGill University, 2014), 47–48.

[34] R. Smith, *Chinese Maps*, 25. The reference to Emperor Wu consulting "ancient maps and books" comes from the *Shiji*. See *SJ* 123.3173: 天子案古圖書. Before his ascension to the imperial throne, the first emperor of Han, Gaozu 高祖, while at war with the Qin, was also

maps were intertwined; for Michael Lackner, the image may just serve as a "short, compact way of reproducing the word."[35] Thus images are expressing something beyond the image, beyond the visual alone.

Toward the beginning of his treatise on maps, Joseph Needham maintains that *tu* covers "any kind of diagram or drawing, so that in cases where a book disappeared at an early time, it is not possible to be sure whether the *thu* which it was said to have had were really maps." He thereupon follows with a now troublingly antiquated, utterly unjustified suggestion "that the pictographic character of Chinese encouraged the idea of mapping."[36] Needham crudely divides premodern cartography into the rational and nonrational, "scientific, or quantitative, cartography" and "religious, or symbolic, cosmography," with the early imperial Chinese over their history being more committed to pursuing the former than their contemporary European counterparts.[37]

Even when we discount Needham's archaic characterization, a further complication in assessing the meaning and use of *tu* is that, in its terrestrial, as opposed to celestial, employment, it could refer either to what might be recognizable as a geographic map or a more abstract terrestrial scheme. Applied by Vera Dorofeeva-Lichtmann to her analysis of the *Shanhaijing*, a terrestrial scheme organizes a terrestrial surface according to a collection of structural principles: "symmetry and equilibration of constitutive elements, completeness of structure, prominent centrality, demarcation of the center and peripheral layers, and orientation to cardinal directions." A terrestrial scheme "conforms to a pattern which establishes a well-balanced hierarchy of space."[38] The earliest references to a "sub-class of 'conventional terrestrial representations'," *ditu* 地圖, according to Dorofeeva-Lichtmann, appear in the *Zhanguoce*, the *Zhouli*, and the *Guanzi*. Whether *ditu* referred specifically to geographic maps is not certain, for a comparison of its use to that of *tu* in the above texts, Dorofeeva-Lichtmann asserts, reveals no precise definitional distinction, with *di* often being omitted in constructions in which the referent appears to be a geographic map. Dorofeeva-Lichtmann concludes: "All this

---

said to have been interested in Qin *tu* and documents, for various reasons: to know the places where access for and obstruction to movement were, population numbers, and generally strong and weak areas, such as where commoners were suffering. See *SJ* 53.2014. Emperor Guangwu of the Later Han was also cited to have more specifically consulted (*an* 案) *ditu*. *HHS* 10A.410: 十五年，帝案地圖.

[35] Michael Lackner, "Diagrams as an Architecture by Means of Words: The *Yanji tu*," in *Graphics and Text in the Production of Technical Knowledge in China*, ed. Francesca Bray, Vera Dorofeeva-Lichtmann, and Georges Métailié (Leiden: Brill, 2007), 353.

[36] Needham and Wang, *Science and Civilisation in China*, vol. 3, 498.   [37] Ibid., 500.

[38] Vera V. Dorofeeva-Lichtmann, "Conception of Terrestrial Organization in the *Shan hai jing*," *Bulletin de l'École française d'Extrême-Orient* 82 (1995), 62.

indicates that if there were attempts to distinguish maps from schemes, this was effectuated not earlier than the end of the 1st millenium B.C. In any case, the difference between maps and schemes was not regarded as significant in Chinese thought and was not rigidly determined."[39]

Not surprisingly, the basic secular purposes of early Chinese maps largely transcend not only temporal but cultural boundaries. Analogues may be found in Hellenistic sources, for example. In the fragment of the geographical survey attributed to Skumnos of Chios, dated to around 85 BCE, Skumnos expounds on the geography of Europe, offering rough distances between recognizable places and landmarks, locations invariably described relative to others, with the addition of a simple cardinal orientation, and often in terms of travel times as opposed to measured distances. Beyond such functional elements, the survey expounds on those features pertinent to human settlement – breeds of domesticated animals, available metals, fresh water sources, weather patterns, and the characteristics of the denizens of the area, often represented in a jaundiced, unflattering light.[40]

Those aspects that Skumnos underscores also accord quite closely with those in the geography composed by Strabo,[41] or any number of other ancient Greek geographical descriptions. Like Chinese maps (or almost any map, even current ones), reliability decreases with distance from inhabited areas, as Strabo himself complained of the specifics offered by Putheas about Thoulê.[42] Jacob points out that though Strabo was interested in how to draw small-area, chorographic maps, going so far as to copy instructions about how to draw them, his *Geography* is "a literary description of the world, not a map, and this description relies on traditional patterns: catalogues of place names, terrestrial or maritime itineraries." Strabo's text thus is "a literary geography that did not rely at all on map-making but on the compilation of a library."[43] Only when terrestrial

---

[39] Dorofeeva-Lichtmann, "Conception of Terrestrial Organization in the *Shan hai jing*," 62n26.

[40] Irby-Massie and Keyser, *Greek Science of the Hellenistic Era*, 127–128.

[41] Ibid., 133–134.

[42] Associatedly, monstrous exaggerations also increase with distance. With the ancient Greeks, for instance, the farther away, the more disfigured the described ethnicities, such as those in Libya and India. Debbie Felton also mentions that "Herodotus often matches his increasingly uncertain information with increasing distance from the Graeco-centric world." Felton, "Rejecting and Embracing the Monstrous in Ancient Greece and Rome," 123n85.

[43] Jacob, "Mapping in the Mind," 26. Greg Woolf deems most of what was in Strabo's geography "too imprecise or of limited relevance, either to soldiers or traders. At best it reflects a general sense that conquest and trade were among the uses that might be made of alien territory." Greg Woolf, *Tales of the Barbarians: Ethnography and Empire in the Roman West* (Malden, MA: Wiley-Blackwell, 2011), 86.

locations are verified mathematically, Strabo posits, with reference to celestial positions, are the locations reliable.[44]

With Heron and Ptolemy, both of Alexandria of the first to second century CE, mathematical geography is introduced. In modern scholarship, it is to this brand of geographer that the celebrated Jin dynasty cartographer Pei Xiu 裴秀 (224–271 CE) is repeatedly compared. Both Heron and Ptolemy endeavored to plot terrestrial locations in relation to celestial positions and phenomena. Heron, for instance, ascertained longitude using Hipparchos's calculations of the lunar eclipse, a method also known to Ptolemy.[45] In their geographical exegeses, we thus see attention directed away from anthropocentric details largely relating to settlement or travel toward impersonal calculations using celestial data. Accurate calculations, still specifically couched in terms of travel, become the major concern, with geometric analysis as the tool.

For Ptolemy, mathematical calculations are the province of geography, in contrast to earlier chorographic representations, such as those of Strabo and Skumnos. According to Ptolemy, geography "is a representation in picture of the whole known world together with the phenomena which are contained therein." Small-area, chorographic maps, by contrast, select "certain places from the whole to treat by themselves more fully, even dealing with the smallest details, such as harbors, villages, districts, tributaries, and such like."[46] According to Needham, like Ptolemy, Pei Xiu was interested in mathematical geography, yet his writings also evidence some concern with cultural features. However, Pei Xiu's compositional guidelines did not appear to influence the constitution of most imperial Chinese maps. Even after the arrival of Western surveying techniques brought to China in the Qing dynasty by the Jesuit priests, Chinese maps remained, to use Ptolemy's contrast, quite chorographic in character.

In both early Chinese landscape painting and mapmaking, the representation of space "changed with vantage point and time," and, consequently, "no abstract geometrical system governed space, and points within it were not definable or delimitable in any absolute terms."[47] By

---

[44] Irby-Massie and Keyser, *Greek Science of the Hellenistic Era*, 133.   [45] Ibid., 136.
[46] Ibid., 145.
[47] Cordell Yee, "Cartography in China," in *The History of Cartography*, vol. 2, bk. 2, *Cartography in the Traditional East and Southeast Asian Societies*, ed. J. B. Harley and David Woodward (Chicago: University of Chicago Press, 1995), 144. Michael Sullivan's work reinforces this: He notes that landscapes on early Chinese painted lacquer objects have a continuous, shifting point of view, with no attempt at any true single standpoint. This continuous, shifting point of view "is to be a characteristic of all later landscape painting." In late Zhou art, he observes, "successive planes are simply placed one above

contrast, in the post-Renaissance European perspective, space becomes static, bounded, measurable, as particulate, made up of a coordinate system of points, "each of which has its own discrete identity and can be treated objectively from a single vantage point."[48] Most premodern imperial maps – even perhaps the map offered to the Qin emperor by Jing Ke 荊軻 – were largely meant to diagram the location of human and natural resources, transportation avenues, and natural boundaries preventing or abetting movement, such as mountains and riverways. Distances were thus more likely represented in terms of time and ease of movement, not in terms of actual surveyed measurement.

As it appears there is almost no evidence that the maps were composed of anything more than from secondhand reports or travel accounts, they were readily available to distortion and prevarication. These compositional limitations continued to beset the late imperial, early modern era. The prominent Song mathematician and early scientist Shen Kuo 沈括 himself wrote in his *Dream Pool Essays* (*Mengxi bitan* 夢溪筆談) that a topographical map he made while a government official sent to inspect the frontier was created not by using careful survey measurements but from personal explorations of the mountains and rivers.[49] A later cartographer of the fourteenth century, Zhu Siben 朱思本, in creating his map of China, used "older maps, literary sources, and the results of personal travel," hardly a model of scientific cartography.[50]

But we must make a further distinction relating to the temporal measurements recorded in imperial Chinese maps. Clearly, it was not distant time that was mapped. Rather, it was the recent memorialized time that was the object of the map, with relative distances and locations all askew. What was to be read in the map were the general pathways of spatial possession, the roads to administrative supervision of extraction of resources, and thus the general political possession of the area.[51] It is

---

the other with no overlapping." Michael Sullivan, *The Birth of Landscape Painting in China* (Berkeley: University of California Press, 1962), 19, 24.

[48] Yee, "Cartography in China," 145. In premodern Chinese maps, angles, and thus directions, may be reliable, but not the distances between positions. As in medieval European maps, "relative sizes usually depended less on actual size than on the emphasis that the artist chose to give to the depicted objects: the important figures and features ... important places ... were magnified ... Space, in other words, was 'naive' or discontinuous." Ronald Rees, "Historical Links Between Cartography and Art," *Geographical Review* 70, no. 1 (1980), 66.

[49] 予奉使按边，始為木圖，寫其山川道路。其初遍履山川，旋以麵糊木屑寫其形勢于木案上。*Mengxi bitan* 夢溪筆談, 25.12; in *Siku quanshu* 四庫全書. See also Needham and Wang, *Science and Civilisation in China*, vol. 3, 580.

[50] Needham and Wang, *Science and Civilisation in China*, vol. 3, 551.

[51] As De Weerdt points out, Pei Xiu stressed administrative points of emphasis in the creation of his map, points of emphasis that connect to a historically embedded sensibility

a mélange, a "bricolage" of travel reports and observations thrown together in a visually unframed schema.[52]

In sum, the early Chinese map is at base a text, sharing resonance with travelogues such as the *Huayang guozhi* 華陽國志 (*The Chronicles of Huayang*) or the *Shuijing zhu* 水經注 (*Commentary on the "Classic of Waterways"*), save in graphic form, grossly tracking not static geographic relationships but human movement through space. The Chinese maps are reading the world as comprehensible ciphers rather than as an object, capturing vectors of movement rather than geometries of sight, meaningful action symbolically represented.[53] Their readers then would then presumably focus not so much on the measurements of surveyors but the experiences (fabricated or not) of its occupants, deciphering the map as a diagrammatic exposition of lived space, a schematic argument of domination and exploitation, coordinated to an explicit administrative narrative. Similar to how the European Middle Ages employed diagrammatic illustrations to expound theoretical ideas, the Chinese administrators employed mapped diagrams to expound the incessantly colonizing logic of hegemonic expansion and command.[54]

---

of empire, and associated it with the "Tribute of Yu." He explained that his map "showed the location of contemporary administrative units, jurisdictional boundaries and transport routes in the context of the topographical features – such as mountains, rivers, marshes, lakes and former administrative place-names – described in 'The Tribute of Yu'." De Weerdt, "Maps and Memory," 150.

[52] In this regard, my analysis concurs with Hsu and Martin-Montgomery's "emic" reading of the Mawangdui garrison map (Map 1). On their interpretation, the map is a layered composite of three ephemeral maps, marking three points in time surrounding a military campaign. See Hsin-mei Agnes Hsu and Anne Martin-Montgomery, "An Emic Perspective on the Mapmaker's Art in Western Han China," *Journal of the Royal Asiatic Society* 17, no. 4 (2007). In this way, to quote Jacob, "the drawing as object cannot be dissociated from the drawing as process." Jacob, *Sovereign Map*, 38.

[53] Pickles, *History of Spaces*, 81. Interestingly, this conception of mapmaking shares certain sympathies with Renaissance sensibilities. According to Alpers, in the Renaissance's reading of Ptolemaic writings on mapmaking, the Greek word *graphō*, the "graphic" – the common meaning of which is "to write, draw, or record" – is rendered as *descriptio*; a graphic thus is associated with a description that renders the narratively recorded space visually present, illuminating the invisible through a graphic illusion. Alpers, *Art of Describing*, 135–136.

[54] On this medieval sensibility, see Michael Evans, "The Geometry of the Mind," *Architectural Association Quarterly* 12 (1980). Lackner, referencing Evans, states: "From a comparative perspective, it can be said that the Chinese *tu* as tools for textual analysis are not a singular phenomenon; the use of diagrammatic illustrations to expound theoretical ideas was characteristic of the European Middle Ages (Evans 1980) as well . . . We also find . . . that the image could serve as a short, compact ways of reproducing the word." Lackner, "Diagrams as an Architecture by Means of Words," 353. One might even propose, following Jean Baudrillard, that the map precedes territory and thus is the very definition of the real: "it is the map that precedes the territory . . . it is the map that engenders the territory and if we were to revive the fable today, it would be the territory

Mensuration and Accuracy in Early Chinese Cartography

At the beginning of the preface to a famous map Pei Xiu produced, the "Yugong diyu tu" 禹貢地域圖 (A map of the area of the levies of Yu), he complains about the quality of early maps, saying that none give "anything like a complete representation of named mountains and large rivers." Their arrangement is "rough and imperfect," rendering them unreliable. In Needham's translation, Pei Xiu's final estimation is vitriolic: "Some of them contain absurdities, irrelevancies, and exaggerations, which are not in accord with reality, and which should be banished by good sense."[55] Unfortunately, Needham's rendition of this passage takes some liberties, employing stronger language than is completely justified by the Chinese. More literally translated, the representational "forms" are said to be "rough" or "crude," not having been thoroughly "examined" (*shen* 審). What Pei Xiu actually speaks of are prevarications ("absurdities," *huang* 荒/謊), extraneous matters (*wai* 外), distortions (*yu* 迂), and exaggerations (*dan* 誕), not in regard to "reality," per se, but to received documentation, reports, or just personal experience. Finally, he does not say such "should be banished by good sense" but instead that, upon deliberation with others, they would not be selected – for use, one presumes. The crux of the problem therefore is not necessarily the level of skill their creators displayed but that what they sketched may – perhaps intentionally – have not been metrically reliable markers of the physical space they were meant to represent.

There have been repeated efforts, particularly among recent Chinese geographers (though also among Western geographers and historians, notably Joseph Needham, Mei-ling Hsu, and Hans Bielenstein), to locate the areas imperial Chinese maps appear to designate and to demonstrate the metric accuracy of the represented geographic features. Needham announces that "during the whole of the millennium when scientific cartography was unknown to Europeans, the Chinese were steadily developing a tradition of their own, not strictly astronomical, but as quantitative and exact as they could make it."[56] By the beginning of the Han,

---

whose shreds are slowly rotting across the map." Jean Baudrillard, *Simulations*, trans. Paul Foss, Paul Patton, and Philip Beitchman (New York: Semiotext(e), 1983), 2.

[55] 惟有漢氏輿地及括地諸雜圖 ... 亦不備載名山大川。雖有粗形，皆不精審，不可依據。或荒外迂誕之言，不合事實，於義無取. *Jinshu* 晉書, 35.1039; Needham and Wang, *Science and Civilisation in China*, vol. 3, 539. Needham's translation, and thus interpretation, has had a profound impact on the representation of Pei's criticisms of earlier cartographic activity. Hilde De Weerdt, for instance, adopts Needham's interpretation (or one very similar) of Pei's guiding principles, and criticisms, without comment. See De Weerdt, "Maps and Memory," 150.

[56] Needham and Wang, *Science and Civilisation in China*, vol. 3, 525. Nathan Sivin and Gari Ledyard critique this "positivistic" attitude, arguing that the framing of premodern

Needham reports, the Chinese "were in possession of the simple and ancient survey instruments which had been known to the Babylonians and Egyptians";[57] as mentioned above, in the *Shanhaijing*, Yu's aide, "Youth Dozen," was said to have used counting-rods to "pace out the size of the world." Yet too often, as John Pickles complains, the history of maps is captivated by a "history of scientific advancement and individual achievement; too focused on technical progress and the progress of 'accurate representation.'"[58]

Such pretensions can readily be seen in certain of Mei-ling Hsu's assertions about the Qin and Han maps from Fangmatan and Mawangdui. Following Cao Wanru, Hsu avers their geographic features "are located fairly accurately ... Intricate river systems are shown ... Although no map scale is given on any map, the fair presentations in the maps suggest that some surveying and/or field checking must have been

---

Chinese maps as being part of an evolutionary development toward the more modern, scientific map "tend to stress documents and 'achievements.' This is particularly true in the People's Republic of China, where the official view of history makes science an unproblematically progressive force, and where the imperatives of nationalism prod historians to find Chinese technical priorities. The result of this scientism has naturally been an emphasis on geographic information, accuracy of scale, and elaboration of map signs. There has been little attention to the socioeconomic, aesthetic, and moral dimensions." Nathan Sivin and Gari Ledyard, "Introduction to East Asian Cartography," in *The History of Cartography*, vol. 2, bk. 2, *Cartography in the Traditional East and Southeast Asian Societies*, ed. J. B. Harley and David Woodward (Chicago: University of Chicago Press, 1994), 28. Arguing in a similar vein against the assertion that the appearance of the grid implied the rise of a more mathematical approach to map construction, Yee has contended that premodern Chinese maps were often made in close consultation with secondary reports, whether written or oral. See Yee, "Cartography in China," 126.

[57] Needham and Wang, *Science and Civilisation in China*, vol. 3, 569.

[58] Pickles, *History of Spaces*, 13. It is true that there is evidence in the historical record that terrestrial maps sometimes, if not often, were subjected to administrative reconfirmation. See, for instance, Chen Shou 陳壽, *Sanguozhi* 三國志 (Beijing: Zhonghua shuju, 1982), "Weishu" 24.692: 今二郡爭界八年, 一朝決之者, 緣有解書圖畫, 可得尋案摘校也. The text speaks of administrative borders as being unclear, sometimes requiring official intervention for their clarification, using textual and graphic implements. However, in the earliest complete legal code, that of the Tang, though there are articles pertaining to the corruption of documents and the intentional alteration of characters, there is nothing pertaining to the alteration of sketches or maps, of *tu*. This in itself should be indicative, for if so much care was taken for sketches to be accurate, and thus reliable, why wouldn't their corruption or intentional alteration be subject to punishment? Indeed, it is curious, if accuracy were an ideal, why there was not more discussion in the received literature about measuring geographical terrain, especially since the techniques and need were present. For codes pertaining to the management of documentary corruption, see *The Tang Code*, Articles 369, 374, 387, 417, 420, and 438 in *Tanglü shuyi* 唐律疏議 (Nanjing: Nanjing shifan daxue chubanshe, 2007), 799–801, 810–811, 829–830, 872–873, 876–877, 901–902; translated in *The T'ang Code*, vol. 2, 431–432, 440–441, 454, 479–480, 483, 499–500. But as an anecdote about Kuang Heng in the *Hanshu* indicates, an anecdote I shall discuss later in this chapter, there is indeed sometimes concern with the corruption involved in using a flawed map. See *HS* 81.3346.

done prior to mapping. This was definitely the case for the Han maps."[59] The source of her certainty for this is ultimately unclear, for as Hsing I-tien has acknowledged, there remains substantial disagreement concerning the areas represented by the maps; the maps are merely suggestive. There are still more than four or five asserted identifications of the areas represented by the Qin and Han maps.[60]

In the Qin Fangmatan diagrams, the graphic features, the drawn lines themselves do not conclusively render them identifiable as maps, since their representations are far from precise. They could in reality have been merely artistic representations, for some nonadministrative purpose. Only upon referring to the text surrounding the depictive features, combined with our knowledge of the tomb's owner being a government official, can we begin to believe that they may have been meant to serve as some sort of map. What remains unclear is the process by which they were composed: From whose observations were the maps composed and by what process were they put together? It is not even clear if they were descriptive or prescriptive maps, that is, if they were describing areas already settled or if they were merely recommending areas of potential settlement.[61] In fact, one of the duties of the *sikong* 司空, the "Minister of Works," as prescribed in the *Liji* was to measure territory to determine

---

[59] Mei-Ling Hsu, "The Qin Maps: A Clue to Later Chinese Cartographic Development," *Imago Mundi* 45, no. 1 (1993), 93. For a concurring opinion, see also Helwig Schmidt-Glintzer, "Diagram (*tu*) and Text (*wen*): Mapping the Chinese World," in *Conceiving the Empire: China and Rome Compared*, ed. Fritz-Heiner Mutschler and Achim Mittag (New York: Oxford University Press, 2008), 175–176.

[60] Hsing I-tien, "Cong chutu ziliao kan Qin–Han juluo xingtai he xiangli xingzheng" 從出土 資料看秦漢聚落形態和鄉里行政, in *Zhiguo anbang* 治國安邦 (Beijing: Zhonghua shuju, 2011), 255. Hans Bielenstein also deems the "garrison" map found in the Mawangdui tomb to be metrically inaccurate. While he assents to the determination as to the locale it represents, he propounds, at least the area south of the watershed, that its north–south dimensions are compressed, that the Pearl River delta is moved too far to the west, and the river courses are incorrectly presented. However, the area of southern Hunan north of the watershed that it depicts is, he believes, in close accord with modern maps: "While the central river system on the ancient map is twisted northward in the upstream region, the various rivers are easily identifiable, and the locations of the prefectural cities are roughly correct in their relations to each other." Hans Bielenstein, "Notes on the *Shuijing*," *Bulletin of the Museum of Far Eastern Antiquities* 65 (1993), 264–265. Dorofeeva-Lichtmann agrees to this general estimation of the inaccuracy of Chinese maps: "The majority of Chinese global maps, as well as the great bulk of local maps made before the influence of European science, are known for their striking lack of precision from the point of view of modern cartography. Distortion of Chinese maps is considered to result from their intention to transmit more a certain *spatial idea* or *viewpoint* than geographic facts." Dorofeeva-Lichtmann, "Conception of Terrestrial Organization in the *Shan hai jing*," 61.

[61] In Benjamin Orlove's formulation, such would be the signs of a "proleptic narrative." See Benjamin Orlove, "The Ethnography of Maps: The Cultural and Social Contexts of Cartographic Representation in Peru," *Cartographica* 30, no. 1 (1993), 37–38. Thanks to Robert Rundstrom for this reference.

where to locate villages and settle the population.[62] According to Hsing I-tien, the Fangmatan and Mawangdui maps were in all likelihood principally employed to represent administratively the location of populations relative to waterways and mountains.[63]

The following passage in the *Suishu* 隋書 (*The Documents of the Sui Dynasty*) may give a sense of the standard purpose of early imperial maps: "[The former] monarch measured territory for the administration of villages, assessed land areas to settle people, totaling the productive capacity of the lands and reckoning the profits of the mountains and marshes."[64] In the *Suishu*, we also have an instance of craftsmen being sent to inspect the canals and survey advantageous terrains.[65] Yet, as emphasized previously, from almost every indication in the histories, the surveys were not carefully measured but rather based on subjective, general observations. Deng Ai 鄧艾 (d. 264 CE), a Wei-era administrator, reputedly "estimated the heights and distances, measuring by fingerbreadths, before drawing a plan of the place and fixing the position of [military barracks]."[66] Needham insinuates that these measurements were associated with offensive military endeavors, but from the passage's context, it seems more likely they bore upon the defense of already established settlements. Furthermore, far from being an indication of careful surveying, as Needham intimates it is, the estimates seem actually to be hastily made, based on a quick subjective survey, not a more labor-intensive mathematical one.

---

[62] See *Liji* 禮記, "Wangzhi" 王制: 司空執度, 度地居民, 山川沮澤, 時四時, 量地遠近, 興事任力。凡使民, 任老者之事, 食壯者之食. *Liji jijie* 禮記集解, 358. James Legge's translation: "The minister of Works with his (various) instruments measured the ground for the settlements of the people. About the hills and rivers, the oozy ground and the meres, he determined the periods of the four seasons. He measured the distances of one spot from another, and commenced his operations in employing the labour of the people. In all his employment of them, he imposed (only) the tasks of old men (on the able-bodied), and gave (to the old) the food-allowance of the able-bodied." *Li Chi: Book of Rites*, 1:228.

[63] Hsing I-tien, "Cong chutu ziliao kan Qin–Han juluo xingtai he xiangli xingzheng," 257–258. Others, such as Helwig Schmidt-Glinzer, argue for a possible military employment of the Fangmatan maps: "The fact that we find among the overall sixty-one marked locations several passes and other strategic points suggests that the maps served military purposes." Schmidt-Glintzer, "Diagram (*tu*) and Text (*wen*)," 174.

[64] 王者量地以制邑, 度地以居人, 總土地所生, 料山澤之利. Wei Zheng 魏徵, *Suishu* 隋書 (Beijing: Zhonghua shuju, 1973), 24.671. For a comparative example of an early survey, see Fang Xuanling 房玄齡 et al., *Jinshu* 晉書 (Beijing: Zhonghua shuju, 1974), 26.779.

[65] 已令工匠, 巡歷渠道, 觀地理之宜. *Suishu*, 24.684.

[66] 鄧艾每見高山大澤輒規度指畫軍營處所. Needham and Wang, *Science and Civilisation in China*, vol. 3, 571–572. See Li Fang 李昉, *Taiping yulan* 太平御覽, 335.2a; Chen Shou, *Sanguozhi*, 28.775. In the *Sanguozhi*, the relevant sentence reads as follows: 每見高山大澤, 輒規度指畫軍營處所.

Again, according to Ptolemy's classic definition, the early Chinese terrestrial maps are not geographic, maps of the known world, but chorographic, maps of small areas. For Ptolemy, the final aim of chorography was to create "recognizable images of the visible features of single parts of the *oecumene*, the inhabited world . . . A field of vision was thus opened up to the work of the chorographer, who had to demonstrate the skill of a draftsman in rendering ports, countries, villages, rivers, and streams."[67] According to Ptolemy's definitions, chorography differs from geography in that chorography "selects certain places from the whole." The task of geography, by contrast, is "to show the known habitable earth as a continuous unit, how it is situated and what is its nature; and it deals with those features relevant to be mentioned in a more comprehensive and general description of the earth, such as gulfs, the larger towns and nations, and the principal rivers."[68]

In the West, Ronald Rees observes, prior to the European Renaissance "there was no terminology to distinguish clearly between maps and paintings." The first professional European cartographers were actually pictorial artists "who had engaged in the work of copying, decorating, and even compiling maps."[69] A beginning attempt at defining the difference between maps and landscape paintings in representing "place" perhaps might be drawn from Edward Casey's distinction: "maps are practical in orientation, seeking to *guide or induce action* in the viewer. In contrast, paintings aid us in appreciating the world, and rarely demand more than eye movement. Maps aim to represent accurately the features of the world, whereas landscape paintings 'attempt to convey the sensuous aspects of environing place-world.'"[70] Yet, as Natasha Heller perceives, these distinctions do not hold in many Chinese terrestrial maps. The map of Mount Wutai 五臺山, as depicted in Mogao 莫高 Cave 61 in Dunhuang in western China, is, Heller declares, "a hybrid of these two types of representation."[71] Maps might represent any number of experiences, sensuous or otherwise, recalling past journeys or suggesting future ones.[72] Regardless of its function, a map is a supervenient addition to discourse, to more fundamental, basic discursive descriptions or notations.[73] The *tu–wen* interrelationship is

---

[67] Nuti, "Mapping Places," 90.

[68] Irby-Massie and Keyser, *Greek Science of the Hellenistic Era*, 145.

[69] Rees, "Historical Links Between Cartography and Art," 60, 62.

[70] Natasha Heller, "Visualizing Pilgrimage and Mapping Experience: Mount Wutai on the Silk Road," in *The Journey of Maps and Images on the Silk Road*, ed. Phillipe Forêt and Andreas Kaplony (Leiden: Brill, 2008), 29.

[71] Heller, "Visualizing Pilgrimage and Mapping Experience," 30.   [72] Ibid., 31.

[73] Florian Reiter remarks that in many compendia of *tu*, whether they are religious diagrams or geographic maps, "the text itself is the nucleus of the book, and the t'u simply illustrate it . . . Actually most maps (ti-t'u) in the [late imperial] gazetteers serve similar purposes.

dynamic, as Guolong Lai's analysis of diagrams from the early Han evinces, with a *tu*, "map" or "diagram," either "substituting, supplementing, or illustrating a text (*wen*)."[74] This accords with Cordell Yee's claim that Chinese maps are primarily textual because they are drawn largely on the basis of textual sources and "the text complements spatial information on the map."[75]

For geographers and historians of science, maps are produced by the surveying gaze, whether collected from secondhand reports or firsthand observation, often composed by artisans employed for such a purpose. And indeed, we have incidents in the Chinese standard histories of such activities, as discussed earlier. However, premodern Chinese maps, because of their general metric inaccuracy, are often compared to landscape paintings. According to Rees, such is in keeping with cartography's "prescientific" phase: "Mapmaking as a form of decorative art belongs to the informal, prescientific phase of cartography. When cartographers had neither the geographical knowledge nor the cartographic skill to make accurate maps, fancy and artistry had free rein."[76] If little careful surveying of a landscape was involved, the "view," the "gaze" is almost always from unelevated ground, not a "bird's-eye view" at all.

The surveying gaze in early Chinese maps is almost certainly low.[77] Unlike in those from post-Renaissance Europe, we have no sense of horizon. The maps often have essentially a boundless, unframed space. The order of the frame is based on human measure, the perspectival view of the landscape,[78] except that we have no human figures by which to estimate the direction with which the survey was taken or the relative area

They support in an artistic way the respective text." Reiter, "Some Remarks on the Chinese Word *t'u*," 312. Reiter's prioritizing text over illustration is reversed in Richard J. Smith's explanation of early cartographic norms. He writes: "The foremost map-maker of the Sui and Tang periods was the eighth-century scholar, Jia Dan. He is particularly well known for making explicit one of Pei Xiu's implicit assumptions – that written texts are a valuable complement to any map. In Jia's words: '[When depicting things such as] mountains and rivers, one must talk of heads and tails and sources and reaches. On a map, these things cannot be completely drawn; for reliability, [therefore,] one must depend on [appended] notes.'" See R. Smith, *Chinese Maps*, 26–27.

[74] Schmidt-Glintzer, "Diagram (*tu*) and Text (*wen*)," 172. See also Guolong Lai, "The Diagram of the Mourning System from Mawangdui," *Early China* 28 (2003), 45. Indeed, in the 《歷代地理指掌圖》, the map is explicitly described as complementing the text: 「圖也者，所輔書之成也。」 See *Song ben li dai di li zhi zhang tu* 宋本歷代地理指掌圖, 2.

[75] De Weerdt, "Cultural Logics of Map Reading," 247.

[76] See Alpers, *Art of Describing*, 126.

[77] For the craftsmen of Chinese maps, the representing eye is located on the very picture surface itself. Whether the territory was surveyed or not, the viewer's position is included within the surveyed territory. Alpers, *Art of Describing*, 138.

[78] For a discussion of the artistic framing of maps, see Alpers, *Art of Describing*, 144.

covered by the survey. As with landscape paintings, Chinese maps do not render their landscapes immediately recognizable from the removed, "God's eye" perspective. The maps do not situate their lands carefully. Instead, Chinese maps offer a description of lands possessed (and thus display the marks of possession) rather than lands known.[79] Rather than reflecting, or mirroring, a stable, unified visual territory, they were more likely, to borrow Svetlana Alpers' eloquent phrasing, the "unframed sequence of ... vistas successively viewed."[80]

All of this is just further evidence that the early Chinese terrestrial map is a rough pictorial illusion, an illusion of comprehensive space that is merely a composite aggregate.[81] In Europe, it is only with the "privileging of vision" in the Renaissance that a shift occurred "from 'reading the world as an intelligible text (the book of nature) to looking at it as an observable object (a secular autonomisation of the visual) ...' an emphasis that enabled a 'new world' to be seen and made."[82] In accordance with this, the geographer David Harvey defines the development of modern cartography as the institutionalized practice of

locating, identifying and bounding phenomena and thereby situating events, processes and things within a coherent spatial frame. It imposes a spatial order on phenomena. In its contemporary manifestation, it depends heavily upon a Cartesian logic in which *res extensa*[e] are presumed to be quite separate from the realms of mind and thought and capable of full depiction within some set of coordinates (a grid or graticule).[83]

It should be abundantly clear that the norms of such mapping sensibilities naturally cannot, and should not, be applied to premodern Chinese maps.

The Aesthetic Similarities Between Landscapes and Maps

In accord with the central aim of marking borders or boundaries, the essential function of early Chinese terrestrial maps is to describe and, when occupied, divide and label terrain – a feature not definitive of the early landscapes. But there are various aspects that are shared by early landscapes and maps. One is the fact that both often express a dynamism, an active flow of line and the arrangement of space that goes beyond any simple, realistic description. A second shared feature is an emphasis on

---

[79] Needham poses the false dichotomy between "literary-descriptive and more practical and cartographic" maps, the latter appearing more frequently from the Southern Song onward. See Needham and Wang, *Science and Civilisation in China*, vol. 3, 518.

[80] Alpers, *Art of Describing*, 62. With this phrase, however, Alpers is not describing a map but seventeenth-century Dutch peep-boxes.

[81] Alpers, *Art of Describing*, 62.   [82] Pickles, *History of Spaces*, 81.   [83] Ibid., 81–82.

a focal point, with the placement (or an intentional erasure) of what is in the center being significant. Third, both early maps and landscapes use symbols to express power and hegemony, with landscapes expressing such in a more encoded, subtle fashion.[84] In maps, even the metric grid is an expression of power, the display of the extent of a terrain that can be measured and quantified. The arrangement of space in maps is meant to heighten this sense of hegemony, as it did in imperial landscapes. In the landscapes, mountains and trees metonymically stand for the power of the court and the empire at large.[85] Finally, underlying the presentation and organization of the conspicuous features of early landscapes and maps are not only general spatial relations but a directional sense and a marking of their sacrality. Temples, "*feng*"ed spaces, sacred natural bodies (mountains, rivers, etc.) are made salient. But directionality and relationality – whether the cardinal directions, or the relations between natural or man-made objects – are also emphasized in both.

All of these features highlight the importance of relative placement. For both early landscapes and maps, locality and location – generally speaking, emplacement – are crucial; it is through the deciphering of these relative placements that landscapes and maps make sense and become legible. Maps and landscapes are to be read, not just simply viewed. In the landscapes, for instance, one reads features of majesty and aggrandizement; in the maps, one reads similarly – though to different purposes – in the tracings of hegemonic power represented in riverways, townships, mountainous boundaries and their relative locations. Both also intentionally exaggerate power or its lack by highlighting powerful places.

But there are naturally some functional distinctions. In early maps, regions are regularly supplied with locale names, to render the impression, true or not, that the administration hegemonically occupied the area. Textual labels of hegemonic power are frequently employed in early maps, whereas in traditional landscapes, there is little of the sort. These labels are important for the legibility of power relations within the maps. The scope of a map is also usually broader than that of a landscape. Finally, in a map, human movement – or its possibility – is the operative concern, whereas in an early Chinese landscape, it is usually not, with certain exceptions, such as pilgrimage landscapes.

Ideally, maps should be spatially homogenous, with no point spatially distorted in emphasis. But in reality, designing a chorographic map

---

[84] See Martin Powers, "When Is a Landscape Like a Body?" in *Landscape, Culture, and Power in Chinese Society*, ed. Wen-hsin Yeh (Berkeley: University of California Press, 1998).

[85] See Lewis, *Construction of Space in Early China*, 157–158.

weaves together multiple, experientially separate perspectives, offering the illusion of an integrated, homogenous space. Cosgrove explains:

Each chorography is a bird's eye view of a small part of the earth's surface, cleverly combining different viewing positions. In addition to seeing the territory mapped out at a consistent scale, permitting accurate measurement of the distances between points, the observer gains a visual impression of distance and topography, as if looking [through] a picture or window frame at landscape scenery. As in painting, the frame itself serves as an ordering device, structuring and composing its contents. Achieving the effect of distance depends upon sophisticated technical coordination of perspectival geometry.[86]

The construction of early landscapes involves a single viewer, and not the making of an abstracted, redacted, "syncopated" composite of multiple viewings gathered from others, as happens in maps.[87] The experience captured in landscape painting is not the experience of multiple viewers, for the landscape's ostensible purpose is not, like the map's, to capture a simulacrum of an objective representation. It is this single authorial viewpoint, of the drawer or painter, as with Xie He, that is at the core of the earliest Chinese discussions of painting.

Thus, in its fundamental process of composition, a landscape painting, integrating the viewpoint of one artist into a frame, is not the process of composing a map.[88] However, when landscapes integrate the movement and perspectives of multiple viewers, as they may in, for instance, the paintings of Buddhist travelers, they involve, in their record of journeys and experiences, more of the integrated mapping consciousness than single-viewer landscapes may (see Map 2).[89] A map's basic function is interactive in a way the landscape is not – the questions it is meant to be asked and to answer, present and future, presumably by multiple unrelated and mutually disinterested users, are unlike those asked of and answered by the landscape – if the answering of questions is even a function of painterly landscapes. Nevertheless, the earliest Chinese landscapes and maps share an affinity in that, as Patrick Crowley remarks relating to

---

[86] Cosgrove, *Geography and Vision*, 24–25.   [87] Alpers, *Art of Describing*, 58.

[88] "The map has an immediate instrumental value, and its drawing, while it is being done, accompanies, reflects, and completes a discourse in the act of being enunciated. In all likelihood we imagine the birth of cartography in Greece as the drawing in sand of a geometrical figure, of a circle, figuring the celestial sphere or the surface of the terrestrial disk, before the eyes of a group of attentive students." Jacob later states, maps have a "performative power": "All that is important is the intellectual concentration of those who draw the figure and those who look at it." Jacob, *Sovereign Map*, 38–39.

[89] See Heller, "Visualizing Pilgrimage and Mapping Experience."

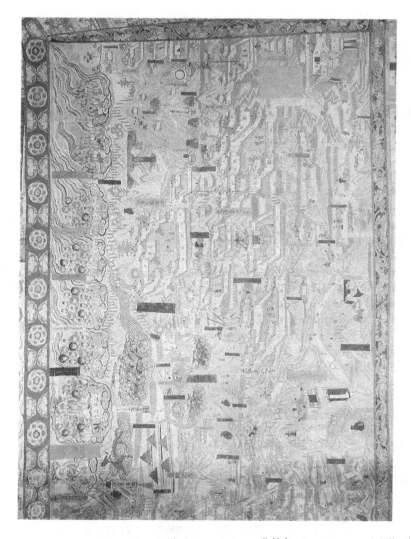

Map 2 Wutaishan 五臺山. Cao Wanru 曹婉如, Zhongguo gudai ditu ji: Zhanguo – Yuan 中國古代地圖集，戰國—元 (Beijing: Wenwu chubanshe, 1990), image 38

Roman artworks, both "effectively diagram the gaze through the manipulation of composition and ornament."[90]

[90] Patrick Crowley, "Picturing the Gaze in the Greco-Roman World," 22, unpublished paper. Cited with permission of the author.

The first extant treatise on landscape painting is from the Six Dynasties period, an essay by Zong Bing 宗炳 (375–443 CE), "An Introduction to Painting Mountains and Rivers (Landscapes)" 畫山水之序, an essay that, according to Ping Foong, "defined landscape painting's primary purpose as a medium for accessing the numinous powers attributed to mountains." The landscapes were objects "on which one's mind might lodge temporarily to arouse the *shen* 神 and *ling* 靈 and thus to identify with the mental state achieved by religious adepts."[91] By the Northern Song dynasty, Foong states, "Contemporary writers explain mountainous imagery – awe-inspiring depictions of towering and immovable formations – as representations of the emperor and as allusions to his inexorable ruling powers."[92] Indeed, Munakata Kiyohiko, Foong points out, insisted that Zong was not "arguing for the efficacy of all landscapes represented pictorially but of *sacred mountains* in particular."[93] Such painterly emphasis on the efficacy of sacred mountains and the connection of natural to monarchial power tallies with the monarchial appropriation of mountains as sites of visualized, and envisioned, domination. Through his visualizations, the ruler proleptically travels, touring lands he has already successfully brought into his sovereign realm and lands he aims to bring under his control. In ritual, the envisioned becomes bodily movement, the proleptic finds physical expression. When the ruler physically ascends a sacred mountain and performs sacrifices there, his envisioned sovereignty is symbolically effected. Ritual is thus one potent mechanism for extending sovereignty, a way that the envisioned becomes enacted. In this context, the power of vision is thus the potential power of travel, the road, the *dao* 道, a sanctified means to extend sovereignty, the sovereign's very paces the physical assertion of his claims.

As artistic media, early maps used stock representational conventions. In several of the earliest archaeologically excavated exemplars of terrestrial maps, those from Fangmatan and Mawangdui, dark undulating lines were used to express what appear to be riverways and mountain ranges, while boxes and text were utilized to locate specific areas and populations (see Map 3). There was no attempt at anything akin to a detailed, scrupulous realism. What appear to be representations of riverways regularly break off into only two main branches and the thickness of the lines were often unvaried across the branchings, giving no sense of topography, which would be more accurately indicated with the variation of the width of the waterway as it travels across the terrain. Because boxes and text were the location marks, settlements were not precisely indicated, as they might have been,

---

[91] Ping Foong, *The Efficacious Landscape: On the Authorities of Painting at the Northern Song Court* (Cambridge, MA: Harvard University Asia Center, 2015), 17.
[92] Foong, *Efficacious Landscape*, 3.   [93] Ibid., 17n15. Italics mine.

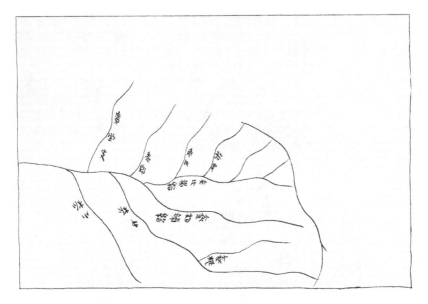

Map 3 Fangmatan 放馬灘. Cao Wanru 曹婉如, Zhongguo gudai ditu ji: Zhanguo – Yuan 中國古代地圖集，戰國—元 (Beijing: Wenwu chubanshe, 1990), image 7

with dots. Representations of mountain range elevations were formulaically and repetitively represented. Other geographic features, many of those listed as important to commanders in the *Guanzi* – such as roadways, bridges, passes, walls, administrative borders, forests, cultivated areas, the sizes of the population centers, canals, and desert areas – were left off. Thus, their representations are crude, rough, of limited use. The perspective of mountains, for instance, is almost uniformly in profile, not planar.

These stock features create only an illusion of reality; indeed, they could have been borrowed (and possibly were) to depict any number of areas.[94] Many of these stock conventions, devices, and absences are part of later maps and landscapes. The problem for analyzing the conception of maps is just this bipolar state, with the map governed both by artistic norms involved in sketching or painting and by mensurative norms involved in close, reflective representation. Maps were clearly perceived as being "sketched" or

[94] Jacob makes a similar remark relating to Hartmann Schedel's *Nuremberg Chronicle* of 1493, of which a number represented different cities using the same plates: "The same plates were at times used to depict different cities. The link of the plate with the place-name is a fiction, at the edge of plausibility." Jacob, *Sovereign Map*, figure 40.

"painted."[95] And yet, landscapes are from an unelevated, more horizontal visual standpoint, usually encouraging one point of reference, the
artist's; maps, with their inherent vertical imbrication of multiple unelevated perspectives, offer multiple journeys and visual imaginings.[96]

François Jullien contests that any idea of Chinese painting, and thus
drawing, is about depiction, about rendering the object fully and completely,
to the extent that the eye is deceived by its false realism. To render the object
fully and completely was more the aim of European painters. According to
the famed Renaissance painter Alberti, European painting is to "represent
things seen":

Above all, because the thing seen occupies a place, the painter must begin by "circumscribing" that place, delimiting its surface by outlining its form. That form is defined
by its referent; it has a model and a previous existence in nature. It is not defined in the
first place by the system of tensions in which it is caught and which makes it come
about, both animating and deploying it, as is the case for the Chinese painter.[97]

The standard by which all European painting is measured is its ability to
mirror. Thus the mirror is, in the European tradition, "the painter's master
and guide." The reflection of the mirror is the content of the painting, the
painted image is the accurate reflection of nature.[98] This emphasis on the
reflection of reality is seen also in the close connection between Dutch
painting and cartography, as illustrated in Jan Vermeer's *Allegory of
Painting*, in which the map that forms the background "is dominated by an
emblematic title inscribed in capital letters, to serve as a lesson to the painter:
DESCRIPTIO."[99] For Jullien, the art of European cartography is an exact

[95] See *Song shi* 宋史 (Beijing: Zhonghua shuju, 2007), 493.14173: 詔長吏察其謠俗情偽，
并按視山川地形圖畫來上.; *HS* 59.2657: 謁大將軍光，問千秋戰鬭方略，山川形勢，千
秋口對兵事，畫地成圖，無所忘失.

[96] "The map ... brings increased reality and authority to speech. It offers the subject the
anticipated and imagined experience of a space and a pathway. More precisely, it invites
whoever looks at it to be positioned as the subject of the statement. As an abstract and
mobile operator, the subject is allowed, through his imaginary and projective itinerary, to
orient and to articulate dynamically the juxtaposition of places and points of reference.
The map thus appears as a means to control the development of a verbal interaction, to
allow the introduction of new discursive objects, digressions, and connected bits of
information, yet at the same time it retains the possibility of returning to the principal
thread of the narrative." Jacob, *Sovereign Map*, 36.

[97] François Jullien, *The Great Image Has No Form: On the Nonobject Through Painting*
(Chicago: University of Chicago Press, 2003), 179.

[98] In a footnote, Jullien quotes from Alberti's *On Painting*: "No one is clearer than Alberti in
summing up painting's aim as the representation of objects: 'The function of the painter
is this: to con-scribe with lines and to tint with colour on whatever panel or wall is given
him all the bodies given so that, at a certain distance and in certain position determined by
the central focal point, everything you see appears in the same relief and seems to have the
same aspect as the bodies given.'" Jullien, *Great Image Has No Form*, 179.

[99] Jullien, *Great Image Has No Form*, 181.

art, defined by surveying, as opposed to pictorially, loosely representing. In Dutch art, the quintessential art of the real, true reflection, *landschap*, "landscape," "designated both what the surveyor measured and what the artist represented." In these mapped landscapes, Jullien observes, the objects and details of the landscape are "so many reference points for the drawing of the site, and are meticulously recorded."[100] This, naturally, was not the case in early China.

Aesthetic Compositional Norms in Early Chinese Maps

As elaborated in the previous section, early maps share many commonalities with landscape paintings – their representations are often guided as much by aesthetic considerations as mensurative ones. We see in their almost monotonous regularities, whether in the spare sketches of Fangmatan or the more rococo extravagant undulations scrolling in every direction throughout the Mawangdui and later Song maps, a repeated stressing, with a modicum of decorative flourish (e.g., the symmetry of the diffusion, the hash marks on the faces of mountains), of their artistic pretensions. But chorographic maps train the gaze with a purpose that is less accidental and personal than in landscape paintings. Furthermore, also unlike landscape paintings, as underscored in the previous section, there is often more than one perspectival "eye" captured in chorographic representations. Different viewing positions are blended into one frame of reference.

If expertly done, with the differences carefully obscured, the map reader perceives believable distances across relative points and thus an impression of distance and landmasses, with means and obstructions to travel portrayed. Yet such is extremely hard to achieve, and most early terrestrial maps fail to blend their representations. For many, including most early Chinese maps, it is uncertain how much consistency was even attempted, and thus whether these maps were expected to be reliable for the purposes of movement and location, for whatever ends. I would hazard that there are ample clues in the early texts that visual representations of space were never expected to be metrically accurate, and that metric accuracy was almost impossible to achieve. This is not simply because of any possible technological absence, conceptual or instrumentational, but because there was no trust in the transfer and sources of sensitive information.

---

[100] Ibid., 182.

I have argued in previous work that such was the case for much "factual" information in the early period.[101]

Natural features pictorially dominate the composition of the terrestrial maps we have, though experiential perspectives inform both their composition and use. In essence, as argued earlier, the pictorializations are the shadows of memory, of previous trackings in time, with their natural features themselves represented iconically, disseminating "countable units whose recurrence plots the space and creates a graphic rhythm of its own."[102] On these early maps place is only a relative position, reachable from another designated point. Since the natural features are represented iconically, in a stylized fashion, it is the marked places that root travel and the possessive intentions of the state. Places indicate occupation; before these marks of travel and occupation, the spaces on the map are unpossessed and, being unpossessed, basically unknown for the state.

A close analysis of various premodern exemplars reveals various other compositional norms. Both traditional Chinese landscapes and cityscapes reveal a curious blend of horizontal perspective flattened into a two-dimensional plane (in profile) governed by an elevated vantage point.[103] In cityscapes, instead of depicting the tops of the buildings, as would be appropriate if such were viewed from the vertical, the buildings are viewed from a distance as if from a street level, most often with their fronts shown, though sometimes with their sides (see Map 4). But such a blending of the horizontal face with a vertical perspective is also obvious with the portrayal of mountains, or, indeed, of any vertically projecting object, including walls and human figures (see Map 5). Frequently, the elevation of the structuring vertical gaze is pronounced, the distance extended to the point where the features on the map are rendered in miniature, even though their horizontal face is preserved, such as in the map of Mount Wutai discussed previously. In the maps from Mawangdui, the regular waves on top of which a cluster of three shaded circles rest have been hypothesized by Mei-ling Hsu as representing mountains. If so, the merging of the horizontal with the vertical gaze was over the centuries a regular feature of Chinese chorographic maps.

This, however, is not a compositional method limited to the Chinese. We can also see it in European maps, such as the seventeenth-century Dutch maps by Claes Visscher[104] and Georg Markgraf.[105] But the objects

---

[101] See Olberding, *Dubious Facts.*   [102] Jacob, *Sovereign Map,* 175.

[103] Robert Harrist, Jr., also notes that this combination of aerial and profile views has been in use in Chinese cartography since at least the second century BCE. Robert Harrist, Jr., *Painting and Private Life in Eleventh-Century China: Mountain Villa by Li Gonglin* (Princeton, NJ: Princeton University Press, 1998), 93–96.

[104] Alpers, *Art of Describing,* 160.   [105] Alpers, *Art of Describing,* 162.

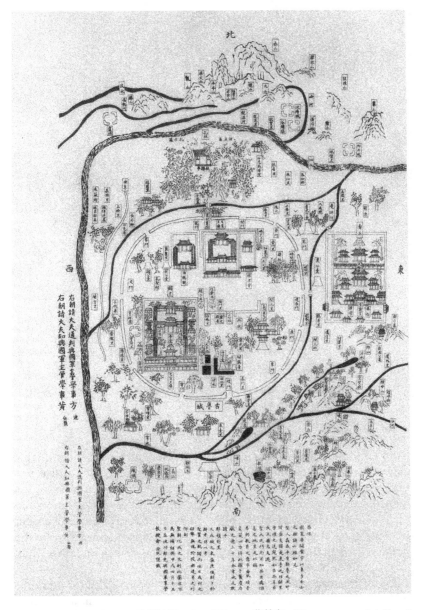

Map 4 Luguo 魯國(宋). Cao Wanru 曹婉如, Zhongguo gudai ditu ji: Zhanguo – Yuan 中國古代地圖集，戰國—元 (Beijing: Wenwu chubanshe, 1990), image 51

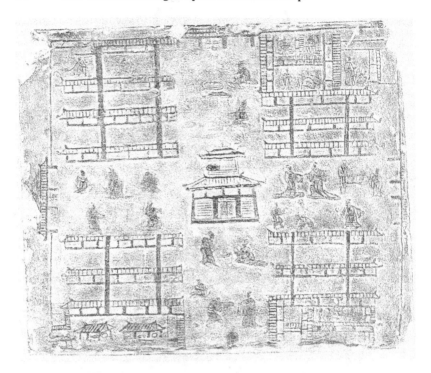

Map 5 Shijin 市井圖 (東漢). Cao Wanru 曹婉如, Zhongguo gudai ditu ji: Zhanguo – Yuan 中國古代地圖集，戰國—元 (Beijing: Wenwu chubanshe, 1990), image 35

in the Chinese maps do not appear to be so much easily identifiable landmarks, "marks on the land (as if to guide travelers),"[106] as features to regularize and organize the interpretation and implementation of the mapped space for the viewer of the map. Indeed, the marks that would individuate and clearly identify objects in the maps are often quite absent (see Map 6). Rather, regular, organized use of space appears to be the operative organizational principle, an aesthetic principle rather than a mensurative one.

The two features that are most often somewhat individuated and thus noticeably irregular are the pathways, of water or people, in addition to strategic or administrative land boundaries; in other words, lines of movement or power, features that are open to, or can bring about,

---

[106] Alpers, *Art of Describing*, 142.

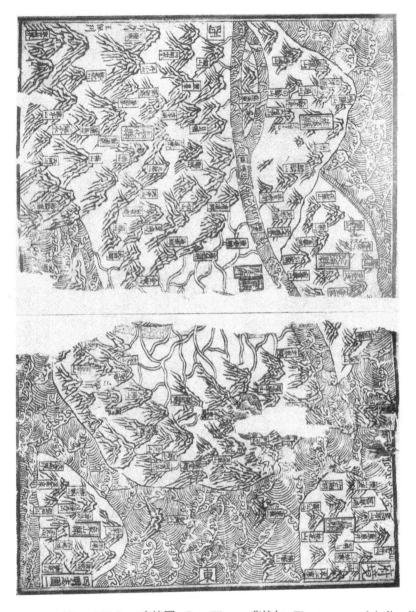

Map 6 Fujing 府境圖. Cao Wanru 曹婉如, Zhongguo gudai ditu ji: Zhanguo – Yuan 中國古代地圖集，戰國—元 (Beijing: Wenwu chubanshe, 1990), image 130

transformation. Yet the individuated features are not their detail; instead, it is in their outlined course and direction. Even then, the outlined forms are crude and simplified, blockily rendered, with only a few bends and swerves to give them individuated curvature.

Maps are thus a reflection of power relations, strategic relationships, distorted as they are through the secondhand reportage that informs their composition. The map is an illusory combination of contingent knowledge, in which there is no true sense of vertical space but only an illusion of verticality. The horizontal space represented is distorted, either extended or contracted over a visual plane of arbitrary size (delimited by the physical size of a strip of wood or a piece of silk). The contingent knowledge of the map "may be seen as embodied, locally constructed, and re-presented as oppositional yet complementary positionings in shifting fields."[107]

The Mensurative Composition of the Map

At present, the earliest excavated artefact that can definitively be identifiable as a *tu* is the bronze-inscribed plan for the mortuary monument of King Cuo (興+昔) of Zhongshan 中山, dated to 310 BCE. In the inscription attending the diagram, for the first time, Behr observes, *tu* denotes a mental activity rather than a static physical object.[108] The planning of the spatial arrangement of the mortuary site indicated in the diagram utilized various arithmetic and geometric devices to give a scaled layout of the site, and is claimed to be the earliest diagram using numerical scale markings in the world.[109] However, the diagram is not realized in the physical layout of the site, for whatever reason. As Sun Zhongming 孫仲 明 notes, in the map there are five designated halls (*tang* 堂); at the site are only two that have been found. Only the king's mount and one large mound at the eastern side, that for Queen Ai 哀后, were discovered.[110]

Nevertheless, employing both the remarks on measurement and the comparative lengths and placement of the lines in this clearly prescriptive diagram, we see that the relative lengths of the lines in some cases somewhat approximate the stated arithmetic relations. In the map, two primary units of measurement were used: *chi* 尺 and *bu* 步. When *chi* was

---

[107] Pickles, *History of Spaces*, 30.   [108] Behr, "Placed into the Right Position," 119.
[109] Yang Xinhe 杨新河, "Zhongguo faxian shijie zuizao de ditu" 中国发现世界最早的地图, *Keji chao* 科技潮 1 (1998).
[110] Sun Zhongming 孫仲明, "Zhanguo Zhongshan wangmu Zhaoyutu ji qi biaoshi fangfa de yanjiu" 戰國中山王墓兆域圖及其表示方法的研究, in *Zhongguo gudai ditu ji: Zhanguo–Yuan* 中国古代地图集：战国—元, ed. Cao Wanru 曹婉如 et al. (Beijing: Wenwu chubanshe, 1990), 1.

used, the arithmetic relation between line and stated measurement were often close. For instance, regarding the three large central "halls" (*tang*) and two small end "halls," the printed proportional dimensional ratio is 200:150 *chi*, or 5:3.75; the ratio of the area of the drawn spaces is, according to Sun Zhongming, 5:4. Similarly, the stated areas of the "halls" to the "temples" is 200:100 *chi*, or 2:1; the drawn ratio is also 2:1. However, when *bu* is the unit of measurement, the accuracy of the ratios falls.

Examination and analysis of the mensurative composition of early Chinese maps is complicated by the choice of norms with which we may pursue the analysis. Modern graphic information systems analyses may be fruitfully applied to maps composed using metrically accurate surveys, and, so Agnes Hsu and Anne Martin-Montgomery have demonstrated, could also be applied to those that did not, if there are sufficient recognizable data points with which one can establish the general frame of the map before adding a "warp" to distend the rest of the map to fit with other recognizable features.[111] With any such metrically irregular map, geographer Robert Rundstrom has outlined, "the ability to recognize point similarity rests to a large extent on the ability to recognize their relative position." Deciding which specific locations to record in the examination of positional overlap depends on the "visual recognition of characteristic line crenulations and relative feature positions."[112] From his analyses of twentieth-century Inuit maps, Rundstrom cautions against two probable sources of error in recognizing and recording homologous points: poor point selection, resulting in "undue clustering and/or dispersal of points," which can be avoided by "careful point selection procedures," and scale error – bias in the map projection – which is unavoidable.[113]

The Inuit maps share a vital similarity with early Chinese maps: their creation was based on the needs of relative location and navigation between points. In Rundstrom's account, "Maps of a single feature, such as a river or coastline segment, were usually provided in response to a navigational inquiry about a particular route or path ... Other Inuit maps served as responses to a more general geosophic inquiry about the characteristics of a network of linear features (two or more coasts or rivers), or the overall landscape of a region."[114] A further interesting

---

[111] See Hsu and Martin-Montgomery, "Emic Perspective on the Mapmaker's Art in Western Han China."

[112] Robert Rundstrom, "Maps, Man, and Land in the Cultural Cartography of the Eskimo (Inuit)" (PhD diss., University of Kansas, 1987), 87–88.

[113] Rundstrom, "Maps, Man, and Land," 90.

[114] Ibid., 103. See also Jacob, *Sovereign Map*, 40.

similarity is the inconsistency of map scale. As noted earlier in this chapter, scholars of early Chinese cartography, such as Mei-ling Hsu, applaud what they see as the general metric accuracy of early Chinese maps.[115] For instance, with regard to the Mawangdui maps, Hsu points to cartographer Tan Qixiang's appraisal of their scale as being extraordinarily accurate: "According to Tan, the map scale within the command area varies between 1:150,000 to 1:200,000 ... Perhaps the intended scale is 1:180,000, or 'one inch to ten miles' in Han units. If this is true, the map's scale factor (error) ranges from 0.9 to 1.2 with 1.0 being perfect. Given the fact that all modern maps have some amount of distance distortion, the scale error of this restored antique map is remarkably small."[116]

Rundstrom's examination of Inuit maps demonstrates that theirs, too, without any modern surveying techniques, could achieve such scales, but their scales varied from point to point across the map "by at least 1:50,000, and a few by as much as 1:100,000." It is not clear how consistent the scale is across all points on the Han map either, and we are not certain about the exact location displayed by the Han maps. If what Yee has noticed about the inconsistency of scale across even later imperial Chinese maps has any bearing, it would be extraordinary if Han-era maps were consistently scaled.[117] A key question, then, is whether the level of accuracy within the Han maps, whatever it was, indicates the use of surveying techniques. Not if the Inuit maps are any indication. The Inuits "didn't do anything but practice dead-reckoning from their boats. They were extremely good at it . . . because their very lives often depended on it."[118] Like the Inuit sketches, the Han-mapped sketches could very well have been composed without detailed survey data. And if they were, it is not clear how *intentionally* accurate they were, rather than being illustrations of the fact that careful spatial appraisals, as with the Inuits', not infrequently render areas with relative accuracy.[119]

---

[115] In addition to Mei-ling Hsu, see also Wan Fang 万方, "Zhongguo gudi tu – Fangmatan yihao Qinmu chutu ditu". 中国故地图–放马滩一号秦墓出土地图, *Shuwu* 书屋 (2006).

[116] Mei-Ling Hsu, "The Han Maps and Early Chinese Cartography," *Annals of the Association of American Geographers* 68, no. 1 (1978), 47–49. Enno Giele also depends on Tan Qixiang's research in his translation, "The Xiongnu." See, for instance, Ssu-ma Ch'ien, "Xiongnu," in *The Grand Scribe's Records*, ed. William H. Nienhauser, Jr. (Indianapolis: Indiana University Press, 2011), 244nn39, 40, 41, 43, 44, and 245n51.

[117] Yee, "Cartography in China," 29: In pre-twentieth century Chinese maps, "a consistent scale over a whole map is the exception; that the grid found on Chinese maps is not based on a coordinate system but is primarily an aid for estimating distances between points; and even so grids were still not the norm in officially sponsored nineteenth-century maps."

[118] Robert Rundstrom, personal communication, April 10, 2015.

[119] In the same communication with Rundstrom of April 10, 2015, I asked, "[C]ould a careful artisan/administrator who lives near or in the area have a somewhat detailed

The physical limitations of the palimpsest likely also distorted early Chinese maps' framing and composition, whether the compression, straightening and curving, or lengthening and shortening of their graphic components. Media features, according to Rundstrom, seemed to have had an effect on the curvilinearity of represented rivers in Inuit maps.[120] Though Rundstrom does not believe exaggerated scaling to have been the case with the Inuit maps, geographer James Corner asserts that such is often used to give points of emphasis.[121]

Reading Maps

Jacob incisively points out that "[a]t first glance, a map with errors is as much a map as a correct map." Only by reference to externals will a distinction be possible and yet any external reference "is compatible with a broad range of graphic options, schematic or highly sophisticated variants, from the sketch drawn from memory to maps produced by scientific agencies. The map can be held to represent space *only by a social consensus.*"[122]

The optic activity on a diagram, a *tu*, is most commonly described as a simple "looking at" (*jian* 見), though diagrams were also "scrutinized" or "studied" (*cha* 察), and "surveyed" (*guan* 觀). Of course, terrestrial diagrams, or maps, were not simply looked at but utilized and read. In various early imperial historical texts, such as from the *Shiji*, *Hanshu*, and *Hou Hanshu* – and even in the excavated Liye 里耶 strips – there are mentions of *tu* or *ditu* being "referred to" or "consulted" (*an* 案), for various purposes,[123] but there are no descriptions in early Chinese texts of how the maps are actually being perceived, interpreted, and mentally appropriated. This is not a limitation particular to China: Jacob declares that in no ancient Greek source is anyone ever portrayed utilizing a map for a practical purpose.[124] In the early texts there are also no statements

sketch made of that area that would be within a certain 'acceptable' margin of error but that was not based on survey data such that some might conclude it did involve surveys?" Rundstrom answered: "Yes. An experienced person with skills in ... understanding, interpreting, and observing landscapes on the one hand, and in rendering images of those landscapes with the best tools available at the time could do it."

[120] Rundstrom, "Maps, Man, and Land," 132.   [121] Corner, "Agency of Mapping."

[122] Jacob, *Sovereign Map*, 13.

[123] *SJ* 118.3085: 左吳等案輿地圖; *SJ* 123.3173: 天子案古圖書; *HS* 29.1686: 可案圖書, 觀地形, 令水工準高下, 開大河上領; *HHS* 50.1667: 明年, 案輿地圖, 令諸國戶口皆等, 租入歲各八千萬; Chen Shou, *Sanguozhi*, "Weishu" 24.692: 今二郡爭界八年, 一朝決之者, 緣有解書圖畫, 可得尋案摘校也. In Liye strip 412, the pertinent text is as follows: 即令卒史主者操圖詣御史, 御史案讎(=相符合)更并, 定為輿地圖。See the transcription section of *Liye Qin jian* 里耶秦簡 (Beijing: Wenwu chubanshe, 2012), 30.

[124] Jacob, "Mapping in the Mind," 26.

that speak to how accuracy, even if only rough, was assessed and critiqued.

Reading a terrestrial map with thorough comprehension territorializes space, gives it structure. Through the deciphering involved in reading, a map becomes simultaneously illuminated and illuminating. The illusion of a homogenous, coherent space gives the impression of legibility. However, with too much homogeneity in its features – or too much distortion – the map becomes unrecognizable, its features unperceivable, their relationships illogical and illegible. Prior to the identification of the defunct map's delineations, it remains merely a denotatively ambiguous landscape – a rough outline. An attempt to read a defunct map is disorienting; because of its distortions, it effectively *deterritorializes* space. Until the map's reader is able to securely identify its settlements and natural features, its boundaries appear dislocated and confusing. Its symbols, already equivocal though ideally aiming for a mathematically precise univocality, are only imperfect formal designations, designations that are open to political and cultural deformations, as Hilde De Weerdt has illustrated with the general maps of the earliest extant printed historical Chinese atlas, the Song-era *Lidai dili zhizhang tu* 歷代地理指掌圖 (*Handy Geographical Maps Throughout the Ages*): In the general maps, the Sixteen Prefectures lost to the Liao in 938 are still placed within the Chinese empire in maps composed in the 1080s, when the prefectures were still in Liao control. This intentional, political distortion "is illustrated most vividly in 'The Map of Autonomous Jurisdictions during Our Dynasty' ('Benchao huawai zhoujun tu' 本朝化外州郡圖), on which the Sixteen Prefectures, together with other prefectures on the western and southwestern periphery, are designated as jurisdictions that, 'although they pay taxes, population registers are not sent up to the Board of Revenue'."[125] The interpretive complexities brought about by such deformations are further complicated by the various denotative emphases and de-emphases, presences and absences, made across a map.[126]

---

[125] De Weerdt, "Maps and Memory," 163.

[126] John Pickles puts the interpretive problem this way: "the difficulty is precisely where to begin and where to end in reconciling these various responsibilities: how do we understand a text as a whole and how do we understand its parts since all texts have a certain anticipation of their parts from the whole, yet the whole is composed only of parts? Image-event, line-meaning, object-relation, sign-signified, map-world; all are parts-whole complexes of relation and meaning." Pickles, *History of Spaces*, 56. Jacob raises further complications pertaining to its use and thus its legibility: Is the map portable or not, suited to management of space in real time or not? Can it be unrolled or unfolded? If not portable, is it on a wall or a floor? Unscrolling a map renders it viewable "as through a cinematographic process . . . The handling of this kind of map causes space to unwind in the fashion of a symbolic voyage moving in two directions." Folding requires a reduction to make the folded sections of the map contain sufficient interpretable

A good way to understand how maps are read and deciphered is to better understand how they are *misread*, and how maps become defunct and unreadable. All maps have intrinsic preferences, distortive emphases that prioritize one readable feature over another. These distortions affect later scholars' reading of the map, but they also, naturally, affected their contemporary reading. The fundamental question to reading any map is concerned with the point at which it ceases to be seen as a map, ceases to have any comprehensible grammar. Framing the question another way using Jacques Bertin's definition of "efficient,"[127] which speaks to how quickly one perceives the answer to a given question in the source, how efficient were early maps, and to which questions?

Perhaps one of the most detailed expositions of the political entanglements involved in the creation of an interpretable but intentionally distorted map lies in the early Han story of Kuang Heng 匡衡, on whose behalf a "mistake" was created, very possibly with the sanction of higher powers. Following is my translation of the relevant text:

> Originally, Kuang Heng was enfeoffed in the Le'an township of Tong [of the Linhuai Commandery]. The fields of the township were about 3,100 *qing* in area, with the Min field path serving as their southern border. In the first year of the Chuyuan era [the first year in the reign of Emperor Yuan of Han] (48 BCE), the commandery map(s) mistook the Min field path for that of Pingling (which lay further south). More than a decade later, [Kuang] Heng was enfeoffed [as the Marquis of the whole of] Linhuai Commandery, and thereupon the [southern] borders of his fief were in fact

information such as to be legible, if only parts of the map were to be held within the viewer's gaze. "Folding allows the map to be reframed at will. The viewer may fold the map to focus his or her gaze on a narrow territorial zone corresponding to the space that is traveled, that is seen. Or, the viewer may unfold the map to widen the point of view and make distances and contiguities more relative ... Held in the hands, the map is amenable to being turned, oriented, put in front of the panorama sought to be read and in the direction of the route being followed. In certain cases the toponymy has to be read upside-down when the topography is seen according to a preferred orientation." Maps on walls and floors naturally face different interpretative complications. Jacob, *Sovereign Map*, 82, 84, 87–97.

[127] "Efficiency is defined by the following proposition: If, in order to obtain a correct and complete answer to a given question, all other things being equal, one construction requires a shorter period of perception than another construction, we can say that it is more efficient for this question." Bertin, *Semiology of Graphics*, 9. Bertin further expounds on the efficient resolution of a conundrum by an image: "The meaningful visual form perceptible in the minimum instant of vision will be called the IMAGE. In this sense, IMAGE corresponds to 'form' in 'form theory,' to 'pattern' and to 'Gestalt'. A synonym would be 'outline' ... The most efficient constructions are those in which any question, whatever its type or level, can be answered in a single instant of perception, in A SINGLE IMAGE. The image, the temporal unit of meaningful visual perception, must not be confused with the FIGURE, which is the apparent and illusory unit defined by the sheet of paper, by a linear frame or by a geographic border." Bertin, *Semiology of Graphics*, 11.

taken to be the field path of Pingling, thus [formally] allocating [his fief] an additional 400 *qing* of land. Not until the first year of the Jianshi era [the first year of the reign of Emperor Cheng of Han] (32 BCE) did the commandery officially confirm the borders of its enfeoffed domains, submitting to the throne their accountings, adjusting and confirming the map(s), and informing the chancellor's (i.e., Kuang Heng's) office of this.[128] Kuang Heng said to his faithful scribe Zhao Yin, "The recorder Lu Si previously worked in the Bureau for Hortatory Addresses and is practiced in these matters, being knowledgeable about domain borders. Organize and gather the bureau's assistants."[129]

The next year, when the calculations were being made, Kuang Heng asked Zhao Yin about the matter of the domain border: "What does the bureau want?" Zhao Yin said, "[Recorder Lu] Si had the calculations reviewed and ordered [your] commandery to certify the calculations. I fear [your] commandery will not be willing to adhere to the certified [calculations]. You could order your household aide to submit a petition to the throne." Kuang Heng said, "I am uncertain whether it will be undertaken [to certify the calculations]. Why go so far as to submit a petition?" [Kuang Heng] in the end did not report [to the throne] that the bureau called for the review but awaited the bureau to do so. Later [Recorder Lu] Si delegated his subordinate Ming to review the calculations, saying, "According to the old map(s), the south of Le'an township took the Pingling field path as its border and did not follow precedent and take the Min field path as its border. Is there an explanation for this?" The commandery then again allotted 400 *qing* to [Kuang Heng's] Le'an enfeoffed domain. Kuang Heng dispatched his attendant scribe to Tong to receive the more than 1,000 *shi* of the returned field rental payment of grain into his household. Metropolitan Commandant Jun and Chamberlain for Palace Revenues Zhong pursued the matter for the Chamberlain for Law Enforcement and presented their investigative findings: "Heng for being the primary commander overseeing the theft deserves [a penalty of] over ten pieces of gold. According to the *Spring and Autumn*, the many lords may not take over lands; with such [a proscription], [the many lords] will be united and will respect the laws and regulations. Kuang Heng occupies a position among the Three Lords [as chancellor], assists with the government of the state, oversees the accounting books, knows the substance of the commandery's situation, and 'corrected' the borders of [his] feudal domain. The accounting books having been certified, [Kuang Heng] broke the laws and regulations, took over and stole land in order to enrich himself. At this point, Lu Si and Ming bent toward and accorded with Kuang Heng's view, partisanly reviewed the commandery's calculations, wantonly

---

[128] Kuang Heng was elevated to the position of chancellor in 36 BCE, toward the end of Emperor Yuan's reign, maintaining his position until this investigation in 30 BCE, two years after the ascension of Emperor Cheng. See the entry for Kuang Heng in Cang Xiuliang 倉修良, ed. *Hanshu cidian* 漢書辭典 (Shandong: Shandong jiaoyu chubanshe, 1996), 239.

[129] For details about the Bureau for Hortatory Addresses (*zou cao* 奏曹), see Olberding, *Dubious Facts*, 42.

reduced the district borders, satisfying those below and deceiving those above, acting wrongly by taking land to satisfy and enrich a high official. All of this is not proper." Thereupon the monarch accepted the address but avoided administering [the punishment]. Chancellor [Kuang Heng] was reduced to a commoner's status and ended his life at home.

初，衡封僮之樂安鄉，鄉本田隄封三千一百頃，南以閩佰為界。初元元年，郡圖誤以閩佰為平陵佰。積十餘歲，衡封臨淮郡，遂封真平陵佰以為界，多四百頃。至建始元年，郡乃定國界，上計簿，更定圖，言丞相府。衡謂所親吏趙殷曰：「主簿陸賜故居奏曹，習事曉知國界，署集曹掾。」明年治計時，衡問殷國界事：「曹欲奈何？」殷曰：「賜以為舉計，令郡實之。恐郡不肯從實，可令家丞上書。」衡曰：「顧當得不耳，何至上書？」亦不告曹使舉也，聽曹為之。後賜與屬明舉計曰：「案故圖，樂安鄉南以平陵佰為界，不（足）〔從〕故而以閩佰為界，解何？」郡即復以四百頃付樂安國。衡遣從史之僮，收取所還田租穀千餘石入衡家。司隸校尉駿、少府忠行廷尉事劾奏「衡監臨盜所主守直十金以上。春秋之義，諸侯不得專地，所以壹統尊法制也。衡位三公，輔國政，領計簿，知郡實，正國界，計簿已定而背法制，專地盜土以自益，及賜、明阿承衡意，猥舉郡計，亂減縣界，附下罔上，擅以地附益大臣，皆不道。」於是上可其奏，勿治，丞相免為庶人，終於家。[130]

The episode reveals that in the first year of Emperor Cheng's reign, officials in the Linhuai Commandery prepared a document certifying fiscal boundaries – probably for tax purposes – and that Kuang Heng, chancellor since the previous emperor Yuan's reign, was concerned about the new emperor discovering his malfeasance. He thus wished for the recorder Lu Si to correct any document that would leave his fief with the southern border at the Min field path, instead stating that the southern border was at the Pingling field path. Lu Si, apparently concerned he would be punished for this deception, has his subordinate Ming collude with officials in the Linhuai Commandery to again "mistakenly" place the southern border of Kuang Heng's fief at the Pingling field path. But clearly someone in the central court administration had become aware of the fraud and ordered an investigation, which exposed the entire plot and concluded in Kuang Heng's being fined for wrongly expanding the borders of his feudal domain. Though Emperor Cheng accepted the findings, demonstrating he was no longer going to allow Kuang Heng to continue to enrich himself (it is possible he had some knowledge of this prior to the investigation), he did not administer the fine, whether because Kuang Heng could have retaliated in some way or because of Kuang Heng's relationship network. Instead, Kuang Heng simply had to resign from his position at court.

[130] *HS* 81.3346; Wang Xianqian 王先謙, ed. *Hanshu buzhu* 漢書補注 (Beijing: Shumu wenxian chubanshe, 1995), 81.1433b–1434a. I thank Griet Vankeerberghen and Fan Lin for directing me to this passage.

In addition to the fascinatingly intricate complications of Kuang Heng's political intrigue – leaving one to wonder what exactly the emperors knew and when – there are numerous indications of how maps were employed, their level of accuracy, and their legibility. First, most basically, the maps mentioned in the anecdote were created for economic purposes, the older ones preserved along with the newer ones. But these maps either were not so accurately detailed as to make errors manifest or their markings were not always scrupulously cross-checked with other administrative records (including previous maps). Without an external administrative record and accurate detailing, the initial "error" would not have been detected. It is also quite plausible that the marking on the "erroneous" maps of the southern boundary at the Pingling field path instead of at the Min field path was simply accepted because of Kuang Heng's elevated administrative status and connection with Emperor Yuan. The error was only "discovered" after the new emperor took the throne, some sixteen years after the erroneous maps had been made. A further indication of a massive cover-up that may have involved Emperor Yuan himself is the reluctance of the succeeding Emperor Cheng to administer the fine.

If the erroneous maps were legibly detailed, they were nevertheless distorted, never functionally transparent, and thus their error was merely accepted as truth. But furthermore, the use of the word *wu* 誤 may point to a politically flexible notion of truth. Indeed, if my analyses in previous work might bear upon this current instance, there was no real "mistake" about the map at all.[131] Any perception of an error would thus arise from a lack of cognizance of the "truth" of the politicized facts, the truth that the southern boundary, whatever other previous documents stated, was accepted as being at Pingling. The "error" of the "mistaken" maps was thus an error in not openly acknowledging this politically accepted revision. All court officials, including Emperor Yuan, may very well have known the maps were politically distorted. With the additive of this unpublicized information, this intentional distortion, the map becomes

---

[131] Olberding, *Dubious Facts*, 138–143. As I wrote about another episode in which *wu* was used, the error is "akin to the error of a document that 'lacks' complete information: A document is 'lacking' and thus flawed or mistaken." The "error" is not "an objectively incontestable error. It is instead an error of emphasis or of ignorance, a deficiency that allows the original perception . . . to remain basically unaltered. The loose boundaries of the sources of error – that it commonly appears to be treated as stemming from the manner in which information is communicated or received rather than any objective discrepancy between what is perceived and what is the case – permits an expanded boundary on what could have been treated as reliable and useful." Olberding, *Dubious Facts*, 142–143.

more legible. In sum, the issue of error was not one of accuracy but intentional distortion.

Chapter Summary

Though similar in construction to landscapes, early Chinese *tu* were plans of definite spatial consequence, their definition resting not so much on their appearance as on their function and syntax, composed in a way that was legible and efficacious. The pacing out of the territories represented in *tu* likely also signaled a personal or ritual investiture. In both early Chinese landscapes and terrestrial maps, spatial representations changed across their face, of either visual vantage point or temporal relations between locales. Maps thus were prone to distortion or even falsification. Further complicating the maps' legibility is whether their markings of human activity and construction are descriptive or prescriptive. Attempts to precisely articulate and measure the relative spatial locations and the distances between them must thus anticipate embedded challenges and contradictions. These mensurative challenges are further magnified by the aesthetic conventions and features that impacted mapmaking. Stock representational conventions suffuse the early maps, with dark undulating lines used for rivers (or even possibly mountains), and boxes and texts for settlement areas. Further confusing the metrical evaluation of the map is the blending of the vertical and horizontal perspectives, horizontal space distorted, extended or contracted over an arbitrarily sized visual plane. In short, there was little attempt at carefully descriptive realism. To best understand how such maps might have been read or deciphered would involve analyzing how they were misread, and how they became defunct, illegible, to analyze what was regarded as an "error" in the map.

3   Movement and Geography

Though their forms are obscured by a layered, multivocal composition, early maps were, I have been arguing, largely a summation of memory, of lived experience, of permissions and prohibitions of sight and knowledge. Sight and knowledge could be prohibited or permitted directly and physically, by walls and forbidding travel, movement, and also indirectly, by the limitations, occlusions, and distortions of the information one received from locals but also from one's own spies, diplomats, and representatives, whose loyalties (captured in the administrative prizing of *zhong* 忠 or later, in the imperial period, *lian* 廉) might be insecure, open to persuasion and corruption, for even the most banal, trivial, personal reasons. In order to understand most thoroughly how the visualized diagrams could be best deciphered and read, by both their original users and current scholars, we need to better appreciate how the sovereign space they were attempting to trace was fully formed. Doing so, we can better grasp what exactly they were *not* describing, or how their descriptions were distorted and limited, and thus how we need to be careful in taking them, and their visualizations of power networks, at face value. In the following chapters, I explore the internal, external, and transgressive definitions of sovereign space, definitions that lie at the root of how sovereignty was established, extended, curtailed, and ruptured. Naturally, much of this lived use of space cannot be captured on a static diagram or map, a limitation that should give us pause when we analyze early maps. Rather than trying to forcibly excavate the concrete data, to press them into a shape we can metrically recognize and translate, we should treat them as only roughly gesturing toward spatial relationships and even possibly containing locations that are either distorted, perhaps intentionally, or prescriptive.

Martial Lines: The Walling of Sovereignty

The short essay titled "*ditu*" 地圖 in the *Guanzi* 管子 discusses the features of a landscape that all military commanders must thoroughly know, associating these directly with "examining" (*shen* 審) and "understanding" (*zhi* 知) *ditu*, "terrestrial maps." If the succeeding list of features is any indication, some common attributes of early Chinese geographic knowledge are:

(1) its topographical features, including valleys (*gu* 谷), mountains (*shan* 山), hills (*qiufu* 丘阜), and highlands (*linglu* 陵陸);
(2) flora, including grasses (*jucao* 苴草), trees (*linmu* 林木), and rushes (*puwei* 蒲葦);
(3) civil engineering structures, including roads (*daoli* 道里) and walls (*chengguo* 城郭), and settlements (notable townships (*mingyi* 名邑) and abandoned townships (*feiyi* 廢邑)); and
(4) land quality (*kunzhi zhi di* 困殖之地).

The passage concludes by describing the function of this knowledge – to be aware of obstructions and openings, impediments or aids to movement.[1] A passage in the *Hanshu*, in an address by Liu An 劉安 (179–122 BCE), puts it more succinctly: with a map, one surveys major aspects that permit or prevent movement – mountains, waterways, critical points, and barriers.[2] Of course, many of the features listed in the *Guanzi* essay are not included in most extant premodern geographic maps.[3] The features in most premodern maps hew more closely to those essentials remarked by Liu An. Thus we may say that Liu An's contracted list contains the fundamental features highlighted in most descriptions of graphically represented terrestrial space: mountains, waterways, and man-made alterations to the natural landscape, such as roads, walls, and towns.

Pei Xiu, while also giving primary emphasis to named mountains (*mingshan* 名山) and the great rivers (*dachuan* 大川), later in his famous preface catalogs features very much in alignment with those in the *Guanzi*

---

[1] "All military commanders must first examine and come to know maps. They must know thoroughly the location of winding, gate-like defiles, streams that may inundate their chariots, famous mountains, passable valleys, arterial rivers, highlands and hills. They must also know where grasses, trees, and rushes grow, the distances of roads, the size of city and suburban walls, famous and deserted towns, and barren and fertile land. They should thoroughly store up [in their minds] the location of ways in and out of the terrain. Then afterward they can march their armies and raid towns. In the disposition of troops they will know what lies ahead and behind, and will not lose the advantages of the terrain. This is the constant value of maps" 凡兵主者，必先審知地圖，轘轅之險、濫車之水、名山、通谷、經川、陵陸、丘阜之所在，苴草、林木、蒲葦之所茂，道里之遠近，城郭之大小，名邑、廢邑、困殖之地，必盡知之。地形之出入相錯者盡藏之，然後可以行軍襲邑，舉錯知先後，不失地利，此地圖之常也。See *Guanzi jiaozhu*, 2:529–530; *Guanzi*, 391–392.
[2] 以地圖察其山川要塞, *HS* 64.2778.
[3] For a collection of extant pre-Yuan maps, see Cao Wanru 曹婉如, *Zhongguo gudai ditu ji: Zhanguo – Yuan* 中國古代地圖集，戰國—元 (Beijing: Wenwu chubanshe, 1990).

essay: mountains (*shan* 山); waterways such as rivers (*chuan* 川) and lakes (*hai* 海); wet areas such as marshes (*ze* 澤) and bogs (*xi* 隰); relatively even and uneven dry terrain, such as plains (*yuan* 原) and slopes (*bei* 陂); roads (*lu* 路); settlements such as commanderies (*jun* 郡), principalities (*guo* 國), administrative seats (*xian* 縣), and townships (*yi* 邑); and borders (*qiangjie xiangzou* 彊界鄉陬). But here again, as indicated in the descriptives Pei attached to his list of features, these are noted for their permission or hindrance of movement. Pei remarks on whether roads are indirect/curved (*yu* 迂) or direct/straight (*zhi* 直), whether areas are easy (*yi* 易) or difficult (*xian* 險) to traverse, and the distances to be traveled between places (*diyu yuanjin* 地域遠近).[4] These two essays', and Liu An's, significant and characteristic points of emphasis coincide with what is detailed in maps of the later imperial period. For instance, with the Song *Lidai dili zhizhang tu*, "The map of the empire consists at its basic level of an administrative grid, the Great Wall, networks of rivers and mountains, and peoples and states on the periphery whose vague identities define the solidity of the empire."[5]

The fundamental function of most early imperial maps, it seems, was the administration of settled taxable agriculturalist populations, the foreign threats to these administrative polities, and the natural and artificial boundaries, specifically walls, riverways, and mountains, that can serve as defenses against such incursions. Significantly, in the *Lidai dili zhizhang tu*, most of the non-Chinese peoples that had been listed on Jia Dan's 賈耽 (729–805 CE) ninth-century map were not included, with the readers of the map informed that "only those who present a challenge to Chinese sovereignty are to be noted."[6] The Great Wall, along with the above-mentioned mountains and riverways, had become, by the Song, "a part of the empire's timeless base layer," turning into a "naturalized" demarcation of the empire.[7]

The inclusion of the above geographic details in early maps accords with how descriptions of terrain are represented, or recommended, in early canonical administrative and military documents. In the *Sunzi*, for instance, descriptions of terrain are to refer to "the fall of the land, proximate distances, the difficulty of passage, the degree of openness, and the viability of the land for deploying troops."[8] All terrain is thus

---

[4] Fang Xuanling et al., *Jinshu*, 35.1039–1040.
[5] De Weerdt, "Cultural Logics of Map Reading," 255.   [6] Ibid., 253.   [7] Ibid.
[8] 地者，高下、遠近、險易、廣狹、死生也. *Sunzi yizhu* 孫子译注 (Shanghai: Shanghai guji chubanshe, 1984), 78; Roger Ames, *Sun-Tzu: The Art of Warfare* (New York: Ballantine Books, 1993), 103.

definable in terms of its possibilities for action. Without knowledge of the "spatial disposition" or "form" (*xing* 形) of the land, "its mountains and forests, its passes and natural hazards, its wetlands and swamps – you cannot deploy the army on it."[9] The *Sunzi* recognizes that the knowledge of this terrain comes from local reports: "Unless you can employ local scouts, you cannot turn the terrain to your advantage."[10]

These prescriptive recommendations regarding the knowledge, the "mapping" of terrain, find ample exemplars, whether in analytical or historical texts. In the *Guanzi*, we saw the basic concern with movement and profitable allocation of forces and supplies. In the *Huainanzi* 淮南子, terrain is also put in terms of movement, in its direction or prevention. When speaking of the "dispositions of the terrain" (*dishi* 地勢), the *Huainanzi* elaborates only on those features that impact movement, both literally, as with "mountain defiles" (*xialu* 峽路), "marshy passes" (*jinguan* 津關), "great mountains" (*dashan* 大山), and "notable barriers" (*mingsai* 名塞), as well as figuratively, with "dragon and snake coils" (*longshepan* 龍蛇蟠), "trapping umbrellas" (*queliju* 卻笠居), "goat intestine paths" (*yangchangdao* 羊腸道), and "webbed fishtrap gates" (*conggoumen* 蔮笱門).[11] Indeed, the *Huainanzi* is explicit in its connecting mapping to movement, at least in military affairs: "Knowing [which terrain] is obstructed or passable … this is the office of the commandant" 知險易 … 此候之官.[12] A similar emphasis on movement and its obstruction is found in the description of the official charged with handling *tu* in the *Zhouli*, the supervisor of strategic obstructions (*sixian* 司險). This official is enjoined to know about "the obstructions posed by mountains and forests, and by rivers and marshes," as well as of the pathways and roads that cut through them.[13]

---

[9] 不知山林、險阻、沮澤之形者，不能行軍. "Jiu di" 九地, *Sunzi*; *Sunzi yizhu*, 197; Ames, *Sun-Tzu*, 161.

[10] 不用鄉導者，不能得地利. "Jiu di," *Sunzi*; *Sunzi yizhu*, 197; Ames, *Sun-Tzu*, 161.

[11] Liu An 劉安, *Huainanzi jishi* 淮南子集釋 (Beijing: Zhonghua shuju, 1998), 1:15.1073.

[12] Liu An, *Huainanzi jishi* 1:15.1058; see also Andrew Seth Meyer, *The Dao of the Military: Liu An's Art of War* (New York: Columbia University Press, 2012), 104.

[13] 掌九州之圖，以周知其山林、川澤之阻，而達其道路. 設國之五溝五涂，而樹之林以為阻固，皆有守禁，而達其道路. 國有故，則藩塞阻路而止行者，以其屬守之，唯有節者達之. *Zhouli zhushu*, (Beijing ed.) 2:799–800. Haicheng Wang details the importance of the *sixian*, concluding with the hypothesis, "If we take the *Zhouli* to reflect Warring States practice, then we can infer that military maps depicting a state's topographical features were systematically made and collected by state agencies, a point hinted at in other late Warring States texts as well. In one of them, *Han Feizi*, maps are equated with the actual land: 'if (we) present the maps (to the Qin state to pledge subservience), (our land) will be reduced.'" Wang, *Writing and the Ancient State*, 200. Even if Warring States maps were "systematically" made, such does not entail that they were necessarily produced by careful, systematic, metrically accurate surveys, or resulting in metrically accurate maps, as I've argued in the previous chapter.

Even in idealized mapping documents, such as the *Shanhaijing*, there is, as Vera Dorofeeva-Lichtmann states, "*a process-oriented scheme* for moving through the world step-by-step."[14] The location of each mountain in the *Shanjing* portion is organized according to routes, with the location of each mountain "given according to the principle of respective locations, that is with respect to the preceding one along the route, including the precise distance from it."[15] (The *Haijing*, devoted to "fabulous" distant peoples, includes routes in its first four chapters but not in subsequent ones and "the precise distances between locations are never in evidence."[16] This, however, may be due, at least in part, to its alien focus.) Indeed, since Liu Xin 劉歆 (ca. 50 BCE–23 CE), the origins of the *Shanhaijing* were believed to have been the "route notes" made by Bo Yi 伯夷, assistant to Yu. As Dorofeeva-Lichtmann observes, "'Pacing' the routes is attributed to Yu the Great, whereas describing them to Bo Yi." The structuring of space is thus organized around prescribed, repeatable actions, steps and directions taken.[17] Through patterned, defined routes, spatial arrangements receive an earlier iteration in the "Levies of Yu" ("Yugong" 禹貢) chapter of the *Shangshu* 尚書 (*Book of Documents*),[18] but the routes in that chapter are marked only by a few geographical objects, with no other details provided. These routes also are not related to the stipulated terrestrial divisions, that is, the nine provinces and the five zones. By contrast, as Dorofeeva-Lichtmann points out, each route in the *Shanhaijing* "is linked to a certain section of the earth's surface."[19]

At the start of this section, I outlined the *Guanzi*'s recommendations to military commanders to examine *ditu* as rooted in possibilities of movement and maneuver. As also indicated, numerous similar statements are made in the *Sunzi bingfa* 孫子兵法 and other early Chinese works regarding those features of the terrain with which the competent general needs to be familiar. What these share, as with any military map, is a concern for movement and profitable allocation of forces and supplies. But as many specialists of the extant early Chinese maps realize, the forwarding of military agendas and aims were likely not their chief purpose. Rather, the

---

[14] Dorofeeva-Lichtmann, "Conception of Terrestrial Organization in the *Shan hai jing*," 58.

[15] Ibid., 59.   [16] Ibid.   [17] Ibid., 60.   [18] See above, p. 44.

[19] Dorofeeva-Lichtmann, "Conception of Terrestrial Organization in the *Shan hai jing*," 60. Dorofeeva-Lichtmann terms this a "conceptual organization of space." See also Vera V. Dorofeeva-Lichtmann, "Political Concept Behind an Interplay of Spatial 'Positions'," *Extrême-Orient-Extrême-Occident* 18 (1996), 13.

primary purpose of most extant maps, and perhaps of most early maps in general, favored the administration of economic, not military, force.[20] The downplaying of any conceivable military purpose in these maps may owe to the threat inherent in their possession. To possess a map of any real military value was to possess the means to destabilize both the enemy's and one's own political regime. One need only reflect on the story of Jing Ke to understand just how powerful and, even more importantly, how relatively *rare*, the possession of a useful military map was, for the map enabled one to view relationships that were otherwise invisible.[21]

Yet it should be underscored that, as in ancient Greece, in ancient China, maps were not necessary for the organization of space. All that was necessary was the understanding of relative locations. As Christian Jacob declares in his article, "Mapping in the Mind,"

Traveling, exploring, seafaring, war-making, ruling and founding remote colonies did not necessarily imply the use of maps. There is not a single ancient Greek source that depicts someone using maps in a practical situation. Such a fact had two implications. First, 'geographical knowledge' did not depend on maps, but on other media, such as travel reports, sea journeys, and periegeses, descriptions of a particular country. Geography relied on words and discourses, on human memory. Second, maps had other functions: the way they were drawn, the information they encompassed, the way they were diffused, simply did not allow practical and field uses.[22]

In fact, both Strabo's and Ptolemy's works on geography were dependent on travel reports – place names and itineraries, *not* astronomical calculations, for such were basically unavailable.[23] For Jacob, the functional distinction of the map in ancient Greece from the sixth and fifth centuries BCE was this: the map "helped to gather, organize and unify a heterogeneous knowledge about places and tribes, but its purpose was also more abstract and theoretical."[24] Represented geographic, or chorographic (i.e., of a limited region), space is thus a set of "places," a "place" being unitary (a unit) but "invested with understandings of behavioral appropriateness, cultural expectation, and so forth."[25]

---

[20] "The *Kuan-tzu* chapter on ti-t'u clearly shows that maps were used as essential means of administrative control"; Reiter, "Some Remarks on the Chinese Word *t'u*," 313.

[21] For Jing Ke's ruse using a (false?) map of the Dukang 督亢 region of Yan 燕, see *SJ* 86.2532 and 2534.

[22] Jacob, "Mapping in the Mind," 26.

[23] Ibid. See also Irby-Massie and Keyser, *Greek Science of the Hellenistic Era*, 145. Ptolemy recognized that astronomical measurements were preferable but, as there were few of them, had to resign himself to relying on distances measured by traveling on the surface of the earth.

[24] Jacob, "Mapping in the Mind," 29.

[25] Andrew M. Riggsby, "Space," in *The Cambridge Companion to the Roman Historians*, ed. Andrew Feldherr (New York: Cambridge University Press, 2009), 152.

If scheming and planning for future eventualities in keeping with a conceptual, possessive organization of space[26] are basic cognitive activities behind *tu*, a "mapping" or "planning" of movement, references in numerous early Chinese texts concerned with military action most certainly can reveal nuances of its employ, and the employment of maps and mapped terrain in a military context. The *Huainanzi* declares: "That which soldiers secretly discuss is the way of Heaven; that which soldiers diagram (圖) and sketch (畫) are the forms of the earth; that about which they speak openly are human affairs; that which decides the overcoming [of their enemies] are key areas and strategic dispositions."[27] Beyond the obvious connection between mapping and terrain, the parallelism in the passage suggests an initial grouping of hidden plans – the way of Heaven and the forms of the Earth – followed by that which is openly discussed and displayed, namely human affairs and military might. Maps – including military plans and depictions of terrain, and the movements of the heavens, which guide the course of human affairs – are kept hidden, only to be revealed and realized at the proper time and place.

This sentiment accords with the dangers of possessing a map of any real military value, as the story of Jing Ke demonstrates.[28] The greatest leader,

[26] Dorofeeva-Lichtmann, "Conception of Terrestrial Organization in the *Shan hai jing*," 60.

[27] 兵之所隱議者，天道也；所圖畫者，地形也；所明言者，人事也；所以決勝者，鈐勢也。 *Huainanzi*, "Binglüe" 兵略 ("An overview of the military"); Liu An, *The Huainanzi*, trans. John S. Major, Sarah A. Queen, Andrew Seth Meyer, and Harold D. Roth (New York: Columbia University Press), 603; Liu An, *Huainanzi jishi*, 2:15.1081.

[28] Such sentiments are further reinforced by the *Hanfeizi* passage cited by Haicheng Wang mentioned in n13. In it, we definitely see the potency, and danger, in the possession of a map: "When the map [of one's territory] is submitted [to another state, even one presumably offering 'assistance'], territory will be severed off ... Once one's territory is severed off, one's state will also be severed" 獻圖則地削，效璽則名卑，地削則國削. *Hanfeizi jijie* 韓非子集解 (Beijing: Zhonghua shuju, 1998), 19.453; translation mine. The *Hanshu* also remarks that the younger brother of Emperor Yuan (r. 48–33 BCE) was prohibited by the emperor from borrowing materials related to geography (*dixing* 地形) and the location of the state's frontier barriers (*sai* 塞) and natural obstacles (*e* 阨), because these were materials "not appropriate for the many feudal lords and kings" 不宜在諸侯王 under the purview of the emperor. See *HS* 80.3324–3325. Concern over the possession of maps was an explicit concern in the Song dynasty, as Fan Lin has amply demonstrated in her dissertation: "In 1053, Vice Commissioner of the Ministry of Revenue, Fu Yong 傅永 (ca. 11th century), while being sent to the Liao Empire, happened to find out that the Khitan official who accompanied him was not only informed of the recent merger of two Song prefectures, but also had seen a map of Yizhou. The Song government, being highly alert after learning this, immediately sent a secret order (*miyu* 密諭) to the prefectures in Hebei Circuit on the border with the Liao, forbidding the presentation and circulation of prefectural maps among envoys. This rule was once again reinstated two decades later, on the one hand ordering envoys to follow the arrangement that Song had made for them, on the other hand forbidding the Bureau to supply them with maps." Lin, "Cartographic Empire," 107. We can also see this concern in European maps, as Jacob details with respect to a 1575 mapped view of

the mapper of military and political plans, is thus advised repeatedly in the *Huainanzi* not to be seen, to "lodge in the Sourceless" and move "in the Formless,"[29] not to allow himself to be "gauged" (*kui* 揆) or "measured" (*duo* 度).[30] If the leader's plans are ever seen, they will not work, for his "forms" (*xing* 形) will be "regulated" (*zhi* 制), controlled by others.[31] Thus the Way should have no form. Without form, it is not susceptible to schemes and plans: it cannot be "regulated" (*zhi* 制), "measured" (*duo* 度), "deceived" (*zha* 詐), "circumscribed" (*gui* 規), or "disordered" (*lü* 慮).[32] The commander orders the plans of his subordinates but his own plans are not known. His knowledge must be kept to himself. He must

see singularly and know singularly. Seeing singularly is to see what is not seen. Knowing singularly is to know what is not known. To see what others do not is called "enlightenment." To know what others do not is called "spiritlike." The spiritlike and enlightened is one who triumphs in advance. He who triumphs in advance cannot be attacked when he defends, cannot be defeated in battle, cannot be defended against when he attacks.[33]

As I have elaborated elsewhere,[34] in the discussions captured in early Chinese historiographical representations, though geography was an essential concern for military deliberations, whether in the *Zhanguoce* or in the military memorials of the early Han, the geographic details included in the court discussions pertaining to these matters were not precisely represented. Of course, they were not, in gross outlines, utterly inaccurate. The relational positions of the kingdoms of the Warring States, as represented in the *Zhanguoce*, were basically correct. We can see evidence of this in the discussions of troop movements in the *Zhanguoce*, when Zhang Yi 張儀 cautions the King of Wei 魏 that Qin cavalry would only need several days.[35] For Zhang Yi, time, not space, is

Gdansk. Human figures placed in the foreground of an oblique view of the city were included, according to the authors of the volume in which this representation was included, "to prevent the Turks from looking at the city views and getting strategic information about them. They were, so to speak, an iconographic defense against hostile viewers who were forbidden by their religion from looking at human figures." Jacob, *Sovereign Map*, figure 39.

[29] 藏於無原 ... 運於無形. Liu An, *Huainanzi jishi*, 3:15.1080; Liu An, *The Huainanzi*, 602.

[30] 不可揆度者也. Liu An, *Huainanzi jishi*, 3:15.1085.

[31] 謀見則窮，形見則制。 Liu An, *Huainanzi jishi*, 3:15.1093.

[32] Liu An, *Huainanzi jishi*, 3:15.1067.

[33] 夫將者，必獨見獨知。獨見者，見人所不見也；獨知者，知人所不知也。見人所不見，謂之明；知人所不知，謂之神。神明者，先勝者也。先勝者，守不可攻，戰不可勝，攻不可守. Liu An, *Huainanzi jishi*, 3:15.1096; Liu An, *The Huainanzi*, 612.

[34] See Olberding, *Dubious Facts*, particularly chapters five, six, seven, and ten.

[35] "Furthermore, in all directions Your land is level and open to the other feudal lords. Straight roads converge on it as do the spokes of a wheel upon its hub. Not a single [named] mountain nor great river lies athwart them. From Zheng, the capital of Han, to Liang, the capital of Wei, is but a hundred leagues; from Chen, the capital of Chu, to

the metric. As Cordell Yee contends, this temporal sensibility is one of the broad features informing the representation of space that is shared by both early mapmaking and painting. In both

the experience of space was dynamic and fluid, intimately related to one's experience of time. Space, emptiness, was regarded almost as an entity in itself – as such it was boundless and unlimited. Objects could be measured and defined; space could not be so fixed.[36]

With more localized details, however, we find exaggeration, or at least an obvious lack of concern for even a plausible representation of space. Neither distances nor locations were fixed – in truth, distances were readily available to modification. Often, within early Chinese historical narratives, troops flew across vast distances over impossibly short intervals. For instance, in Sima Qian's famously detailed account of the battle of Jingxing 井陘, although he gives the time and place, using his descriptors, it is very difficult to precisely mark the battle's location. The representation of geographic space in the addresses that flesh out the historiographical narrative are similarly imprecise, if not more so. It was not uncommon in the addresses for traversed geographic space to be extended or contracted – or encumbered by insurmountable natural boundaries – to suit the rhetorical needs of the addressor.[37]

An address submitted by Liu An to Emperor Wu of Han highlights the limitations of maps and the risks involved in depending on them to pursue state-sponsored initiatives, particularly military ones. In it, Liu An speaks to the emperor's plans to defend the kingdom of Nanyue 南越 against the repeated onslaughts of the neighboring Minyue 閩越 people, both of whose polities lay adjacent to Liu An's kingdom of Huainan. Highly critical of the emperor's planned military expedition, Liu An's address presents an archetype of geographical description, one common to the early histories. In fact, the address is one of the relatively few instances in the Han histories in which there is a quoted remark about the use of a "ditu" 地圖. In this section of the address, in which Liu An describes in some detail the geographic features of Yue lands, he cautions that any

---

Liang, slightly more than two hundred. A horse might gallop or a man run the distance and not feel weary on arrival in Liang. To the south of Liang are the [frontier marches] of Chu; to the west are the [frontier marches] of Han; to the north are the [frontier marches] of Zhao; and to the east are the [frontier marches] of Qi. On all four sides Wei soldiers stand guard and those defending the wayhouses and border fortresses are on alert" 地四平，諸侯四通，條達輻湊，無有名山大川之阻。從鄭至梁，不過百里；從陳至梁，二百餘里。馬馳人趨，不待倦而至梁。南與楚境，西與韓境，北與趙境，東與齊境，卒戍四方，守亭障者參列. He Jianzhang, *Zhanguoce zhushi*, 2:823; Olberding, *Dubious Facts*, 82. Translation modified.

[36] Yee, "Cartography in China," 144.   [37] Olberding, *Dubious Facts*, 104–105.

expedition in which the soldiers are not aware of the "dispositions" (shi 勢) and "obstructions" (zu 阻) will fail miserably.[38] Even if their lands are conquered, they likely would not be able to be put under the administration of commanderies and districts and thereby be incorporated as part of the imperial "map."

It is at this point in the address that Liu An coincidentally makes his only reference to a map, a ditu, stressing that a map's distances are deceptive. The proximity in mapped distances is an illusion, a dissembling artifice that conceals the actual extension of space, a deception that can easily lead, Liu An insinuates, to careless calculation and underestimation of the time and resources needed to traverse the distance. The referenced map, presumably the emperor's, is further deceptive in its general lack of botanical, zoological, and topographical detail. It appears, from Liu An's speaking of an "investigation" of the map, that only the three major features of early maps, namely mountains, rivers, and strategic defensive positions, were marked. As he admits, it *could not* adequately display other salient details. Because of this limitation, the map, meant to illuminate, in actuality blinds. Its facilitation of physical movement is hampered by its essential, only roughly accurate, abstraction.

Liu An gives a detailed critique regarding the equation of mapped and lived space, warning the emperor that to survey the landscape on a map may seem simple, "but to traverse [its distances] is extremely arduous."[39] The soldiers will be forced to carry chariots across mountain cliffs, drag boats up along rivers "for hundreds or thousands of leagues." These mountains are the boundaries of the known and the visible, the limit between civilization and wild. The mountains are "where the traces of men disappear and carriage roads do not pass through," the line "by which outside and inside are separated in the natural world."[40] The

---

[38] It is here where a distinction made by Plato between the learning drawn through bodily experience, which we can learn through *mimêsis*, and that which is learned through image-making, e.g., the abstraction of mapping, comes to be most conspicuous. Of course, as Plato recognized, bodily experience can convey as much a deception as a clarification. For the distinction, see Allen, *Why Plato Wrote*, 62.

[39] "When one investigates on a map the mountains, rivers, and strategic defensive positions, their distance on the map from each other is only a couple of inches, but the physical space between them is hundreds or thousands of leagues. The obstructing cliffs and the woods and bush cannot be adequately displayed on a map. To survey this on a map seems quite simple, but to traverse it is extremely arduous" 以地圖察其山川要塞，相去不過寸數，而間獨數百千里，阻險林叢弗能盡著. 視之若易，行之甚難. Olberding, *Dubious Facts*, 192–193; *HS* 64A.2778.

[40] Olberding, *Dubious Facts*, 195; *HS* 64A.2781. Scott offers a relevant insight on early states: "[A]lmost any area that was difficult to access, illegible and trackless, and unsuitable for intensive farming might qualify as a barbarian zone." James C. Scott, *Against the*

soldiers will be "hemmed in by thick forest and groves of bamboo" and their boats "will smash against rock" all along the waterways, and the men will not only be imperiled by poisonous snakes and predatory beasts but also by invisible, and unmappable, disease and weather.[41]

Thus even were the map metrically accurate (which it presumably is not), there are features of the landscape, as Liu An stresses, that undermine its efficacy. Liu An clearly demonstrates that, informed even by the best maps, the emperor is woefully "unfamiliar with the terrain of the southern border region."[42] The emperor's distorted view is brought about by the illusion of its vertical location, the illusion of its hanging above the planar frame of the emperor's map. The illusion of this ocular travel upwards brings a dislocation, and a distortion of view and experience. What is most important in all of this is the fact that Liu An's geographic knowledge is more detailed, and thus presumably more accurate (unless his presentation is intentionally distorted or falsified) than the mapped knowledge the emperor has access to. It is this "local" knowledge, this knowledge acquired by personal travel that is the basis for all maps, as I have argued, but it is also the most reliable. Thus Liu An is in essence denying the very efficacy of a map, any map, in strategic considerations. Only with the personal experience of a terrain, he implies, can anyone truly understand the uses and misuses of a map.

Pertaining to the reliability of local knowledge, we make an important qualification: as with any collected information, local knowledge was only as good as its source. If sources were compromised, adulterated, or simply deceptive, as they naturally could be, especially when the inquiry came from unwelcome parties, local knowledge about terrain would likely be incomplete or distorted. Strabo mentions that the unreliability of geographic information was great when gathered about distant lands, as India was for the Greeks:

But it is necessary for us to hear accounts of this country with indulgence, for not only is it farthest away from us, but not many of our people have seen it; and even those who have seen it, have seen only parts of it, and the greater part of what they say is from hearsay; and even what they saw they learned on a hasty passage with an army through the country. Wherefore they do not give out the same accounts of the same things, even though they have written these accounts as though their statements had been carefully confirmed.[43]

Grain: A Deep History of the Earliest States (New Haven, CT: Yale University Press, 2017), 228.

[41] Olberding, *Dubious Facts*, 193; *HS* 64A.2779.   [42] Ibid., 194; *HS* 64A.2781.

[43] *The Geography of Strabo*, trans. Horace Leonard Jones (Cambridge, MA: Harvard University Press, 1930), bk. 15, 3.

In essence, the territorializing efforts of domineering powers to collect information about an area are obstructed by the deterritorializing efforts of local denizens who intentionally offer bad or misleading information.[44]

Chapter Summary

In order to properly appraise early Chinese maps, their current readers would be well advised to remind themselves of the fact that their spatial relationships seem to be based less on precise measurements than rough gestures, drawn from the experiences of those who have traveled the area. Prohibitions and permissions to movement are the primary drivers to the composition of knowledge about terrestrial space. This is demonstrated in emphasized landscape features, whether in the rare essay on maps (*ditu*) – such as found in the *Guanzi* or by Pei Xiu, the celebrated mathematically oriented cartographer – or in remarks by advisors to the throne such as Liu An. The seminal function of prohibitions and permissions to movement is further demonstrated in remarks located in other early Chinese texts with distinctly military or administrative valences, such as the *Sunzi*, *Huainanzi*, and *Zhouli*. Even the geographic idealizations of the *Shanhaijing* follow a process-oriented scheme, a "pacing" of its routes.

Given that the composition of early maps is largely dependent on movement, and thus on travel reports, they are very open to distortion and misappropriation. These compositional operations have epistemic consequences, not simply for how the knowledge produced is used by officials, but why officials need to keep such valuably abstracted knowledge hidden; indeed, how they need to keep all measurable knowledge hidden until it is necessary to disclose. The core of early Chinese sovereignty is vulnerable to the depredations of those who abuse measurement, especially when measurement is governed by the personal travel of those whose reports may be governed by ulterior motives. The early Chinese sovereign thus was required to evaluate and cement geographic relationships in more ritualized, personally inflected ways.

---

[44] See Deleuze and Guattari, *A Thousand Plateaus*, 222, on "deterritorialization."

4 The Perception of the "State": The Internal Definition of Sovereign Space

Particularly in autocratic or monarchic regimes, central governmental powers often appropriate or attempt to neutralize local unauthorized cults and thus local sovereignty, militarily or otherwise. Early China was no exception. But local religious structures are necessary to maintain ideological and cultural dominance. In the place of original local cults, early Chinese authorities – possibly dating back to the Western Zhou period but almost certainly from the Qin and early Han (207/2 BCE–8 CE) periods – installed a system of "altars of soil" (*she* 社). The altars of soil served as imperial "writing" on the space of the land, a legend of its occupation, or intended occupation, just as governmental offices created formal semantico-political connections.[1] Concomitantly, the early Chinese authorities developed and employed the notion of *de* 德, commonly translated as "virtue" but more accurately translated as "charisma" – whether moral, political, or psychological. These ritual structures were employed to extend and solidify the Huaxia 華夏 or "Chinese" sense of territorial sovereignty. This sense of territorial sovereignty was not superficially symbolic but actively manifested in how frontier regions were managed – legally, bureaucratically, and militarily. While *de* was frequently understood as a potential influence beyond the borders of the state, defining in some measure the reach of early China's

---

[1] "In origin these altars were heaped-up mounds of soil. Feudal lords established ritual and political allegiances by mixing a gift of soil from the altar mound of the central ruler into their own mound. The altars of the soil and the grain symbolized the social, political, and religious heart of the feudal state, while offerings to the spirits of the four directions (*fang* 方) served to delineate the borders of each territorial polity and its spirits. Landscapes, their mountains, and their rivers, figured as sacred spaces. They were, as the *Liji* states, able to produce clouds and cause the emergence of wind and rain, and inhabited by 'strange beings' called 'spirits.'" Roel Sterckx, *The Animal and the Daemon in Early China* (Albany: State University of New York Press, 2002), 109. In his *Heaven Is Empty*, Filippo Marsili notes that a passage in "The Hereditary Houses of the Three Kings" ("San wang shijia" 三王世家), the last chapter of the *Shiji*'s "Hereditary Houses" section, explains that the *she* altars "epitomized an old, allegedly Zhou-like, 'feudal', 'devolutionary' conception of space," representing not territory "directly controlled by the emperor, but as the portion of land the sovereign entrusted to the authority of local leaders." Marsili, *Heaven Is Empty*, 197, and *SJ* 60.2115.

informal "soft" sovereignty, it was most regularly used to speak to the area where the central court's administrative apparatus was formally in place and regularly supervised. There was, explicit on the Zhou bronzes, a lineal or administrative connection to the central court, expressed in the possessive "our."[2] Indeed, I hazard that a general clue to the limit of formal administrative oversight is when the sovereign's ritualized power is described as not "reaching" an area, as in this *Zuozhuan* passage: "Jin was located deep in the mountains, a neighbor to the Rong and Di, and was far from the royal house. The king's numinous power did not reach us, and our efforts to subdue the Rong left us no leisure."[3]

Losing the altars of soil, losing *de* was akin to losing the allegiance of the populace. The *she*, symbol of the imperial cult, were designated to the feudal lords in official enfeoffment ceremonies, used to register households, and numerically allocated. These ritual edifices also perhaps were cast as border markers, just as border markers were cast as ritual edifices. The notion of *de* was not merely an ideological or philosophical one, applicable only to recondite intellectual essays or debates on proper leadership, but a spatially active one, one that was extended throughout the sovereign domain. *De* can be associated with the ritualized gaze of sovereignty, a gaze that surveils, literally oversees the movements and activities of its subjects. Correspondingly, the "enemies" or "opponents" (*di* 敵) of the sovereign domain are those who are not affected or swayed by the sovereign's *de*, and thus their areas are *luan* 亂, chaotic, beyond "human" control. The general question for this chapter is how borders are defined and managed, and thus how sovereign space is *strategically* defined in early China. Ritual concepts such as *de* and the assignment of the altars of soil in enfeoffment ceremonies indicate the symbolic establishment of sovereign terrain through sanctified means, rather than merely secular lines or walls.

I've argued that specialists of early China often seem to attempt to define boundaries in a modern mode, whether on map or in text, with a precisely defined line, and treat the wall as the concrete manifestation of this line. In its premodern application, sovereign borders were more aptly defined by the extension of administrative or sociomoral force. Those areas that recognized the sovereign force of the central government, whether by sending tax revenue or obeying administrative edicts meant

---

[2] Wang, "Western Zhou Despotism," 99.

[3] 晉居深山，戎狄之與鄰，而遠於王室，王靈不及，拜戎不暇. *Zuozhuan*, Zhao 15.7a; Yang Bojun, *Chunqiu zuozhuan zhu*, 4:1371; *Zuo Tradition (Zuozhuan)*, 3:1527. This passage puts Jin's cultural connection to the central Zhou order into question, as Qin's cultural connection later would be. The more distant a polity state, the more its cultural allegiances were put in some doubt.

for the realm under control, could be deemed areas "within" the frontier. Military force could buttress such administrative or sociomoral power (and indeed, military force is regularly treated, as Giddens also does, as "the single most essential element of state power"),[4] but military force could not replace it, for if areas far from established settlements were unwilling to submit and had alternate sources of support or were also claimed administratively, however tentatively, by competing powers, these areas could not be held indefinitely. Only when the extraction of resources and the application of administrative control was regularized in an area should that area be deemed a part of the sovereign realm.

Examinations of other early imperial formations, such as the Inca and Egyptian, further confirm the administrative division of internal from external regions. On its southeastern boundary, the Incan empire faced the hostile challenges of the Chiriguano groups. As a military frontier, the southeast served as a barrier; culturally, the southeast also served as a contact zone, an area of socioeconomic complexities that repudiates any exclusionary "line." Like the early Chinese polities, the Inca political economy "was based on tribute collection from peripheral regions and large-scale extraction of goods and services (*mit'a* taxation) from subject populations." Also in common with early Chinese polities, the Inca "relocated ethnic groups (*mitmas*) to new environments, as a way of heading off revolts while creating productive enclaves of specialists, including soldiers and artisans." The imperial core controlled subjects and territories directly, with border regions governed by "intermediate client elites."[5]

In the ancient Egyptian context, specifically the Egypt of the second millennium BCE, we see the symbolic, magisterial underscoring of Egyptian sovereignty in border monuments, a "hyper-Egyptian monumentality."[6] And yet, there was a constant mixture, and sometimes even reversal or obscuration of claimed cultural identity, in order to extend the boundaries of Egyptian sovereignty. In one case, Egyptianized Nubian princes were required to dress themselves in

---

[4] Giddens, *Nation-State and Violence*, 58.

[5] Sonia Alconini, "The Dynamics of Military and Cultural Frontiers on the Southeastern Edge of the Inka Empire," in *Untaming the Frontier in Anthropology, Archaeology, and History*, ed. Bradley J. Parker and Lars Rodseth (Tucson: University of Arizona Press, 2005), 116.

[6] The Egyptian administrator Siamun's lavish tomb in the Nubian frontier area of Tombos, the architecture and arrangement of which was paradigmatically Egyptian, illustrates the assertion of a link to "the powerful colonial core through the construction of impressive funerary monuments." Stuart Tyson Smith, "To the Supports of Heaven: Political and Ideological Conceptions of Frontiers in Ancient Egypt," in *Untaming the Frontier in Anthropology, Archaeology, and History*, ed. Bradley J. Parker and Lars Rodseth (Tucson: University of Arizona Press, 2005), 222–224.

"barbaric" appurtenances, even though they were culturally Egyptian; in another, the king of Babylon Kadashman-Enlil's chariots were placed amid the chariots of Egyptian vassals, "in order that they be not seen separately"; and in a final case the Babylonian king's sister was "mixed in with the Pharaoh's retinue, so that no one could tell her apart from the Pharaoh's lesser wives."[7] Though Stuart Tyson Smith insists that ancient Egyptian borders were "clearly drawn and travel and commerce were regulated in much the same way as a modern nation-state's," from evidence like the above, with regard to its ideologically and even administratively sovereign claims, as in the early Chinese case, inner and outer, though distinguished, were not as discrete as any professed martial boundaries might indicate.[8] Smith asserts this evidence offers the opportunity "to assess the role of ideology in constructing social boundaries that served to legitimate the rule of political elites."[9] For the early Chinese, I argue, the ideological and administrative were mutually reinforcing. A full, robust picture of early Chinese sovereignty needs fuse the two.

As the Incan and Egyptian examples suggest, because of the heterogeneity of the cultures under a premodern sovereign's purview and the difficulties of traversing extensive physical distances, frontier zones were permeable. It is also because of this that symbolic or ritualized assertions of authority were so important in the premodern era. With the modern conception of monarchial sovereignty, Benedict Anderson once observed, the state is

fully, flatly, and evenly operative over each square centimetre of a legally demarcated territory. But in the older imagining, where states were defined by centres, borders were porous and indistinct, and sovereignties faded imperceptibly into one another. Hence, paradoxically enough, the ease with which pre-modern empires and kingdoms were able to sustain their rule over immensely heterogeneous, and often not even contiguous, populations for long periods of time.[10]

---

[7] S. Smith, "To the Supports of Heaven," 228–230.

[8] Ibid., 230. In their monograph, *The Practice of Diplomacy*, Keith Hamilton and Richard Langhorne assert that the Romans themselves "allowed highly porous borders." "It would have been very difficult for a traveller in the second or third centuries to be entirely clear when he was entering or leaving the Roman Empire. And even when he was certain that he must be within it, he would have found a wide variety of local relationships with Rome which were determined by the circumstances in which the area in question had been joined to the Roman Empire. There could be areas of unsubdued tribes, there could be varieties of client kingdoms, there could be provinces which were under senatorial rather than imperial jurisdiction; and on the peripheries, there were kingdoms and tribes which owed a greater or lesser degree of allegiance to Rome, in which there could even be grants of Roman citizenship." Keith Hamilton and Richard Langhorne, *The Practice of Diplomacy: Its Evolution, Theory and Administration* (New York: Routledge, 1995), 12–13.

[9] S. Smith, "To the Supports of Heaven," 230.

[10] Benedict Anderson, *Imagined Communities* (London: Verso, 1991), 19.

Clifford Geertz makes the point even more forcefully in his study of nineteenth-century Bali: there, political organization was not a

neat set of hierarchically organized independent states, sharply demarcated from one another and engaged in 'foreign relations' across well-drawn frontiers ... What it reveals is an extended field of highly dissimilar political ties, thickening into nodes of varying size and strength at strategic points on the landscape and then thinning out again to connect, in a marvelously convolute way, virtually everything with everything else.[11]

Frontiers, in this organizational mode, were "'not clearly defined lines but zones of mutual interest,' not 'the precise MacMahon lines of modern political geography' insulating one 'country' from another, but transition areas, political ecotones through which neighboring power systems 'interpenetrated in a dynamic manner.'"[12] According to Geertz, the contest between polities was less for land than for men, "for their deference, their support, and their personal loyalty ... Political power inhered less in property than in people; was a matter of the accumulation of prestige, not of territory." Disagreements were "virtually never concerned with border problems, but with delicate questions of mutual status, of appropriate politesse ... and of rights to mobilize particular bodies of men, even particular men, for state ritual and what was really the same thing, warfare."[13] In short, it is not so much the terrain itself but population, and its settlement, that is definitive of borders; thus it was, for instance, that Emperor Wen of the early Han (r. 180–157 BCE) was not seriously concerned about the segments of the Chinese population fleeing into the Xiongnu 匈奴 areas, for "they are not sufficiently numerous to increase your population or *broaden your territories*,"[14] the size of the sovereign territory intimately intertwined with the allegiances of the settled population.

---

[11] Clifford Geertz, *Negara: The Theatre State in Nineteenth-Century Bali* (Princeton, NJ: Princeton University Press, 1980), 24.

[12] Geertz, *Negara*, 24.

[13] Ibid. Geertz also relates a humorous anecdote of two princes of south Celebes who were asked where their borders lay. Both agreed the borders of one principality "lay at the farthest point from which a man could still see the swamps" and the other lay "at the farthest point from which a man could still see the sea." Asked whether they had fought over the land between, from which one could espy neither swamp nor sea, one prince responded that they had better reasons to fight than over "these shabby hills."

[14] 亡人不足以益眾廣地. *SJ* 110.2903, emphasis mine. Enno Giele translates this as speaking to the Han population and territories, but shortly before this in the text, in another letter, Emperor Wen states that he would forgive (and thus not pursue the return of) those commoners who had fled to the Xiongnu side, suggesting that those fleeing referenced in this statement were actually from the Han to the Xiongnu side. See Ssu-ma Ch'ien, "Xiongnu," 280.

Many scholars still have not identified the deep connection between sovereign domain and ritual edifices, and some deny the administrative efficacy of the moral norms that are embedded in ritual sensibilities. Nicola Di Cosmo, for instance, cites the lack of any ceremonial or moral justification when the Zhou attacked the Xiongnu as evidence that moral considerations carried little weight and were merely superficial veneers for more opportunistic political calculations. The war waged in the sixth century BCE by Jin 晉 against the Xianyu 鮮虞, a Di 狄 tribe, was an example "of how little propriety and virtue mattered in wars fought against foreigners." The moral issues "allegedly" involved in conflicts between the Han Chinese and foreign tribes "were, at their best, mere pretexts":

Instead, the Chou states found it relatively easy to conduct military campaigns against foreign peoples, sometimes leading to their extermination, because there was no clear moral [proscription] against conquering them. There was, however, a political context that militated against the use of brute force. Less blunt instruments, therefore, such as alliances and peace treaties, were also adopted by the Chou states, though their final aim remained the pursuit of power.[15]

Elsewhere I have addressed the validity of ritual–moral considerations in early Han debates concerning state affairs,[16] but I would like to employ my discussion here to forward another indirectly related hypothesis. Moral considerations, and the ritual sensibilities in which they were embedded, were not illegitimate for conflicts in general – they were only inapplicable to unrecognized or unrecognizable spatiocultural dispositions, spatiocultural formations (*xing* 形). The incomprehensibility of those polities that lacked definite, "settled" boundaries, or whose boundaries were extremely flexible, unarticulated, namely those of the non-Chinese tribes, left the Chinese confused, relatively unwilling, uncertain about the appropriateness of applying or even unable to assume, to affect its normal, conventional moral attitudes, arising from the non-Chinese tribes' seeming unresponsiveness to attempts to "civilize" and "normalize" their lifestyle.[17] It is because of this cultural uncertainty, including the untranslatability of spatial dispositions, that early Han advisors, such as Wang Hui 王恢 (?–80 BCE) and Han Anguo 韓安國 (?–127 BCE), often start from the premise that the Xiongnu, as with other non-Chinese polities – only respond to displays of force: "They will arrive like gale

---

[15] Di Cosmo, *Ancient China and Its Enemies*, 116.
[16] Olberding, *Dubious Facts*, chapter 8, "Moral Norms as Facts."
[17] For instance, see the Han dynasty minister Han Anguo's 韓安國 representation of the Xiongnu as unwilling to recognize imperial traditions and how this connects to managing the threat they pose. *HS* 52.2401; Olberding, *Dubious Facts*, 119–120.

winds and will depart like retracting lightning ... They pursue their prey
following the pastures. They do not stay anywhere for long. It is difficult to
keep them under control," a disposition that causes the Chinese to disrupt
their own settled practices on the border areas, to command the border
commanderies to "let off planting and weaving ... in order to provide
support" for the situation with the Xiongnu.[18] But it's because of their
cultural and thus spatial "formlessness" (*wuxing* 無形), arising directly
from their frequent movement, that any protracted campaign, extension
deep into unknown lands, will be dangerous and very possibly fruitless,
unless the campaign employs the "formlessness" of other tribal polities,
such as the Yuezhi 月氏, in its military, geographically invasive enterprises.[19]

The Power of the Name (*Ming* 名) in Border Formation

In early China, the power of the name intimately involves reputation and
thus efficacious personal power. Scholarship has long recognized this
power in reference to the proper order of social norms, urged by
Confucius in his discussion with his disciple Zilu about "correcting
names," correctly adjusting ritual relationships and behaviors.[20] Less
well recognized is how the power of naming also extended to the formation of territorial relationships and boundaries. In the idealizing *Zhouli*,
among other idealizing texts such as the "Royal Regulations" ("Wangzhi"
王制) chapter of the *Liji*, lands were named as being in certain zones, and
thus to be allocated to those with whom the sovereign had a specified kind
of ritually sanctioned relationship.

Yet the naming power of the sovereign went even deeper, to the actual
naming of the spaces themselves, to what was considered within his direct
sovereign purview, the area of ritual altars, and that which lay beyond this
purview, the area of the "wilds," where sovereign power was less fully
exerted. Indeed, we see a direct assertion of this in a *Zhouli* passage,
from the section on the official in charge of terrestrial diagrams (*tu* 圖),
the *Dasitu* 大司徒, the great officer of conscripted labor. After stating that
the *Dasitu* needs to know the general terrestrial features of the area of
the Nine Provinces, such as mountains and forests, rivers and marshes,
and so on, he is to define the settled areas, regulating them with *feng*
boundaries, and establishing altars of the soil and grain. The following
remark pertains to the describing and designating, "naming" of territories:

---

[18] *HS* 52.2401; Olberding, *Dubious Facts*, 120.

[19] Wang Hui suggests that the costs of military campaigns could be avoided by "supplementing a smaller Chinese force with a group of Yuezhi barbarians." See *HS* 52.2402;
Olberding, *Dubious Facts*, 121–122.

[20] See *Analects*, "Zilu," *Lunyu jijie*, 3:885–896.

[The great officer of conscripted labor] marks off the number of the monarch's cadastral areas (*bangguo*), the areas within the walls and those fields that lay outside the walls. He regulates the cadastral boundaries (*jiang*) of the (monarch's) territories. He digs moats and builds *feng* boundaries for them. He establishes their perimeter ritual earthen platforms in the four directions for the altars of soil and grain and plants trees for the spirits of the agricultural fields.[21] Each uncultivated wilderness area [that is to be planted and made into an agricultural field] is marked by an appropriate tree. With the trees, one designates ("names") the altars of soil and the yet uncultivated wilderness areas. 辨其邦國都鄙之數，制其畿疆而溝封之，設其社稷之壇而樹之田主。各以其野之所宜木，遂以名其社與其野。[22]

Were this the only remark that recommends such a ritual process of naming, we might consider it merely a product of the idealizations of the *Zhouli*. But we see this ritualized process of the naming of territory, and thus the definition of its borders, in other texts, such as the *Book of Lord Shang* (*Shangjunshu* 商君書), a text routinely associated with a purely secularist, hard-nosed mentality. Therein, the author speaks of excellent governance as requiring forming barriers for commoners with rules. Once barriers are formed with rules, the ruler's reputation (his "name") and lands are "created." The text roots the success or failure of territorial and reputational expansion solely in war, but what is more salient for this analysis is how the expansion of reputation and land are conjoined: Breadth of territory is synonymous with breadth of one's reputation, one's "name."[23] When lands were assaulted, it was an assault on one's name, one's reputation, as is insinuated in this passage from the *Zhanguoce*: The Duke of She "augmented his ancestral lords' lands, retaking the area beyond Fangcheng (i.e., beyond the bounds of his state). His *feng* boundaries were not invaded and his reputation was not impugned among the feudal lords."[24] If we can plausibly assert this close

---

[21] 《周禮·地官·大司徒》：設其社稷之壇，而樹之田主 {鄭玄}注：田主，田神。后土，田正之所依也 {賈公彥} 疏：此田主，當在藉田之中依樹木而爲之，故云各以其野之所宜木.

[22] *Zhouli zhushu*, (Beijing ed.) 1:242.

[23] 民本，法也。故善治者，塞民以法，而名地作矣。名尊地廣以至於王者，何故？戰勝者也。名卑地削以至於亡者，何故？戰罷者也 "The root of the people is law. Hence, those who excel at orderly rule block the people with law; then [good] name and land can be attained. When the name is honored and territories are extensive to the point that you become the Monarch, why is that? {It is because of victory in war.} When the name is disdained and the territory is dismembered to the point of perishing, why is that? It is because of defeat in war." *Shangjunshu*, "Hua ce" 畫策; *Shangjunshu zhuizhi* 商君書錐指 (Beijing: Zhonghua shuju, 1986), 107–108; Shang Yang, *The Book of Lord Shang: Apologetics of State Power in Early China*, trans. Yuri Pines (New York: Columbia University Press, 2017), 215–216.

[24] 恢先君以撐方城之外，四封不侵，名不挫於諸侯. Liu Xiang 劉向, *Zhanguoce jianzheng* 戰國策箋證 (Shanghai: Shanghai guji chubanshe, 2008), "Wei wang wen yu mo ao Zi Hua," 威王問於莫敖子華, in Chuce yi 楚策一, 1:808, 812; He Jianzhang, *Zhanguoce zhushi*, 2:524.

association between name and territory, the extent of one's military force, of seemingly secular military constructs, such as walls and barriers, should not necessarily be equal to the extent of one's sovereign purview, for the sovereign's reputational force could extend far beyond these discrete militaristic structures, the reputational force carrying efficacious administrative sway.

More evidence for the power of the monarch's name can be discovered in his prerogative to change place names, not merely for secular administrative purposes but for ritual ones.[25] Indeed, the divide between the administrative and ritual is itself specious, for to make a ritual change was in itself often administrative. Names of spiritually pregnant natural areas, such as mountains, were changed in connection to a new or renewed assertion of sovereignty, as any number of examples in the literature pertaining to "changing the name," *gengming* 更名, of a place will attest.[26] Thus, the "celebrated," "named" mountains were very possibly those whose names had been altered or changed in the imperial arrogation of its ritually significant space. These name changes were not superficial reorderings; they were performative appropriations of space – active, efficacious territorializations. When space was won, the name could be changed; similarly, a name could be changed when space was lost, was "pared away" (*xuedi* 削地). Thus, analyzing instances of this gaining and losing of territory, the powers asserted and the manner in which they were asserted – such as in their renaming – assists in the demonstration of what sovereignty meant, its extension and contraction. Place names changed frequently over time, registering to some extent the vagaries of sovereignty.[27] These frequent changes frustrate the efforts of students of early Chinese geography to resolve spatial relationships.

Such name changes, asserting the extension or contraction of political sovereignty, in the equation of the political with the spiritual,

---

[25] Lewis remarks on this: the ruler was able to "spontaneously apply appropriate names to all things" and thereby claim them and their powers, as Yu did with spirits. Mark E. Lewis, *Writing and Authority in Early China* (Albany: SUNY Press, 1999), 39, 34. This may explain how difficult it can be to precisely determine locations in the early Chinese record. Indeed, locations could have different names for different purposes. Rémi Matthieu has enumerated several issues relating to this. See Rémi Mathieu, "Fonctions et moyens de la géographie dans la Chine ancienne," *Études Asiatiques: Revue de la Société Suisse d'Études Asiatiques* 36, no. 2 (1982), 145–150.

[26] See, for instance, when King Wu of Zhou changes the name of Xing Hill 刑丘 to Huaining 懷寧 just before attacking Zhou 紂, the last king of Shang, as recorded in *Hanshi waizhuan* j. 3; *Hanshi waizhuan* (Beijing: Zhonghua shuju, 2009), 95. Or any number of examples in the *Shiji*, such as in "Qin benji," when Wei takes over the area of Yinjin 陰晉 and renames it Ningqin 寧秦. See *SJ* 5.205.

[27] Ban Gu himself remarks in the "Dili zhi" how often place names changed: 先王之迹既遠，地名又數改易. *HS* 28a.1543.

simultaneously extend or contract ritual and spiritual sovereignty – and cultural definition. To extend an enforcement of ritual space was to extend the enforcement of ritual competences, which as Joachim Gentz observed, determined the "borders" of a ritual system.[28] In the "Royal Regulations" ("Wangzhi") chapter of the *Liji*, we can see that ritual sacrifices to celebrated, named natural areas, mountains and rivers, were territorialized:

> The son of Heaven sacrificed to all the [named mountains] and great streams under the sky, the five mountains receiving (sacrificial) honours like the honours paid (at court) to the three ducal ministers, and the four rivers honours like those paid to the princes of states; the princes sacrificed to the [named mountains] and great streams which were in their own territories.

天子祭天下名山大川：　五岳視三公，　四瀆視諸侯。　諸侯祭名山大川之在其地者。[29]

The extension of one ritual system, by necessity, meant the contraction or obliteration of another, the intentional denigration or even extirpation of a previous cultural hegemony, very likely now deemed "barbaric," foreign, unworthy. The rhetoric of the barbaric was fungible, asserted not so much because of any bright cultural line but in order to intentionally exclude and render impotent, both culturally and politically. As Paul Goldin has noted, Zhou nobles were "conceived as viceregents charged with establishing ritual colonies and serving the king's interests away from the royal center, in the midst of alien populations," to establish "satellite ritual centers."[30] The ritualized act of touring the realm, *xunshou* 巡守, was not simply ritual, it was also politically administrative. Prior to the common, ready codification and dissemination of laws, ritual obligations were somewhat commensurate with legal obligations. In other words, the extension of ritual force is identifiable with the extension of politico-legal force. The ritualizing of space thus had an administrative effect, legal but also military. (Similarly, the assertion of legal force was akin to the assertion of the monarch's ritual, religio-moral power.) Thus passing through sanctified barriers was to pass into a militarily defensible zone; vice versa, passing into a militarily defensible zone was to pass into a ritually sanctified space. It is not for naught that walls and borders were commonly given ritual, religious significance. Yet one should not therefore insist that sanctified space only existed within walled areas. As mentioned in the

---

[28] Joachim Gentz, "Long Live the King! The Ideology of Power between Ritual and Morality in the *Gongyang zhuan*," in *Ideology of Power and Power of Ideology in Early China*, ed. Yuri Pines, Paul R. Goldin, and Martin Kern (Leiden: Brill, 2015), 81.

[29] *Li Chi: Book of Rites*, 1:225, translation modified; *Liji jijie*, 1:347–348.

[30] Goldin, "Representations of Regional Diversity During the Eastern Zhou Dynasty," 36.

above *Zhouli* passage, fields lying outside walled areas were also sanctified, as were, of course, rivers and mountains. Militaristic boundaries,
such as barriers (*sai* 塞), were pragmatically located – in areas that could
offer the greatest military benefit, such as a narrow mountain pass. What
lay outside them may have also be part of a sovereign territory but, for
pragmatic reasons, could not be readily defended with military boundaries. Nevertheless, we might hazard that militaristic boundaries might very
well mark a proximate limit to sovereign space, to what was defensible,
and thus the areas in which sovereign authority, religio-moral or legal,
could reasonably, pragmatically be extended.

We can further perceive the equation of ritual edifices with sovereign
boundaries in the preservation or destruction of the former. Destroying
the altars of soil was analogous with destroying the state and its terrestrial
powers. In other words, to destroy the altars of soil was to efface the
sovereign's power over his borders. Each sovereign presence possessed
altars in their realms, which signified *administratively* their rule, that the
secular administration of the area was subject to their preferences. To
remove, or redistribute, the altars was to redistribute sovereign powers.
Following is an illustrative passage from Cai Yong's *Duduan* 獨斷 (the
first sentences of which are identical with, and thus possibly derive from,
the "Method of Sacrifices" ("Jifa" 祭法) chapter of the *Liji*):

> The altars of soil that the many lords establish for the Hundred Surnames are
> called the state's altars of soil. The altars of soil for the many lords themselves
> are called the lord's altar of soil. With respect to the altars of soil of a fallen
> state, in ancient times, the Son of Heaven took possession of the altars of soil
> of the fallen state and distributed them among the many lords, making the
> altars serve as cautionary reminders for the lords. If the roof obstructs what is
> above, not allowing [the lord] to communicate with Heaven, and a woven
> cover blocks what is below, not permitting communication with the Earth,
> then the lord cuts himself off from Heaven and Earth. Facing the north
> towards the darkness, this expresses the extinction [of the state].

諸侯為百姓立社曰國社，諸侯之社曰侯社。亡國之社：古者天子亦取亡國之社
以分諸侯，使為社以自儆戒，屋之掩其上使不通天，柴其下使不通地，自與天
地絕也，面北向陰，示滅亡也。[31]

Indeed, in the *Zuozhuan* and *Guanzi*, the altars of soil were defined
administratively. In the *Zuozhuan*, the Prince of Qi, requesting
a breadth of territory, asks for it in terms of a thousand *she*: "The Prince
of Qi said, 'From the Ju [boundary] westward, I request to hand over to
you one thousand communities and await your commands.'" By Du Yu's
杜預 calculations, one "community" (the translator's rendition for *she*,

---

[31] Cai Yong 蔡邕, *Duduan* 獨斷. *Sibu congkan* 四部叢刊, 子部, 卷上, 9.

"altar of soil") was twenty-five households.[32] In the "Chengma" 乘馬 chapter of the *Guanzi* 管子, a square of six *li* ("leagues") is equated with a *she* 社.[33] In the *Zhanguoce*, communities associated with altars of soil were offered by Zhao to Qin: "You [Zhao] offered my king [of Qin] two altars of [soil] (fn: two villages, each with its own altar) to help [Qin] defray the cost of sacrifices for her aid."[34] In a further passage from the *Zhanguoce*, Su Qin intimates that the multiplication of altars of soil across an area are a sign of the extension of sovereignty.[35] Even in the military text, *Sun Bin's Art of War* (*Sun Bin Bingfa* 孫臏兵法), territory is associated with its altars: "[F]ailure to gain victory can result in one's territory being pared away and the altars of one's state being put at risk."[36] Concern about losing the altars of soil was concern for sovereign possession, not only morally, but spatially and thus administratively. Indeed, as noted above, altars of soil, *cum* households, could be offered as payment for debts. But an administrative assignment in payment of debt would not just be financial – it also carried essential, nonsuperfluous religious responsibilities, such as paying obeisance and rendering sacrifices to the altars of soil.[37]

---

[32] 「齊侯曰，自莒疆以西，請致千社，以待君命。」 *Zuozhuan*, Zhao 25.6; Yang Bojun, *Chunqiu zuozhuan zhu*, 4:1465; *Zuo Tradition (Zuozhuan)*, 3:1647. See also *Lüshi chunqiu* 呂氏春秋, "Gao yi" 高義: "Our Master Mo Di sent Gongshang Guo traveling to Yue. There Gongshang Guo expounded upon his code of conduct. The king of Yue was so pleased that he said, 'If only your teacher were willing to come to Yue, I would hope to enfeoff him with the former territories of Wu, the banks of the Yin River, and three hundred registered communities [*she*]'" 子墨子游公上過於越。公上過語墨子之義，越王說之，謂公上過曰： 「子之師茍肯至越，請以故吳之地，陰江之浦，書社三百，以封夫子。」 *Lüshi chunqiu jishi* 呂氏春秋集釋 (Beijing: Zhonghua shuju, 2011), 1:514; *Annals of Lü Buwei*, trans. Jeffrey Riegel and John Knoblock (Stanford, CA: Stanford University Press, 2000), 480–481. Inside the temple housing the altar, the names of people were recorded in an administrative document.

[33] 方六里名之曰社. *Guanzi jiaozhu*, 90.

[34] 而賜之二社之地，以奉祭祀. *Zhanguoce*, Qince 2, "Xing shan zhi shi" 陘山之事; He Jianzhang, *Zhanguoce zhushi*, 3:144; *Chan-Kuo Ts'e*, 92.

[35] "Su Qin shui Qi Min Wang": "The families of death-defying warriors offer prayers, groups of these families make offerings to their dead. From the most accessible of the large cities to the smallest districts, altars of soil are set up everywhere and every town big enough to hold market stops its work in order to make offerings to the monarch" 中人禱祝，君醫釀，通都、小縣、置社、有市之邑，莫不止事而奉王. He Jianzhang, *Zhanguoce zhushi*, 1:421.

[36] 戰不勝，則所以削地面危社稷. Out of chapter 2, "An Audience with King Wei of Qi" (*Jian Wei wang* 見威王). See D. C. Lau and Roger T. Ames, *Sun Pin: The Art of Warfare* (New York: Ballantine Books, 1996), 129.

[37] "[The Son of Heaven] orders that the common people not reduce their efforts, to make offerings to August Heaven and the High Thearch, the spirits of the renowned mountains and great rivers, and the four directions, and perform sacrifices to the numinosities of the ancestral altars and the altars of soil and grain, to pray for blessings for the common people" 「令民無不咸出其力，以供皇天上帝、名山大川、四方之神，以祀宗廟社稷之靈，為民祈福。」 (Translation mine.) See *Liji*, "Yue ling" 月令; *Liji jijie*, 1:457; *Li Chi: Book of Rites*, 1:278. See also *Lüshi chunqiu* 呂氏春秋, "Jixia ji" 季夏紀, *Lüshi chunqiu jishi*,

Clearly, *she* were administrative markers, though the details of their application and politico-legal effects are as yet unclear. When one sovereign power overcame another, an assertion of his sovereignty over territorial areas was to destroy, or commandeer, previous altars or delegate their maintenance to his supporters. The spiritual powers of each area were, as Hsing I-tien has observed, a reflection of representational, delegated powers.[38] Sovereigns would regularly perform sacrifices to these altars in their tours of inspection (巡狩).[39] Thus alterations of the sovereign landscape would be reflected in the location and spatial organization of the sacrifices he would perform. As reflected in the quote from the "Royal Regulations" chapter of the *Liji* just above, the primary possession of ritual boundaries could be in the possession of the lords, with the monarch acting as a supervenient power.[40]

Further evidence for the varying ritual influence, and thus sovereign boundaries, of the monarch can be seen in the differing placement of the four marchmounts (*si yue* 四嶽). The ritual power of these mountains would sometimes be in the hand of the "many lords," sometimes in the hands of the son of Heaven.[41] The allegiance between the monarch and his lords was reinforced by the ritual sacrifices to shared spiritual entities. The powers of these sacred mountains would augment the power of the monarch over the governance of his sovereign realm. Such a connection is reflected in a passage from the "Shundian" 舜典 chapter of the *Shangshu*, in which the legendary emperor Shun "deliberated with the [officers of the] Four Peaks—/to open the gates of the four [directions],/to clear the vistas of the four [directions],/to penetrate what could be heard from the four [directions]."[42] Again, this creation of ritual space was akin to the creation of a legal space, for ritual boundaries, like legal ones, asserted

---

2:131; *Annals of Lü Buwei*, 154. This passage demonstrates how common people were compelled to pay obeisance to the altars of soil (among other religious edifices).

[38] In the Shang dynasty, for instance, the spirits of the four quarters were the reflection of the delegated powers for the terrestrial four quarters of the Shang polity. Hsing I-tien 邢義田, "Cong gudai tianxia guankan Qin–Han changcheng de xiangzheng yiyi" 從古代天下觀看秦漢長城的象徵意義, in *Tianxia yijia* 天下一家 (Beijing: Zhonghua shuju, 2011), 88.

[39] For inspection tours in the ancient monarchial Seleucid Empire (311–64 BCE), see Paul J. Kosmin, *The Land of the Elephant Kings: Space, Territory, and Ideology in the Seleucid Empire* (Cambridge, MA: Harvard University Press, 2014), chapter 6.

[40] *Shuoyuan*, "Bian wu" 辨物：使者曰：「誰（守）為神？」孔子曰：「山川之靈，足以紀綱天下者，其守為神。社稷（之守）為公侯，山川之祀為諸侯，皆屬於王者。」 *Shuoyuan jiao zheng* 說苑校證 (Beijing: Zhonghua shuju, 1987), 462.

[41] 名山大川或在諸侯，或在天子. *HS* 25.1206.

[42] 詢于四岳，闢四門，明四目，達四聰. Li Xueqin, *Shangshu zhengyi*, 72; Martin Kern, "Language and the Ideology of Kingship in the 'Canon of Yao,'" in *Ideology of Power and Power of Ideology in Early China*, ed. Yuri Pines, Paul R. Goldin, and Martin Kern (Leiden: Brill, 2015), 142.

an administrative sphere in which outside powers were not permitted to interfere.[43]

Appropriating the Local Spirits

At times however, for some reason, new rulers were unable to appropriate the altars from older sovereign formations.[44] Some, like King Kang of Song, as represented in the *Zhanguoce*, would simply chop up and burn the old altars of soil and grain of conquered territories. As he did so, Kang declared, "I will fiercely force the ghosts and spirits of Heaven and Earth to submit to me!"[45] But others simply worked to appropriate the old altars in a new formation, for, as Michael Puett has argued, "The need to … bring nature deities and Di itself into [the ancestral pantheon] shows … a belief that spirits are *not* inherently inclined to act on behalf of the living."[46] According to the *Shiji* and the *Shangshu*, Tang of Shang had wished to relocate, to remove the altars of soil instituted by the previous Xia rulers, but was unable to.[47] A conquering ruler had to not only conquer politically and administratively, he also had to conquer and/or appropriate religious and spiritual forces, drawing them under his purview, his supervision. As Gilles Boileau has observed, in the early Zhou era contact with natural forces was essential for control of a particular area. Military leaders, such as King Wu of Zhou would perform sacrifices to the natural spirits to appease them before transgressing across their "bodies" in a campaign.[48] In the *Analects*, the sovereign power of a distant

---

[43] For an analysis of ritual rules that illustrates the degree of kinship they share with legal rules, and their adjudication, see Gentz, "Long Live the King!" 82.

[44] An insightful study into the intersection and interaction of colonizing imperial powers and indigenous cultures is Alice Yao, *The Ancient Highlands of Southwest China* (New York: Oxford University Press, 2016). Therein, she reveals how numerous indigenous cultures, with her focus being those of ancient southwest China, adapted their ritual activities in response to the pressures imposed by external colonizing forces, and vice versa, how imperial authority attempted to control or manipulate local ritual authority. See, in particular, chapters 6 and 7. I am grateful to an anonymous reader for recommending this source.

[45] "Song Kang Wang zhi shi": 斬社稷而焚滅之，曰：「威服天下(地)鬼神。」In Song Wei ce 宋衛策, Liu Xiang, *Zhanguoce jianzheng*, 2:1828, 1831; He Jianzhang, *Zhanguoce zhushi*, 3:1219.

[46] Michael J. Puett, *To Become a God: Cosmology, Sacrifice, and Self-Divinization in Early China* (Cambridge, MA: Harvard Asia Center Publications, 2002), 53.

[47] When Tang had conquered Xia, he wished to conjoin the Xia altars with those of the Shang spirits of the soil, but "was unable to do so, and the 'Altars of Xia' was written" 欲遷其社，不可，作夏社. *SJ* 3.96; "Tang shi" 湯誓 in Li Xueqin, *Shangshu zhengyi*, 193.

[48] See, for instance, *Shangshu*, "Wu cheng" 武成: 告于皇天后土，所過名山大川. Li Xueqin, *Shangshu zhengyi*, 291. Gilles Boileau, *Politique et rituel dans la Chine ancienne* (Paris: Institut des hautes études chinoises, 2013), 110. Boileau later also points to the passage in the "Shimai" 時邁 poem where King Wu is stated to have gathered to himself

vassal area was identified with its ruler's performance of the sacrifices to the altars of soil and grain, in an acknowledgment of the dominant spiritual powers of the central ruler.[49] All of this indicates the attempts by the central sovereign authority to either overcome or incorporate potentially contestational or opposing spiritual forces.

If native spiritual forces, and their cults, could not be appropriated, it appears that officials attempted to eliminate them as illicit and subversive, just as the religious traditions of later eras that were not successfully appropriated or integrated into a state apparatus were monitored and, if deemed a threat, suppressed. Such illicit cults were often connected with localized, pre-state power formations, "grounded entirely in local custom or practice. These were organized by 'shamans' or powerful families and dedicated to mountain spirits or to hermits or immortals known only in the locality."[50] From certain accounts of officials tasked with their elimination, we can see that the contest between entrenched, native local powers and the colonizing imperial ones was fierce and difficult to resolve, the commoners practicing the rites of the older cults being treated as manipulated and ignorant. Clearly, the cults, and the concomitant old forms of political power, were at least occasionally able to survive any initial attempts at their extirpation. As Mark E. Lewis notes, "Only mountain cults recorded on official sacrificial registers were licit."[51] Crucial was that the cult was officially sanctioned, a distinction illustrated most pellucidly in the account of a Latter Han official, Song Jun 宋均, where the practice of shamans marrying men and women in an attempt to propitiate certain local mountain spirits was outlawed. Jun released an official order forbidding shamans from continuing this practice and disturbing "good" (liang 良) commoners.[52]

This concern with protecting the "good" commoners points to a moralizing root set in state power. Sovereign entities were, so the Yijing advises, to "observe" the commoners and "implement teachings,"

many of the territorial spirits: 懷柔百神，及河喬嶽. Boileau, *Politique et rituel dans la Chine ancienne*, 111.

[49] *Analects*, "Ji shi" 季氏, *Lunyu jijie*, 4:1132.

[50] Lewis, *Construction of Space in Early China*, 234. The succeeding, supervenient imperial cults would strategically construct a long, "if sometimes imaginary, history of cult and a grounding in the canonical texts."

[51] "In addition to local cults devoted to individuals, many were also dedicated to natural powers. Some of these are described in accounts of officials who attempted to stamp them out." "Such accounts emphasize the regional character of the cults, treating them as extensions of local custom. They ascribe their administration to 'shamans,' who seek to dupe the people for profit." Lewis, *Construction of Space in Early China*, 233. Several accounts of officials censoring local religious practices can be found at *HHS* 41.1397 and 41.1413.

[52] *HHS* 41.1413.

thereby contesting, and suppressing, previous religio-cultural practices.[53] Illicit, extra-state religious activity was seen as interfering with the education into, and exercise of, proper moral principle and salutary ritual behavior. Only the principles and behaviors institutionalized by the state were to be permitted. Not prohibiting extralegal religious activities, as a passage in the *Fengsu tongyi* 風俗通義 warns, can lead to the dissolution of the state and the imperiling of the lord.[54] In the passage, employing shamans and invocators or placing trust in auspicious signs received from the spirit world is in opposition to respecting the "Great Way" and its moral codes. The competition between older localized institutions and newer state-sanctioned ones is further elucidated in the repeated blackwashing of "bewitching" or "licentious" sacrifices, *yin si* 淫祀. Indeed, in James Legge's translation of *Record of Rites* the contrast between state and extra-state religious activity is explicitly counterposed:

> There should be no presuming to resume any sacrifice which has been abolished (by proper authority), nor to abolish any which has been so established. A sacrifice which it is not proper to offer, and which yet is offered, is called a licentious sacrifice. A licentious sacrifice brings no blessing.

凡祭，有其廢之莫敢舉也，有其舉之莫敢廢也。非其所祭而祭之，名曰淫祀。淫祀無福。[55]

Two passages in the *Hanshu* draw a manifest association between such bewitching, licentious sacrifices and beliefs in the powers of shamans and ghosts (*gui* 鬼).[56] Both passages pertain to imperfectly integrated territories in the south, to the areas of Chu 楚 and Chen 陳. Indeed, in a passage from the *Huainanzi*, even the legendary sage rulers, Yao and Shun, "did not make use of shamans' invocations. Ghosts and spirits did not dare to work black magic on them; mountains and rivers did not dare to harm them" 行不用巫祝，鬼神弗敢祟，山川弗敢禍.[57]

Regular travel around the empire and supervising of religious practices (among other aspects of local custom, *su* 俗) was thus required for the state to maintain its hegemonic sovereignty. As stated in the previous section, the practice of *xunshou*, of inspection tours, was both politically

[53] 《易經·觀》, "Da xiang zhuan" 大象傳: "The former kings thereupon inspected the regions, surveyed the common people, and implemented their own teachings" 先王以省方觀民設教. *Zhouyi zhengyi* 周易正義 (Beijing: Beijing daxue chubanshe, 1999), 98.

[54] Ying Shao 應劭, *Fengsu tongyi jiaozhu* 風俗通義校注 (Taipei: Hanjing wenhua shiye, 2003), 322. A similar sentiment can be found in *HHS* 30.3312: 是時桓帝奢侈淫祀，其十一月崩，無嗣.

[55] *Li Chi: Book of Rites*, 1:116; *Liji jijie* 禮記集解, 1:152–153.

[56] *HS* 28B.1666, 81.3335.

[57] *Huainanzi*, "Zhu shu xun" 主術訓 ("The ruler's techniques"); Liu An, *The Huainanzi*, 334; Liu An, *Huainanzi jishi*, 2:693.

and ritually efficacious; the two were intertwined. This practice, as Lewis observes, can be traced back to the Shang: "The idea that the king organized his realm by moving through it was established in the Shang. In this earliest dynasty, the ruler had regularly moved through the landscape of his realm, securing the loyalty of followers who presented offerings and the aid of local gods with whom he renewed ties through sacrifice."[58] To travel the realm and perform sacrifices to the various altars was not simply to connect with them, to reassert their power, but also to repress, to diminish the practice of sacrificing to nonsanctioned altars, by either forbidding it or by appropriating and integrating the illicit. In other words, imperial authorities conquered spirits through vanquishment or possession.

This spatial association with spiritual entities is further reinforced by the repeated prescriptions for lords to sacrifice only to those spirits within their realms. The many lords were to "sacrifice to the named mountains and great rivers within their boundaries."[59] Sacrificing to those ghosts lying beyond one's designated realm, to those that were "not one's own," according to *Analects* 2.24, was to be fawning or presumptuous, an attempt to solicit help when such is not within one's deserts.[60] In his commentary to this passage, Edward Slingerland notes that *gui* 鬼, "ghosts," could refer either to human or nonhuman spectral entities associated with the area.[61] The ghosts associated with natural areas, such as mountains, were sources of territorializing power, to be sacrificed

---

[58] Lewis, *Construction of Space in Early China*, 288. Evidence is also clearly seen in the Zhou bronzes. See, for instance, the Da Yu *ding* 大盂鼎: "Day and night, assist me, the One Man, to govern over the four quarters. For me, you will inspect the territories and peoples that the Former Kings had received" 夙夕召我一人烝四方，越我其遹省先王受民受疆土. Translation in Vincent Leung, *The Politics of the Past in Early China* (New York: Cambridge University Press, 2019), 27–28.

[59] 而諸侯祭其疆內名山大川. *SJ* 28.1357. A similar statement can be found in the *Gongyang zhuan*, except that it underscores the ritual nature of borders by identifying them with *feng* 封: 諸侯山川有不在其封內者，則不祭也. *Chunqiu gongyangzhuan zhushu* 春秋公羊傳注疏 (Beijing: Beijing daxue chubanshe, 1999), 267.

[60] 非其鬼而祭之，諂也. *Analects* 2.24; *Lunyu jijie*, 2:132–134. *Zuozhuan*, Ai 6.4c: "[King Zhao of Chu] said, 'During the Three Dynasties, the commands regarding offerings forbade one to perform sacrifice beyond one's purview. The Jiang, the Han, the Sui, and the Zhang Rivers are in Chu's purview. Banes and blessings do not cross these when they come'" 王曰：「三代命祀，祭不越望。江、漢、睢、漳，楚之望也。禍福之至，不是過也。」 *Zuo Tradition (Zuozhuan)*, 3:1867; Yang Bojun, *Chunqiu zuozhuan zhu*, 4:1636. (For discussion of this *Zuozhuan* passage and the ritual prohibition, see Boileau, *Politique et rituel dans la Chine ancienne*, 110.) "Ji fa" 祭法 in *Liji*: "He by whom all under the sky was held sacrificed to all spirits. The princes of states sacrificed to those which were in their own territories; to those which were not in their territories, they did not sacrifice." 有天下者祭百神。諸侯在其地則祭之，亡其地則不祭 *Li Chi: Book of Rites*, 2:203; *Liji jijie*, 2:1194.

[61] *Analects* 2.24, *Confucius Analects*, trans. Edward Slingerland (Indianapolis, IN: Hackett Publishing Company, 2003), 16; *Lunyu jijie*, 1:133–135.

to by the sovereign leaders of the realm. Thus it is to nonhuman "ghosts" that the Ji clan is performing the *lü* 旅 sacrifice on Mount Tai 泰山, an arrogation of an aristocratic prerogative to which, Confucius protests, the head of the Ji clan, being a minister and not a lord, had no right. Because Mount Tai straddled the border of the states of Lu and Qi, it would receive sacrifices from the rulers of both.[62] For the *Analects*, territorial allegiances, and thus territorial sovereignty, are associated with territorialized sacrifices. Subjects residing within or pledging allegiance to a territory were subject to the territorial sacrifices, to the powers of the associated territorial spirits.[63]

As Vera Dorofeeva-Lichtman has pointed out, these prescriptions are at work even in the idealized itineraries of the *Shanhaijing*. With its system of itineraries marked by mountains, and mountain spirits, a sovereign space is established: "In contrast to the extant versions of the Nine Provinces, the system of itineraries lays special emphasis on local spirits. In particular, an itinerary encompasses mountains that share the same guardian spirits."[64] The itineraries are, therefore, delineated according to the spatial dispersion of divine powers and represent a sacred space. This notion of a spiritually sanctioned space defining an idealized realm is further confirmed, Dorofeeva-Lichtmann notes, by the repeated assertions of support given to the sage king Yu in many recently found manuscripts from the Warring States through the early Han dynasty.[65] Lewis concatenates such idealized prescriptions with actual ones, specifically the sacrifices made by the First Emperor "to important regional gods, most notably the Eight Spirits in Qi ... He also performed the *feng* and *shan* sacrifices on Mt. Tai and Mt. Liangfu ... Finally, he standardized the cults to major mountains and rivers, deciding which natural features throughout the empire would receive sacrifice."[66] Upon the First Emperor conquering other states, he commenced a sacrificial tour, ascending the named mountains, memorializing and monumentalizing his sacrifice with inscriptions to glorify his achievements, as well as to proclaim his aspirations, employing a classicist moral vocabulary, in contradiction to his anti-classicist portrayal in the *Shiji*.[67] In places, he

---

[62] *Analects* 3.6, *Confucius Analects*, 18–19; *Lunyu jijie*, 1:151–153.

[63] 且在邦域之中矣，是社稷之臣也. *Analects* 16.1, *Confucius Analects*, 191; *Lunyu jijie* 4:1132.

[64] Dorofeeva-Lichtmann, "Ritual Practices for Constructing Terrestrial Space (Warring States–Early Han)," 596.

[65] Ibid.

[66] Lewis, *Construction of Space in Early China*, 173. See *SJ* 28.1367–1368, 1371–1374.

[67] A translation and interpretation of various inscriptions can be found in Kern, *Stele Inscriptions of Ch'in Shih-huang*.

also made sacrifices to regional spirits, particularly those eight spirits located in Qi, where the center of the heavens came together. As with Yu in his post-diluvian tour, the Qin emperor first set off east, then south.[68]

In both idealized and actual realms then, sovereign power depended on the ruler's "ability to recognize local spirits and the offerings that suited them."[69] The idea of moving through his realm to organize it was, Lewis observes, established in the Shang: "In this earliest dynasty, the ruler had regularly moved through the landscape of his realm, securing the loyalty of followers who presented offerings and the aid of local gods with whom he renewed ties through sacrifice."[70] Touring was the concrete manifestation of the monarch's spiritual paces metaphorically paced out in the mapping dances mentioned earlier.[71] Through his tours and inspections, the monarch personally territorialized the realm. In the Qin and Han, emperors regularly renewed ties by traveling the empire offering sacrifices to existing nature cults, reflecting "the features of natural geography and the cultic practices that had evolved in past centuries."[72] As with the Shang, the repeated "inspections" of the cultic sites outside its core area served to reinstitute, to reinvest imperial sovereignty broadly.

These reinstitutions of sovereignty by offering sacrifices and attending to local nature cults throughout the realm are further illustrated in the inspection tours of the sage emperors Shun and Yu, which, like the tours of the Qin emperor, followed a generally clockwise path. In the "Shundian" chapter of the *Shangshu*, Shun's tour, occuring once every five years, went east in the second month, south in the fifth, west in the eighth, and north in the eleventh. On his tour, Shun journeyed to the dominant mountains, "where he presents an offering to Heaven and sacrifices to the hills and rivers." Thereafter, Shun performed a set of regulative governing acts, acts asserting sovereignty – instituting standardizations of measures, a regulation of the calendar, and so forth.[73]

---

[68] For Yu's travels, see Dorofeeva-Lichtmann, "Ritual Practices for Constructing Terrestrial Space (Warring States–Early Han)," 602–608.

[69] Lewis, *Construction of Space in Early China*, 292.   [70] Ibid., 288.   [71] See above, p. 46.

[72] Lewis, *Construction of Space in Early China*, 173.

[73] Robert Campany, *Strange Writing: Anomaly Accounts in Early Medieval China* (Albany: State University of New York Press, 1996), 107. A similar tour is prescribed in the *Liji*, "Wangzhi": "In the [fifth] month, (the son of Heaven) continued his tour, going to the south, to the mountain of that quarter, observing the same ceremonies as in the east. In the eighth month, he went on to the west, to the mountain of that quarter, observing the same ceremonies as in the south. In the eleventh month, he went on to the north, to the mountain of that quarter, observing the same ceremonies as in the west" 五月，南巡守，至于南嶽，如東巡守之禮。八月，西巡守，至于西嶽，如南巡守之禮。十有一月，北巡守，至于北嶽，如西巡守之禮。 *Li Chi: Book of Rites*, 1:217–218; *Liji jijie* 1:329. Another reference to such regulations is made in the *Baihutong*: "On behalf of Heaven

A similar assertion of sovereignty is pursued by Yu, described in the *Yuejueshu* 越絕書, when Yu goes on a royal progress through Dayue.[74]

All of this, as Robert F. Campany notes, is "inseparably linked with the system of imperially sponsored local temples and shrines by which the Han and later dynasties sought to implant their authority among the gods and spirits of particular places."[75] Again, these tours were not simply to assert imperial sovereign authority by requesting the assistance of local powers but also to assert an unquestionable dominance over such local powers, a dominance that expresses itself singularly in an episode in the *Shanjing*, in which conflict arises between a high celestial god and a mountain deity. As Lewis states, this conflict "recapitulates the relation between the imperially sanctioned cults and those dedicated to lesser mountains by the cities and towns in their locality."[76] Worship of local *gui* and other nature spirits was thus a contestational ritual activity. The *Zhouli* puts it bluntly: imperial authorities in essence "took over" local ghosts and spirits to assert their dominance over the denizens of that area.[77]

The envisioning of the extent of one's realm asserts itself in the appropriation of natural spirits. The ritual gazing of the monarch from a mountaintop in the *wang* 望, or "gazing afar" sacrifice is an expression of at least an aspirational possession of the realm that can be gazed upon. Gilles Boileau defines the "gazing afar" sacrifice as an offering to "numerous important points that one looks upon."[78] Newell Ann van Auken, in an article on the word, declares that *wang* was only used in received texts to denote a sacrifice to mountains and rivers. The earliest appearance in

---

the King goes along [the roads] to guard and shepherd his people. After the spiritual power [proceeding from his possession] of the Way has brought about general peace [the King] fears that the distant regions have not yet in the same way been affected [by his influence] as the nearer, and that among the hidden and secluded [worthies] there are some who have not yet received their proper positions; therefore he makes a point of personally performing [the task of inspection], which is the highest [expression of his] care and esteem for the people. [On his Tour of Inspection] he examines the rites and music, rectifies the rules and measures" 為天下循行守牧民也。道德太平，恐遠近不同化，幽隱有不得所，考禮義，正法度. *Po Hu T'ung: The Comprehensive Discussions in the White Tiger Hall*, trans. Tjan Tjoe Som (Leiden: Brill, 1952), 495; *Baihutong shuzheng* 白虎通疏證 (Beijing: Zhonghua shuju, 1994), 298.

[74] 及其王也，巡狩大越，見耆老，納詩書，審銓衡，平斗斛. Li Bujia 李步嘉, ed., *Yuejueshu jiaoshi* 越絕書校釋 (Beijing: Zhonghua shuju, 2013), 221.

[75] Campany, *Strange Writing*, 106.

[76] Lewis, *Construction of Space in Early China*, 292.

[77] 國索鬼神而祭祀，則以禮屬民. *Zhouli zhushu* 周禮注疏 (Shanghai: Shanghai guji chubanshe, 2011), 303.

[78] "offrande sacrificielle aux '[nombreux points éminents que l'on] regarde.'" Boileau, *Politique et rituel dans la Chine ancienne*, 111.

extant received literature is the "Yaodian" 堯典 chapter of the *Shangshu*. In a *Zuozhuan* passage, the *wang* sacrifice denotates the boundaries of an area, "and by extension to the sacrifice offered to the spirits associated with rivers (and elsewhere, mountains) that marked these boundaries."[79] These sacrifices, van Auken agrees, are associated with a surveying activity, looking over a vista that the monarch possesses, or even aspires to possess.[80] In van Auken's research, the sacrifice appears in no text prior to the Warring States period, and is best understood as "derived from *wanq* 'look into the distance', which by the Warring States period had taken on the added meaning of a sacrifice performed to those mountains and streams that demarcated the boundaries of a ruler's dominion."[81] Martin Kern's analysis of the "Shundian" chapter adds further support to van Auken's claim, pointing out that in the "Shundian" Shun begins his rule by offering the *wang* sacrifice to the mountains and rivers to express his "sovereignty over the entire realm."[82] This equation between the *wang* sacrifice and the extent of sovereignty accords with an explanation of the "threefold gazing afar" (*san wang* 三望) sacrifice found in the *Gongyang zhuan*. This sacrifice is made to Mount Tai, the Yellow River, and the Eastern Sea, because these mountains and waterways "can give water to an area of up to one hundred *li*." The Son of Heaven "makes sacrifices according to their range."[83] If the explanation of the *Gongyang zhuan* is indicative, the *wang* sacrifice has everything to do with the ability of the sovereign to provide for his people, literally and metaphorically described in terms of the water these natural spaces, and his ritual control over them, can provide. It is to the lord's virtue (*de* 德) that the spirits respond. A symbiotic relationship is present between spiritual powers and worldly moral-political powers. Control over the spirit world is thus deemed a moral-political issue.[84]

---

[79] Newell Ann van Auken, "The Etymonic Determinatives of Wanq (望, 朢)," *Journal of the American Oriental Society* 122, no. 3 (2002), 525.

[80] Van Auken, "The Etymonic Determinatives of Wanq (望, 朢)," 526.

[81] Ibid. The recent discovery of the Chengwu manuscript, which makes mention of the *wang* sacrifice, augments van Auken's findings. See Xinhui Luo, "Omens and Politics: The Zhou Concept of the Mandate of Heaven as Seen in the Chengwu 程寤 Manuscript," in *Ideology of Power and Power of Ideology in Early China*, ed. Yuri Pines, Paul R. Goldin, and Martin Kern (Leiden: Brill, 2015), 51. See also Li Xueqin 李学勤, ed., *Qinghua daxue cang zhanguo zhujian* 清华大学藏战国竹简 (Shanghai: Shanghai zhongxi, 2010), 135–139.

[82] Kern, "Language and the Ideology of Kingship in the 'Canon of Yao,'" 136.

[83] Gentz, "Long Live the King!" 89–90.

[84] For an explicit connection between the spiritual and moral-political powers, see *Liji* 禮記, "Liqi" 禮器: "The gentleman has ritual propriety, thus those outside [his circle] are in harmony [with him] and those on the inside [his circle] do not resent him. Among people, there are none who do not embrace his humanity and the ghosts and spirits indulge in his virtue" 故君子有禮，則外諧而內無怨，故物無不懷仁，鬼神饗德. *Liji jijie*, 3:624.

Virtue (*De* 德) Tied to Territorial Sovereignty

It is in discussions of the power and effects of the lord's virtue that we may see most persuasively its symbolic marking of aspirational or actual acquisitions of new lands. Actions involved in manifesting virtue were the spur to manifesting Zhou sovereignty in non-Zhou lands. The virtuous action of the Zhou ruler won over the high Shang *di* 帝 spirit, revealing both the religious force of Zhou virtue and, concomitantly, the ritual markings of sovereign possession.[85] New acquisitions were, as within acquired territory, marked by a ritual acknowledgement. To win over the high Shang *di* spirit was to proclaim sovereignty over the newly acquired territory. Proclamations of sovereignty required the appropriation of, or domination over, the spirits holding dominion over the territory. In other words, spiritual and profane sovereignty were intertwined.

These concerns with "winning" over the alien other were conspicuous down into the early imperial era. The celebrated early Han minister Jia Yi's own recommendations when dealing with the Xiongnu, mentioned earlier, make heavy use of the territorializing concept of *de* 德, "charisma." According to Jia Yi, a distinction between kings and emperors resides in that for which they do battle. Kings do battle for *yi* 義, "righteousness" or "ritual propriety," a norm that pertains to lower order of nobility; emperors, or more properly "thearchs," do battle for *de*.[86]

De has a long history as a central concept in Chinese literature. Its first appearance is in oracle bone inscriptions. David Nivison states that its appearance usually was connected to the monarch's power to affect or be affected by a certain event or chain of events. In one particular representative inscription, the monarch's *de* is said to have been magnified by his willingness to sacrifice himself on behalf of another who was ill. The monarch's willingness to sacrifice himself causes the spirits to "approve" the monarch's *de*. There is a certain give-and-take mechanism at work here: the monarch places himself "at risk" on behalf of another and, as a result, "receives" an augmentation of his *de*. This "debt of gratitude" is something that Nivison believes took on special import for Chinese society, by way of socialization and social pressure, until it came "to seem to

---

[85] See "Kang gao" 康誥 ("The announcement to Prince Kang"), Li Xueqin, *Shangshu zhengyi*, 14.359–360. See also the "Jun Shi" 君奭 chapter. Li Xueqin, *Shangshu zhengyi* 尚書正義, 16.444. The notice of acknowledgment and encouragement of "virtue" by the Shang *di* spirit is also present in the Xing-*zhong* and Shi Qiang-*pan* Zhou bronze inscriptions. See Zhang Guiguang 張桂光, ed., *Shang Zhou jinwen moshi zongji* 商周金文摹釋總集 (Beijing: Zhonghua shuju, 2010), 1:10175 (Shi Qiang-*pan*) and 2:00251 (Xing-*zhong*).

[86] 王者戰義，帝者戰德. Jia Yi 賈誼, "Xiongnu" 匈奴, in Jia Yi, *Xinshu jiaozhu*, 4.135.

be an ambient psychological force."[87] In short, *de* is a relational notion, one that is only in effect when the possessor of *de* is in some kind of reciprocal association, whether it be with another person, or, as is sometimes the case, with "heaven" (*tian* 天), a concept that formally commands the allegiance of the empire. Furthermore, it speaks to one's (potential) conduct, one's bearing in the course of one's activities.

The later attribution of specific and purely behavioral modifiers to *de* in Western Zhou bronzes is consistent with its previous usages in the oracle bone inscriptions. According to Donald Munro, *de* as it appears in the Western Zhou bronzes often seems to be presented as a notion involving a principle of personal activities that are pursued in accordance with certain communally accepted, socially beneficial standards. A further Zhou contention was that *de* was congenital, derived from one's ancestors, from one's parents, or, in some instances, from heaven itself. This, however, was not a consistent belief: "[the] belief in the innateness of [*de*] was never consistently held by the early Chinese. There are constant references to the obligation individuals felt to imitate the [*de*] of their ancestors, which would be unnecessary if it were innate. Also, people are continually exhorted to 'change their [*de*]' or to 'make [*de*] their standard.'"[88] Such exhortations are in line with the notion of *de* as a disposition, or a way of conducting oneself in view of certain stable norms. As a dispositional notion, it involves a process of mimesis. It seeks to reflect, to capture through close mimicry, or emulation, a pattern of relating to others and to one's general environment.

Though its usage in the bronzes and early texts may not immediately recommend *de* to bear upon concerns of the establishment of spatial sovereignty – and many clearly do not – there are any number of passages that suggest just this. As various passages in pre-Qin texts indicate, including the following from the *Zuozhuan*, possessing *de* was requisite for acquiring and maintaining sovereign territory: "Since ancient times it has been true that one cannot achieve true security by relying on natural defenses and horses. For this reason the former kings cultivated their reputation for virtue [*de*] in order to bring ritual entertainment to the spirits and the human ancestors. One never hears of their having devoted themselves to natural defenses and horses."[89] The implication in this passage is obvious: to secure one's territories, ritual, spiritual

---

[87] David Nivison, *The Ways of Confucianism* (Chicago: Open Court, 1996), 25.

[88] Donald Munro, *The Concept of Man in Early China* (Stanford, CA: Stanford University Press, 1969), 101.

[89] 恃險與馬，不可以為固也，從古以然，是以先王務脩德音，以亨神人，不聞其務險與馬也. *Zuozhuan*, Zhao 4.1b; Yang Bojun, *Chunqiu zuozhuan zhu*, 4:1247; *Zuo Tradition (Zuozhuan)*, 3:1364–1365.

relationships are more important to maintain than military ones. *De* furthermore was important for the expansion of one's sovereign domain. The emphasis in manifold texts on the need to *shi de* 施德 or *bu de* 布德, to "disseminate virtue," gives *de* a clearly spatial effect. Not infrequently *de* is said to be "disseminated" throughout the entire realm, All-Under-Heaven, suggesting that the dissemination of *de* may actually be defining expansionist tendencies, or the maintenance of a territorialized sovereignty. Even if we were to translate this as broadly effecting a moral influence, it is one that must be maintained for a spatialized sovereignty to be kept. Disseminating *de* was akin to, and was commonly spoken of in tandem with, offering material benefits to one's potential or current allies.[90] Indeed, gifts without *de* – for instance, those coming from merchants – were potentially a politically destabilizing force. As Tamara Chin evidences in her study of economic transactions between the Chinese and non-Chinese over the Han dynasty, with commerce replacing tribute, there is an increase of mobility and a concomitant decline in loyalty to the state. The accumulation of private wealth emboldens people to challenge the state, while trafficking with foreign peoples weakens nationalistic allegiances. In its chapters on alien peoples, Sima Qian's *Shiji* insinuates the breakdown of easy nationalistic divides by describing "both frontier and central regions in terms of their customs (*su* 俗) and

---

[90] This is manifestly present in the advice offered to Emperor Wu of Han by Liu An 劉安 with respect to the emperor's desire to subject southern Yue peoples. Liu An offers a choice, for the emperor to either succor the new Min–Yue regent with *de* and gifts, encouraging the regent to govern in accord with Chinese norms or kill him and install another. The aim was very plainly an extension of spatial sovereignty: "Were Your Majesty to desire to have him come and reside in the Central States, then dispatch important officials to interview him. By displaying virtue and bestowing rewards, You can then draw him to You. In this situation, he will assuredly succor the young and support the old among his people and respond to Your sagely virtue. If Your Majesty has no use for him, then preserve their severed lineage (by installing another from his family on the Yue throne), restore their fallen state, install their king and lords, and thereby show support for the Yue people. In this situation, the Yue will certainly pledge to be boundary servants, and for generations they will provide tribute and service. Your Majesty, by means of an inch-square seal with its twelve-foot cord would pacify and console the areas beyond the borders. Without the labors of one infantry soldier, without the dulling of one spear, might and virtue will both emanate forth" 陛下若欲來內，處之中國，使重臣臨存，施德垂賞以招致之，此必攜幼扶老以歸聖德. 若陛下無所用之，則繼其絕世，存其亡國，建其王侯，以為畜越，此必委質為藩臣，世共貢職。陛下以方寸之印，丈二之組，填撫方外，不勞一　卒，不頓一載，而威德並行. *HS* 64A.2782–2783; Olberding, *Dubious Facts*, appendix F, section H, 196. In a series of recommendations about how the monarch should conduct himself to win over his common people, speaking to various internal dispositions and states, the *Xunzi* declares that the highest attainment of virtuous conduct is a "generosity" or "abundance" (德行致厚), aligning it with a giving mindset. See *Xunzi*, "On Honor and Disgrace" ("Rong ru" 榮辱), Wang Xianqian, *Xunzi jijie*, 1:59; *Xunzi: The Complete Text*, trans. Eric L. Hutton (Princeton, NJ: Princeton University Press, 2014), 25.

products."[91] Thus, the *Shiji* occludes distinctions that earlier had pronouncedly separated internal from external. According to Ban Biao, coauthor of the *Hanshu*, this diminution of the power of the state in favor of the marketplace made the *Shiji*'s "Account of the commodity producers" (*Huozhi liezhuan* 貨殖列傳) threatening to the state's order.[92]

A sense of the monarch's ritual charisma, his ritual "power" was deemed crucial for a population's political adherence. When the population, as with the Xiongnu, were not sufficiently affected by the monarch's *de*, the monarch's claims to hegemony were weak. One might plausibly argue that the affective power of *de* was merely symbolic, that its powers could be reduced to more secular, less vaporous advantages. But then comments, as in the *Book of Lord Shang*, which contrast *de*, a ritually instantiated strength against a physical strength, *li* 力, would seem oddly put.[93] If there is no power to *de*, there is no need to contrast it at all.

As a passage in the *Shenzi* 慎子 states, one's *de* is grounded in the lack of doubts toward one, in the solidity of one's reputation for certain conduct and action.[94] The passage in the *Shenzi* links virtue to administration, not just to general conduct, as do manifold examples in another "legalist" text, the *Hanfeizi*.[95] Such connections between *de* and administration are found elsewhere, even in the classical Confucian corpus, where one might expect *de* to be discussed exclusively on a more general, nonadministrative plane. Mencius, for instance, is focusing on administrative concerns when he forwards the injunction, "Honor the worthy and nurture the talented so that Virtue may be made manifest."[96] *De* pertains immediately to the proper administration of sovereign territory – and to its successful extension. Confucius of the *Analects* ties *de* to spatial sovereignty in his contrast of the "gentleman" or "exemplary person" (*junzi* 君子) and the "petty person" (*xiaoren* 小人): exemplary persons "cling" to

---

[91] Tamara Chin, *Savage Exchange: Han Imperialism, Chinese Literary Style, and the Economic Imagination* (Cambridge, MA: Harvard University Asia Center, 2014), 150.

[92] Chin, *Savage Exchange*, 146.

[93] "In general, the governance of the enlightened ruler depends on strength and not on virtue" 故凡明君之治也，任其力不任其德. "Cuo fa" 錯法 ("Implementing laws"), *Shangjunshu zhuizhi*, 66. This pairing opposes military or legal strength against ritual strength. Elsewhere, *The Book of Lord Shang* tries to subsume ritual strength under legal–military strength. See "Qinling" 靳令 ("Making orders strict"): "(Legal–military) strength gives birth to (political) force, (political) force gives birth to fearsomeness, fearsomeness gives birth to virtue, virtue is [thus] borne of (legal–military) strength" 力生彊，彊生威，威生德，德生於力. *Shangjunshu zhuizhi*, 82.

[94] *Shenzi*, "De li" 德立; *Shenzi jijiao jizhu* 慎子集校集注 (Beijing: Zhonghua shuju, 2013), 47–51.

[95] See, for instance, "Er bing" 二柄, in *Hanfeizi jijie*, 39–42.

[96] 尊賢育才，以彰有德. *Mengzi zhengyi* 2:843; *Mencius*, trans. Irene Bloom (New York: Columbia University Press, 2009), 6B7, 139.

de, while petty people cling merely to land.[97] This spatial sensibility is reinforced in other of Confucius's remarks, such as when Confucius gnomically, pithily quips that people with *de* are sure to have neighbors.[98] The spatial sensibility of this remark tallies with a passage from the *Zuozhuan*, in which the Yi 夷 barbarians have a *de* that is "irrepressible" or "insatiable" (*wu yan* 無厭). Because of this, an envoy declares, "My ruler, having failed to defend the altars of [soil and grain], is now cast out upon the moors. He has sent his lowly servant to report this emergency and to say this: 'The disposition [*de* 德] of the Yi barbarians is insatiable. Should they become your neighbors, my lord, then they will be a threat on your [boundaries].'"[99] The spatial sensibility of Confucius's remark also tallies with the defining of cultivating the ancestors' virtue by perfecting all of the aspects of territorial governance necessary to withstand "unexpected" assaults, whether from within, or without.[100]

A famous passage from the *Zuozhuan* directly connects *de* to territorial sovereignty, replete with symbolic meaning pertaining to the preservation, maintenance, and extension of sovereignty. Therein, legendary bronze cauldrons that were "lost" in the Si River 泗水[101] at or just before

---

[97] 君子懷德，小人懷土. *Analects* 4.11, *Lunyu jijie*, 1:250–253.

[98] 子曰：「德不孤，必有鄰。」*Analects* 4.25, *Lunyu jijie*, 1:279–281.

[99] 寡君失守社稷，越在草莽，使下臣告急曰：「夷德無厭，若鄰於君，疆場之患也。」*Zuozhuan*, Ding 4.3f; Yang Bojun, *Chunqiu zuozhuan zhu*, 4:1548; *Zuo Tradition (Zuozhuan)*, 3:1760–1761.

[100] See *Zuozhuan*, Zhao 23.9; Yang Bojun, *Chunqiu zuozhuan zhu*, 4:1447–1448; *Zuo Tradition (Zuozhuan)*, 3:1624–1625.

[101] The *Mencius* explicitly mentions the Si as one of the rivers having been regulated by Yu. It was also a meeting place for twelve lords with the Zhou monarch, as well as the place where Zhang Liang 張良 was said to have met an old man, likely a spirit attached to the river, who gave him secret teachings. The *Lunheng* relates that Confucius was buried on the shores of the Si River. If these mentions are any indication, clearly the Si, as with many other rivers, had ritual significance. See "Teng wen gong shang": "[Yu] deepened the beds of the Ju and the Han, and raised the dykes of the Huai and the Ssu to empty them into the River. Only then were the people of the Central Kingdoms able to find food for themselves" 決汝、漢，排淮、泗而注之江，然後中國可得而食也. *Mengzi zhengyi* 1:377; *Mencius*, trans. D. C. Lau (New York: Penguin Books, 1970), 102. *Hanshi waizhuan* 10.6: 泗水上有十二諸侯皆來朝. *Hanshi waizhuan*, 341; for the reference to Zhang Liang walking along the Si River and meeting Lord Yellow Stone (*huangshigong* 黃石公), see *Lunheng*, "Ziran" 自然, "Siwei" 死偽, and "Jiyao" 紀妖, Wang Chong 王充, *Lunheng jiaojian* 論衡校箋 (Hebei jiaoyu chubanshe, 1999), 1:594, 685, 705. In the "Jiyao" mention, Wang Chong explicitly states Zhang Liang was sauntering along the Si River in Xiapi 下邳 (常閒從容步游下邳泗上). In the version found in *Qianfulun*, "Zhishixing" 志氏姓, Zhang Liang meets with the "spirit person" Lord Yellow Stone in Xiapi, but does it does not specify more exactly where; Wang Fu 王符, *Qianfulun jianjiao zheng* 潛夫論箋校正 (Beijing: Zhonghua shuju, 1985), 446. In the *Shiji* version of this story (at *SJ* 55.2034), Zhang Liang is said to have been walking "across a bridge in Xiapi" 下邳圯上, but does not specify where or across what river. However, according to current reconstructed maps of the late Qin period, Xiapi lay alongside the Si River; Tan Qixiang 谭其骧, ed., *Zhongguo lishi ditu ji* 中國歷史地圖集

the Qin unification – bronzes that, according to Sima Qian's *Shiji*, the First Emperor of Qin was eager to retrieve – were connected implicitly to *de*, the claim to ritually sanctified sovereignty over the realm.[102] The size and weight of the cauldrons were dependent on the *de* of the sovereign who possessed them, their size inversely proportionate to the *de* of the possessor.[103] When the possessing sovereign had great virtue, the cauldrons were heavy but small; likewise, when their possessor had limited virtue, they were light but large. This would suggest that the cauldrons' size, a metric visually associated with power and strength, was a false signifier, a simulacrum of power that was not truly representative. Instead, the cauldrons' true signifier of power was not immediately perceivable – their power was only demonstrable through an intimate personal interaction, an exertion of muscular strength against the cauldrons themselves. Without such interaction, one would be deceived, believing the power of the cauldrons, and by association their possessor, was greater than it actually was. As with the cauldrons, to know the power of the monarch, one needed to be intimately aware of his inner qualities, qualities that require more intimate perceptual skill, akin to knowing his *de*, rather than any immediately perceivable, superficial display.

The cauldrons' connection to territorial sovereignty was pictorially represented in the casting of images of "creatures" (*wu* 物), such as "the sprites of the hills and waters," based on the representations of men traveling from afar (*yuanfang* 遠方), from beyond the limits of the near and known. Again, their power of representation required a personal viewing, a personal interaction with the cauldrons. Their pictorially represented "knowledge" was said to be of assistance to commoners who wished to venture out into the wilds, the area of the unknown, the untamed, the areas lying outside alluvial plains, outside of state administration.[104]

(Beijing: Zhongguo ditu chubanshe chuban, 1982), 7–8, 5/8). *Lunheng*, "Shu xu" 書虛：《傳書》言：孔子當泗水之葬. Wang Chong, *Lunheng jiaojian*, 2:126.

[102] 始皇還，過彭城，齋戒禱祠，欲出周鼎泗水。使千人沒水求之，弗得. See *SJ* 6.248.

[103] 楚子伐陸渾之戎，遂至於雒，觀兵于周疆。定王使王孫滿勞楚子。楚子問鼎之大小、輕重焉。對曰：「在德不在鼎。昔夏之方有德也 … 桀有昏德，鼎遷于商，載祀六百。商紂暴虐，鼎遷于周。德之休明，雖小，重也。其姦回昏亂，雖大，輕也。天祚明德.…. *Zuozhuan*, Xuan 3.3; Yang Bojun, *Chunqiu zuozhuan zhu*, 2:669–671; *Zuo Tradition (Zuozhuan)*, 1:600–601.

[104] "The hundred things were therewith completely set forth, and the people thus knew the spirits and the evil things. That was why when the people entered rivers, marshes, mountains, and forests, they would not meet what could harm them, and the sprites of the hills and waters could not get at them" 百物而為之備，使民知神姦，故民入川澤山林，不逢不若，螭魅罔兩，莫能逢之. *Zuozhuan*, Xuan 3.3; Yang Bojun, *Chunqiu zuozhuan zhu*, 2:669–671; *Zuo Tradition (Zuozhuan)*, 1:600–601.

These penumbral areas – the rivers, marshes, mountains, and forests – nonarable areas lying around an alluvial center, "fiscally sterile areas beyond the core that would not normally repay the cost of governing them,"[105] had to be pictographically mapped before they were deemed "safe" for those timid farmers who had not proceeded into such wilds. To enter into a "barbarian" wild was to leave the known, to leave the epistemically and, more importantly, fiscally mapped. Yet, as James C. Scott intimates, an unstated, associated concern lying beneath the surface was with the attractions of the nonstate areas. Portraying them as replete with monstrous beings was a symbol of the state's trepidation toward the appeal of these wild, "barbarian" areas, whether they were partly incorporated into the state's administrative structures or not. As Scott points out,

The very act of establishing a state and its subsequent enlargement was itself typically an act of displacement ... Many of a state's adjacent barbarian populations may well have been, in effect, refugees from the state-making process itself ... once states were created ... there were frequently as many reasons for fleeing them as for entering them.[106]

This tale of the state's parental, patronizing education of its population about the monstrous beings in order to relieve their fears derives, in fact, from the state's insistence on its knowledge about these penumbral realms. Translating the living wilds into recognizable forms worked to assert a shadowy sovereignty in areas in which the state's sovereignty was, in all truth, quite vulnerable. Residents of these areas often chose to keep distance from the state's apparatuses, areas that Scott labels "shatter zones," where the state's surveillance mechanisms were weaker, less invasive. Such explains why those engaged in illicit activities would flee beyond established surveillance boundaries:[107] "Becoming a barbarian was often a bid to improve one's lot."[108] Indeed, "the sprites of the hills and waters" mentioned above were very possibly those native naturalistic forces that the monarchial regimes sought to subjugate in their incorporative ritual activities, activities I discussed previously. One might argue that the monstrous beings of the wilds appearing in other early texts, such as the *Shanhaijing* or *Mutianzizhuan* 穆天子傳, were similarly challenging apparitions, natural forces contending against state power.

---

[105] Scott, *Against the Grain*, 220.   [106] Scott, *Against the Grain*, 231.
[107] For instance, Hou Ying 侯應 observes to Emperor Yuan 元 of Han that "If a gang of men broke the law, and were in a tight spot, they could flee out past through northern frontier (to become bandits) and then could not be controlled" 群輩犯法，如其窘急，亡走北出，則不可制. See *HS* 94B.3804; Olberding, *Dubious Facts*, 211.
[108] Scott, *Against the Grain*, 232.

To recapitulate, early monarchs utilized various methods to mark their areas of sovereignty. One was to establish settled populations, administratively taxable and legally formalizable units; another was to build edifices, such as walls, roads, or fences; a third was to mark or repurpose the use of sanctified living spaces. These methods sometimes overlapped, with a natural landmark – a mountain or river – being resanctified, reclaimed for the monarchial cult, marked as the site of monarchial influence, as opposed to simply that of local hegemonic forces. In the *Houhanshu*, we see the emperor visiting local cult areas, ostensibly with the aim of observing and regulating them. Monarchial control over religious activities had everything to do with the assertion of his sovereignty over the area. In the *Yuejueshu*, Yu deputizes nobles as the agents of his sovereign powers on the top of a sacred mountain, Maoshan 茅山, in the frontier region of Dayue, giving noble titles to those who had *de*. Upon the conclusion of the ceremony, Yu metonymically takes full command of the region by renaming the sacred mountain Kuaiji 會稽, or "Meeting Mountain," to proclaim his command.[109] His hegemonic aspirations are reasserted in the very next sentence, with Yu, when going through his royal progress through Dayue, meeting with elders, collecting poetry (and thus possible sources of complaints about local corruption), reviewing steelyards and scales, and standardizing the *dou* and *hu* measures.[110]

The employment of the altars of soil to exhibit sovereignty was another means by which landscapes were resanctified, repurposed to monarchial ends. As mentioned, the altars were assigned to those "enfeoffed" with that territory. Space was defined by the area over which such sanctified administrative power could be exercised. Again, the monarch's spatial sovereignty was not defined by landscape so much as his sway over the population, by whether the population in the area, including and most importantly those deputized to govern the area, obeyed assigned rules and laws.[111] As Lewis declares, "Any suggestion of the cultural or political autonomy of regions was anathema to advocates of the imperial order,

---

[109] "When [Yu] arrived in Dayue, he climbed Maoshan (Reed Mountain) and held a great meeting there, at which he gave noble titles to those who had been virtuous, and enfeoffed those who had merit. Then he changed the name of Maoshan to Kuaiji (Meeting) [Mountain]" 到大越, 上茅山, 大會稽, 爵有德, 封有功, 更名茅山曰會稽。Li Bujia, *Yuejueshu jiaoshi*, 221; *The Glory of Yue: An Annotated Translation of the Yuejue shu*, trans. Olivia Milburn (Leiden: Brill, 2010) 224. In an annotation to her translation, Olivia Milburn observes that changing of names of mountains, akin with changing names in general, was to reappropriate the power associated with it, in this case its localized power, and thus its use by local cults.

[110] 及其王也, 巡狩大越, 見耆老, 納詩書, 審銓衡, 平斗斛. Li Bujia, *Yuejueshu jiaoshi*, 221.

[111] As Jia Yi writes, without agreement from those lords who administer the areas, the monarch's laws are basically void: 「陛下即不為千載之治安, 知今之勢, 豈過一傳再

and many policies – most notably the forced resettlement of leading families in the capital region – were instituted to eliminate bearers of distinctive regional cultures. This criticism of local culture took the form of attacks on the inevitable limits, and frequent evils, of 'custom' (*su* 俗)."[112]

Thus a substitute ritual regime subject to central authority had to be instituted by the central government. "Barbarian" culture was deemed a spur to criminal deviance, to a rejection of sovereign Chinese authority. The submission of regional culture to central authority figures prominently in the "Treatise on Geography" ("Dili zhi" 地理志) in the *Hanshu*.[113] Annexing regional nature cults and reclaiming mountains and waterways was crucial for the maintenance and expansion of the imperial cult. Without such annexation, regional powers could challenge the central court. As the *Hanshu* warned about Henei, "their customs encourage an inflexible strength, so there are many powerful families who encroach and seize land. They treat kindness and ritual as unimportant, and are fond of dividing property while [their parents are] still living."[114] Losing these ritual altars, therefore, was directly related to losing sovereign domain. One might even speculate that the loss of ritual altars was as key to the waning of one's sovereignty over a domain as the forfeiture of the territory itself. In the *Mozi*, the last king of Shang, Zhou, became so dissolute that a red bird alighted on the soil altar on Mount Qi, proclaiming the rise of Zhou sovereignty.[115] The key to this sovereign power was exemplified in the powers of *de*.

For the "cultured" early Chinese, not only were the barbarians rude in appearance, they were uncultured in manners. This tallies with the move to "ritualize" the non-Chinese populations, upon their submission.

傳哉。諸侯猶且人恣而不制，豪橫而大強也，至其相與，特以縱橫之約相親耳。漢法令不可得行矣。」 "Yi rang" 益攘, Jia Yi, *Xinshu jiaozhu*, 56–57.

[112] Lewis, *Construction of Space in Early China*, 190.

[113] "Ban Gu's discussion of regional customs and character frequently mentions the tendency to establish powerful lineages that buy up land, form political cliques, and develop alliances, having recourse to violence to further their ends." Lewis, *Construction of Space in Early China*, 220.

[114] 故俗剛彊，多豪桀侵奪，薄恩禮，好生分. *HS* 28.1647; Lewis, *Construction of Space in Early China*, 220–221.

[115] "A red bird holding in its beak a baton of jade alighted at the altar of the Zhou state in the city of Qi and proclaimed: 'Heaven orders King Wen of Zhou to attack Yin [i.e., Shang] and take possession of its state.' Taidian journeyed to pay his respects to the Zhou ruler, the river cast up its chart, and the land brought forth the 'riding-yellow' beast" 赤鳥銜珪，降周之岐社，曰：「天命周文王伐殷有國。」泰顛來賓，河出綠圖，地出乘黃. "Condemnation of Offensive Warfare," *Mozi*, "Against Offensive Warfare" lower section (*Fei gong xia* 非攻下); Mo Di 墨翟, *Mozi xiangu* 墨子閒詁 (Beijing: Zhonghua shuju, 2001), 151–152; *Mozi: Basic Writings*, trans. Burton Watson (New York: Columbia University Press, 2003), 60–61.

Without such, they are "rude," culturally (and politically) unrecognizable, "rebellious," dangerous. To ritualize them, to ritually "encode"
them is, in essence, to bring them within the cultural and *spatial* purview
of Chinese sovereignty. Such requires their reeducation, the elimination,
or at least incorporation of their own cultural and religious traditions,
including their spaces, particularly their sanctified ones, into the Chinese
sovereign realm. These practices, I argue, clearly undermine the persistent contemporary impulse to divide secular and sacred realms, to separate
the "factual" and "moral," to secularize all governmental administration
and its effects, textual or otherwise.

Chapter Summary

To expand his territory, the early Chinese sovereign was obliged to
neutralize or eliminate previous indigenous ritual formations, replacing
or supplementing them with an imperial cult, installing a system of *she*,
"altars of soil." These altars were the territorializing marks of occupation.
Aligned with these altars was the concurrent institution of the notion of
de, the political charisma to which subservient areas owed allegiance.
These two ritual structures – one concrete, the other conceptual – actively
affected territorial administration. The limitations of the sovereign's ritualized power, of the power of his "name" or reputation, were a clue to the
limits of the central court's formal administrative oversight. Distinctions
between "internal" and "external" areas were in fact not so much militarily defined as administratively. But because of the frontier zones' cultural
heterogeneity (and physical distance), it was difficult for the sovereign to
maintain unalloyed control over them.

To extend or maintain his ritualized influence, the early Chinese sovereign exerted his prerogative to ritually change place names (*gengming*)
and engaged in ritualized tours of inspection (*xunshou*). Through such
activities, the monarch territorialized his realm, personally responding to
any challenge to his sovereign authority. Spatial organizations required
repeated spiritual reinvestitures and restrictions on how and to which
spirits subservient lords were to offer sacrifice. Sacrificing to spirits lying
beyond one's terriorial bounds was illegitimate, a subversive attempt to
extend the subservient lord's ritual – and thus administrative – structures
beyond established limits. It was the sovereign's singular prerogative to
use his virtuous charisma, his *de*, to win over the alien spirits of newly
acquired territories, those "barbarian" areas in which sovereign power
was most vulnerable and tentative.

5   The Perception of the "Enemy": The External Definition of Sovereign Space

In this chapter, I examine the conceptualization of state borders, specifically how these borders were defined by the state's and the sovereign's sense of, and reaction to, that which bounds – their neighbors, with whom they most often are in competition. This conceptualization is noticeably reflected, in some measure, in political discussions of the *xing* 形, that is, the "form" or, more precisely, "spatial disposition" of a bounded area. I contend that, from the Warring States to the Han era, the sense of neighbor, and thus of boundary and "spatial disposition," necessarily shifted. Consequently, the sense of what the state was, in contrast and contestation, changed at its most fundamental level. This shift reveals the underlying dynamic of what external force does to a sovereign boundary. When the state's focus is on competitors who are largely seen as culturally commensurate, the terms of engagement and the perception of territory and sovereignty are significantly distinct from when the state's focus is on competitors who are seen as culturally incommensurate. The establishment of sovereign boundaries almost inevitably anticipates the defense against, or an intention toward, future predatory colonization and possession of a competing polity sharing one's sovereign boundary. When the sovereign boundary faces a polity that does not share, for instance, a similarly ritualized administrative state structure, the terms of engagement and rendering of territory in military or diplomatic interface can alter substantially. Thus, when a Chinese polity defeats another with a similarly ritualized administrative apparatus, the release of territory by the defeated polity is semantically different in terms of its political structure from when the defeated is a non-Chinese polity for which territory has an administratively distinctive semantic inflection. This is not to say that non-Chinese polities cannot develop commensurate, recognizable administrative apparatuses; naturally they can. But their ritual, cultural dissimilarities often preclude their being treated as peer polities, deserving of equal status and ritually grounded diplomatic treatment, even when their knowledge of ritual structures is substantial.

Defining Spatial Disposition (*Xing* 形)

From the inscriptional evidence of the Zhou bronzes and Warring States bamboo manuscripts, prior to the Warring States period, the common term referencing the abstract notion of "form" or "spatial disposition," *xing*, was not in use. In the Zhou bronzes, only its earlier variant with the knife signific, 刑, was used. And, indeed, even in the Warring States bamboo texts, this earlier variant was by far the more common, the meaning of which could be defined as "punishment," "law," or the more general "model."[1] In the *Shuowen*, the definitions of the two variants are hardly associable, 刑 defined as "cutting the throat" (*jing* 到), or, more generally, "corporally punishing," while 形 is defined as "image" (*xiang* 象). Only the even less common form of *xing*, 型, is defined in the *Shuowen* as anything close to "law," specifically, "the method of casting objects." In his comments to the definition of 型, the Qing-dynasty commentator Duan Yucai 段玉裁 remarked that 型 was graphically substitutable by 刑 and, moreover, could be extrapolated to mean something akin to "model." Similarly, in his comments to the definition of 形, Duan Yucai also remarks that 形, as defined, has been written with both 型 and 刑.[2]

Review of various classical texts clarifies a number of salient definitive features of the use of the most common, and latest, form of *xing*, 形: The perception of *xing* depends almost solely on vision (or a simulacrum of vision, such as a kind of conceptual comprehension), as opposed to touch or hearing, its perception repeatedly contrasted with that of the voice or sound.[3] It is applied to that which has shape, or even merely a potential shape, and is an encompassing concept, meaning the shape is closed and inclusive, or at least reflective, of that which lies within it.[4] Thus, the *xing*, the externally perceived "form" or "spatial disposition," of the body is reflective, or inclusive, of the activities inside it, its internal features;[5] the

---

[1] Schuessler, *A Dictionary of Early Zhou Chinese*, 688–689.

[2] Xu Shen, *Shuowen jiezi zhu*, 182b, 424b, 688b.

[3] A common phrase from early Chinese texts definitively displaying this contrast is the following: 聽於無聲, 視於無形. For instances of this phrase, see *HS* 94B.3816; *Lüshi chunqiu* 18/2, 18/3 "Zhong yan" 重言, "Jing yu" 精諭, *Lüshi chunqiu jishi*, 2:481, 482; *Annals of Lü Buwei*, 446–447, 448–449; *Liji*, "Quli shang" 曲禮上, *Liji jijie*, 1:21, *Li Chi: Book of Rites*, 1:69.

[4] Boundedness as a defining feature of *xing* can be found in the "Great Treatise" ("Xici" 繫辭) of the *Zhouyi*, in which that which lies "above," abstracted from *xing* is the "formless" *dao*, while that which lies below, or is derived from *xing*, are "objects of use" (*qi* 器). As stated in various other texts, for instance the *Lüshichunqiu* and *Daodejing*, *dao* cannot be given permanent shape. By logical extension, *xing* not only can be, but is fundamentally defined by such. See *Zhouyi: The Book of Changes*, trans. Richard Rutt (New York: Curzon, 2002), 408–433.

[5] The somatic body's *xing* is where evidence of the body's expression – coloration, propensities, qualities, emotional characteristics, etc. – are manifest. *Xing* is what is externally perceived. See *Mengzi*, "Gaozi xia": "That which is located within must display a 'form' without" 有諸內必形諸外. *Mengzi zhengyi*, 2:831. In this passage the effect that one

xing, the "form" or "spatial disposition," of the state (*guo* 國) is inclusive of its internal features, sociopolitical, geographic, and economic.[6] Furthermore, with regard to the state's "spatial disposition," it is affected, strengthened or weakened, by that which is adjacent, that which joins to its borders, as the body is affected by that with which it comes into contact.[7] The boundaries of a spatial disposition, again whether somatic or statist, are thus definable and somewhat definite. In the case of the body, it lies at the edge of what is perceived as part of the body: the skin, the hair. With the state, its boundaries can be defined concretely, or somewhat abstractly: walls, the placement of soldiers, or as I contend, the use of certain accepted rituals or other cultural conventions. Even the spatial disposition of the land, that is, "territory," *dixing* 地形, appears at times to be an inclusive concept, not, as various translations might lead one to believe, identifiable simply with an empty landscape, with unoccupied geography, but actually *inclusive* of the resources on it.[8] Attacking

person has is manifest, can be *seen* in the behavior of others, whether in the general way people perform or how a ruler's conduct will be changed by virtuous ministers.

[6] As the *Xunzi* states, "The manner in which a true king establishes regulations is that he observes [spatial dispositions and propensities] and then establishes regulations for implements. He weighs up distances and then sets gradations in tributes" 彼王者之制也，視形埶而制械用，稱遠邇而等貢獻. See "Zhenglun" 正論, *Xunzi: The Complete Text*, 189, translation modified; Wang Xianqian, *Xunzi jijie*, 2:329.

[7] See, for instance, *Zhanguoce*, "Gong zhong shi Han Min zhi Qin qiu Wusui" 公仲使韓珉之秦求武隧: "Attendant Tang spoke to Duke Zhong, saying, 'Han serves Qin. Han's seeking [the area of] Wusui is not what my ramshackle village (my state) despises. If Han were to have acquired Wusui, its [spatial disposition] could then bolster Chu's'" 「唐客謂公仲曰：『韓之事秦也，且以求武隧也，非弊邑之所憎也。韓已得武隧，其形乃可以善楚。』」 He Jianzhang, *Zhanguoce zhushi*, 3:1062. Chao Cuo 晁錯 formalizes this sensibility with his statement that the "spatial disposition" of the Chinese is defined by how they manipulate their external opponents, by pitting them against each other. (以蠻夷攻蠻夷，中國之形也.) What is also noteworthy is that the description of the "spatial disposition" of the enemy appears to be a thinly veiled dismissal of the potency of the non-Han opponents to the Chinese empire: "Uniting the small (e.g., the various foreign tribes) to attack the great (e.g., the Chinese empire) – this is the [spatial disposition] of the enemy state (i.e., the Xiongnu state)" 合小以攻大，敵國之形也. See *HS* 49.2281; Olberding, *Dubious Facts*, 186.

[8] In *Sunzi bingfa*, there are ample prescriptions, and proscriptions, concerning the use and misuse of territory, and being cautious with regard to that which bounds and defines it. For instance, in "Nine Contingencies" (*jiu bian* 九變) the reader is warned not to engage with certain roadways, armies, walled cities, territory (*di* 地), or commands from the ruler, all of which are *definiens*, culturally or concretely, of the state. 途有所不由，軍有所不擊，城有所不攻，地有所不爭，君命有所不受. If the general is not "fully conversant with the advantages" to be garnered from these nine contingencies, even if he knows the spatial disposition of the land, inclusive the population upon it, he will not be able to gain the "advantages of Earth" 將不通于九變之利者，雖知地形，不能得地之利矣. *Sunzi yizhu*, 157–158. In the chapter, "Forms of Terrain," which pertains to the spatial disposition of the land (*dixing* 地形), the text defines the terrain in tactical terms, in terms of possibilities of movement, of engagement, access, and egress: "Kinds of terrain include the accessible, that which entangles, that which leads to a stand-off, the narrow pass, the precipitous defile, and the distant"

"territory" is attacking the very constitution of the state, its organization and rituals included. The spatial disposition of the state, inclusive of its terrain, is thus defined as a totality, something that can be ruptured or destroyed, when surrounding, confrontational force is applied.[9] In consequence, when the state has its resources and borders demolished, inclusive of or even defined by their cultural and ritual aspects, the state loses its disposition, becomes, in essence, formally unrecognizable. In sum, it becomes without disposition, without a recognizable, or recognizably territorialized administrative disposition (*wuxing* 無形).[10] The state's "territory," conceptually, thus can be closely analogized to the body, in both its make-up and the reasons for its dissolution.

Indications of Neighborly Relations Through the Use of *Xing*

If the political application of *xing* can be reflective of activity both internal and external to the state,[11] it can be a lens through which we perceive how the state conceives itself, and what action the state deems necessary to take to preserve its spatial disposition. As we shall see, the employment of *xing* tallies with other notional and concrete indications of types of separation of the internal, ritually and administratively recognizable self (*nei* 內) from the external, ritually and administratively alien other (*wai* 外). Naturally, the actual divide was not always sharply maintainable, not from the administrative vantage, at minimum. The notional divide was often more of a rhetorical device rather than a defensibly

---

地形有通者，有挂者，有支者，有隘者，有險者，有遠者. *Sunzi yizhu*, 174. Each of these descriptive specifications of terrain are defined not in terms of the topographical or natural features but with regard to its effects on the engagement with an enemy force. For instance, with regard to the more concrete definition, the precipitous defile, the text advises that "if we can occupy it first, we must take the high ground on the sunny side and await the enemy. Where the enemy has occupied it first, quit the position and withdraw, and do not follow him." See Ames, *Sun-Tzu*, 134–136, 146–151. See also the beginning of Liu An's address to Emperor Wu of Han: "Of those who are not familiar with the terrain [*dixing* 地形] of the southern border region, many consider Yue to have numerous people and a powerful military that could pose problems for the border cities." *HS* 64A.2781; Olberding, *Dubious Facts*, 194–195.

[9] *Zhanguoce*, "Chu wei Yongshi wu yue" 楚圍雍氏五月: "Chu will use three states to plot an attack against Qin. In such a case, an attack on Qin's spatial disposition has been made" 是楚以三國謀秦也。如此則伐秦之形成矣. He Jianzhang, *Zhanguoce zhushi*, 3:1009).

[10] "As a state, Zhao has a spatial disposition which survives only if it is allied with Wei; if not, it will fall" 國形有之而存，無之而亡者. He Jianzhang, *Zhanguoce zhushi*, 3:1077.

[11] It deserves to be noted that the notion of *xing* in the *Zhouli* is part of the title of the official, the *Xingfangshi* 形方氏, the "master of the spatial disposition of the realm," who is in charge of the management of the realm's territory: 形方氏：掌制邦國之地域，而正其封疆，無有華離之地. *Zhouli zhushu*, (Beijing ed.) 2:884.

substantive one. The administrative, and indeed ritual, distinctions were not as clear-cut as internal state discussions of them would necessarily support. Depending upon the organization and cultural self-identification of the other, the administrative and ritual distinctions were sometimes relatively slender, whether between the Shang and Zhou or the Han and Xiongnu polities. Nevertheless, the sensibility of a "form" or "spatial disposition" helped shape how the state pursued policies toward its own and other external peoples. Thus there is use in analyzing how the term has been employed, especially in the Han era, in which the term sees widespread employment in various literati texts and in which the Han state's major alien nemesis, the Xiongnu, is disparaged as not being an equal, neither in its organization nor in its traditions.

If we accept the text of the *Zhanguoce* as representative of late Warring States culture, we can see that the spatial disposition of the state was open to contestation and reformation. In one of two passages mentioning the spatial disposition of the state (*guoxing* 國形), Chen Zhen 陳軫 remonstrates with the king of Qin, whose troops are attacking Jing, part of the state of Han, even after Han has "sliced off" (*ge* 割) and given land in the Nanyang 南陽 area to Qin.[12] Relevant for this analysis is the fact that the spatial disposition, the *xing*, of the state can be affected by attacks on it: it can be altered and reduced by external activity.[13] These reductions and alterations, however, are not simply by area, but by population, and thus effective sovereignty, as sovereignty is most defined by power over others. Again, territory is not simply identifiable with a geographic area – empty, unoccupied land did not efficaciously add to a state's territory – but was primarily defined by the population and resources it inhered. Again, to attempt to overcome a state is to attack its very constitution, its administrative organization and ritual apparatuses included. It is thus that to destroy a state's altars of soil and grain are in essence to destroy the state. Indeed, the territory of a state could be non-contiguous, found partly within the realm of another state.[14]

These basic features of the state evoked by the political use of *xing* were also preserved in other addresses and essays representative of the Warring

---

[12] Perhaps somewhat notably, there is no talk in the *Zuozhuan* of "slicing off" land from a state.

[13] "If the spatial disposition of a state is not suitable [for defense], one retreats. If diplomatic relationships are not fraternal, one slices off [land]. These days [land is] sliced off and diplomatic relations are still not familial, [Han troops] retreat and [your] troops do not stop [advancing]. I, Your servant, fear that there will [soon] be nothing in the area east of the mountain from which to retreat or which can be sliced off [to give you]." 國形不便故馳，交不親故割。今割矣而交不親，馳矣而兵不止，臣恐山東之無以馳割事王者矣。 *Zhanguoce*, "Qin gong Xing" 秦攻陘, He Jianzhang, *Zhanguoce zhushi*, 3:981.

[14] 秦、韓之地形，相錯如繡。He Jianzhang, *Zhanguoce zhushi*, 1:172; *Chan-Kuo Ts'e*, 106: "The territory of [Qin] and Han are mixed together like a tapestry."

States period. According to a *Guanzi* essay, "Conversations of the Lord Protector" ("Ba yan" 霸言), states can positively alter or augment their spatial dispositions, their *xing*, only if they are savvy about manipulating or simply subjecting their neighbors and taking action against distant threats.[15] Conversely, small states show weakness, and compromise their spatial dispositions by "conserving" their "resources and serving the strong so as to avoid offending them."[16] Augmenting or contracting spatial dispositions is not equivalent to simply augmenting or contracting one's land space, one's geography, as I have stressed; it is to strengthen or weaken one's sovereign position over the occupied territory from which one can collect state revenue. There is, according to this *Guanzi* essay, no way to positively affect the spatial disposition of one's state, and thus the potential for self-defense and expansion, if one's affairs are in disarray.[17] The early Han minister Chao Cuo 晁錯, in an address to Emperor Wen 文 of Han, evinces closely similar sentiments to the above *Guanzi* passage, in places almost verbatim, suggesting the Han address borrowed text from a source akin to the *Guanzi*. The spatial disposition of enemy states and small states is defined the same in both, though in Chao Cuo's address, the enemy is more explicitly the non-Chinese tribes, and the spatial disposition of the Central States, also defined in the *Guanzi* essay, is reframed to refer clearly to their non-Chinese adversaries.[18] (In the *Guanzi*, the reference is to "those who border the four seas" 負海, that is, those bordering distant lands.)

From an analysis of the political uses of *xing* in these texts, we can extract the following points about the attitude late Warring States and early Han states held toward their neighbors: Like other closed, discrete spatial forms, such as the physical body or a grouping of military troops, the state's spatial disposition is (1) dependent on the internal arrangements and disposition of its components, much as the physical body is dependent on the internal arrangement and disposition of its organs, broadly defined, and the military grouping on the internal arrangement and disposition of the soldiers and armaments; (2) capable of being

---

[15] "To subjugate the near and use force against the far is a [spatial disposition] distinguishing a state belonging to the king" 服近而彊遠，王國之形也. *Guanzi*, "Ba yan" 霸言; *Guanzi jiaozhu*, 1:479; *Guanzi*, 365, translation modified.

[16] 折節事彊以避罪，小國之形也. *Guanzi*, "Ba yan"; *Guanzi jiaozhu*, 1:479.

[17] "From ancient times to the present, there has never been a state that, after having first incited trouble, flouted the times and altered its spatial disposition, in order to establish merit and their name. There is no state that has not been defeated after having previously incited trouble, flouted the times and altered its spatial disposition" 自古以至今，未嘗有先能作難，違時易形，以立功名者。無有常先作難，違時易形，無不敗者也。*Guanzi*, "Ba yan"; *Guanzi jiaozhu*, 1:479, 481. Translation mine.

[18] See *HS* 49.2281; Olberding, *Dubious Facts*, 186–188.

apportioned off, cut into, weakened, or demolished; (3) is weak or strong depending on how it deploys its internal resources; (4) is a physical, spatially locatable formation, whose primary physical feature is that it is visible; (5) is affected, strengthened or weakened, by that which is adjacent, that which joins to its borders, as the body is affected by that with which it comes into contact.

We can learn more about the spatial disposition of the state by action on it, such as invasion and visitation. From the organization and effects of such activities, we can thoroughly trace any distinctions between the spatial dispositions of pre-imperial and early imperial China. Without the sense of a bright line to define a border – and thus no easy equation of a wall, natural or artificial, with a border – the spatial disposition of the state will be intimately connected to these activities. If the invasion or visitation, such as that by alien powers, threatened the identity and even the administration of the state, the activity would be viewed in a different light from that which was merely a military incursion or diplomatic visitation by a cultural peer. The descriptive jaundice of these activities is most forcefully captured in the sense of who was an "enemy," or "adversary" (di 敵). Indeed, the spatial disposition, or lack thereof, of an adversary impinged epistemically on how and where the state could fight. For instance, the formation of the appearance of a state-like apparatus not only affected the Central States treating the Xiongnu as an "adversary" but the Xiongnu likewise treating the Central States as one.[19]

The Boundary and the Other

For the deep, concrete concatenation in the early Chinese consciousness between boundary and state, particularly when the boundary is shared with a ritually unrecognizable, culturally incommensurate, "non-peer" polity, the common symbolic referent in distinguishing one from the other is the wall.[20] Perhaps reflective of its symbolic

---

[19] This is evident from when the Han began perceiving the Xiongnu organization as a adversarial "state," a designation the Xiongnu simultaneously applied to the Han. See *SJ* 110.2890: 然至冒頓而匈奴最彊大，盡服從北夷，而南與中國為敵國. A passage from the *Qian Han ji* from Xuandi's 宣帝 reign also deserves mention. The text speaks to how the Xiongnu could be treated by the emperor as "servants" (*chen* 臣), defining their status as an "enemy state" as based in their not following the proper ritual codes: 三年春正月，行幸甘泉宮，郊泰畤。匈奴呼韓邪單于為郅支所破，遂稱臣，來朝。上議其儀，丞相霸、御史大夫定國議以為「聖主先諸夏而後夷狄，其禮儀宜如諸侯王，位次（其）〔在〕下。太子太傅蕭望之議曰：「單于夷狄禮儀非正朔所加，故稱敵國」 *Liang Han ji* 兩漢紀 (Beijing: Zhonghua shuju, 2002), 20.356.

[20] See *Shijing*, "Da ya" section, "Ban" 板: "Good men are a fence;/The multitudes of the people are a wall;/Great States are screens;/Great Families are buttresses;/The cherishing of virtue secures repose;/The circle of [the king's] Relatives is a fortified wall./We must

import, "the word for city and wall are the same, 城, not only for provincial capitals or large cities but every community, even small towns and villages."[21] For the Chinese, protected settlements were indicators of the realm of the civilized. To step outside protected settlements, to step outside the "four corners," was to enter the barbarian wilds. As Liu An declared about the barbarous "Yue" peoples, "The territories of the Yue lie beyond the four corners and their common people clip off their hair and tattoo their bodies. One cannot put it in order with the laws and regulations of a civilized nation."[22] Inscribed and defined by bounded space, the known world was separated into zones, the innermost zone being the "royal zone," the outermost, the "zone of wastelands," uninhabitable and thus unworthy of defense, occupied by uncultured, wild barbarians. Even Emperor Wen of Han adjures, the boundary symbolized by the Great Wall has deep cultural, and economic, consequences:

According to the decree of the former emperor, the land north of the Great Wall, where men wield the bow and arrow, was to receive its commands from the *Shanyu*, while that within the wall, whose inhabitants dwell in houses and wear hats and girdles, was to be ruled by us; thus might the countless inhabitants of these lands gain their food and clothing by agriculture, weaving, or hunting; father and son live side by side; ruler and minister enjoy mutual security; and all forsake violence and rebellion.[23]

not let the fortified wall get destroyed;/We must not let [he that is] solitary (i.e., the monarch) be consumed with terrors" 价人維藩、大師維垣、大邦維屏、大宗維翰、懷德維寧、宗子維城。無俾城壞、無獨斯畏. *The Chinese Classics: The She King*, trans. James Legge (Hong Kong: Hong Kong University Press, 1960), 503; *Maoshi zhengyi* 毛詩正義 (Beijing: Beijing daxue chubanshe, 1999), 1151–1152.

[21] Joseph Needham, *Science and Civilisation in China*, vol. 4, *Physics and Physical Technology*, pt. 3, *Civil Engineering and Nautics* (New York: Cambridge University Press, 1971), 42–43. Of course, this linguistic equation is not quite true. No city walls have yet been discovered in the excavations around Xianyang, for whatever reason, whether they were never there (which would seem exceptional), or they were completely razed, the evidence of their foundations lost over time. I thank Griet Vankeerberghen for pointing this out. Regardless, the common conceptualization of an early Chinese city was one that was defined in part by a wall. One need only note again that the word for diagram, as W. Behr mentions, the *wei-*□ enclosure around *bi* 啚, which, put together, form the character *tu*, is, in the case of *guo* 國 in Warring States inscriptional texts, "coreferential with the top part of *yi* 邑," iconically signifying a walled city, "according to a widespread paleographical consensus." Behr, "Placed into the Right Position," 115.

[22] 越, 方外之地, 劗髮文身之民也。不可以冠帶之國法度理也. *HS* 64A.2777; Olberding, *Dubious Facts*, 192.

[23] 先帝制: 長城以北, 引弓之國, 受命單于; 長城 以內, 冠帶之室, 朕亦制之。使萬民耕織射獵衣食, 父子無離, 臣主相安, 俱無暴逆. *SJ* 110.2902; Sima Qian, *Records of the Grand Historian: Han Dynasty*, trans. Burton Watson (New York: Columbia University Press, 1993), 146.

The aggressively protective function of the wall was bound up in the sense of the encroaching chaos of the outside, of the extraliminal, the beyond. As the *Guanzi* states,

> The main city wall must be well constructed, the suburban walls impenetrable, village boundaries must be secure on all sides, gates kept closed, and residential walls and door locks kept in good repair. The reason is that if the main walls are not well constructed, rebels and brigands will plot to make trouble. If suburban walls can be penetrated, evil fugitives and trespassers will abound. If village boundaries can be crossed, thieves and robbers will not be stopped. If gates are not kept closed and there are passages in and out, men and women will not be kept separated. If residential walls are not solid and locks are not secure, even though people may have rich possessions, they will not be able to protect themselves. Now, if powers [i.e., those constituting spatial and strategic dispositions 形勢] do not permit wrongdoing, wicked and depraved men will become honest.[24]

To be cast out of the boundaries of the city was, as in classical Greece, to be exiled, without support or protection, without friend or family.[25] But in this passage, the liminal border lies not merely between the civilized interior and the barbaric exterior. In an arresting addition to a naturally parallel list of rebels/brigands, evil fugitives/trespassers, and thieves/robbers, the boundaries between male and female are cited, presumably, given the syntactic parallel, as consequential as, if not more than, the boundaries proffered by main walls (*da cheng* 大城), suburban walls (*guo zhou* 郭周), and village boundaries (*li yu* 里域) listed just prior. Accentuating this contrast is the succeeding reversion to the consideration of the securing of physical and economic borders, as the main and suburban walls and village boundaries secured. This interjection of a sociocultural, sexual boundary clearly informs the interpretation of the overarching function of the listed boundaries.

Following from my arguments in Chapter 2 regarding the likely general inaccuracy in the delineations of early Chinese sovereign space, a more fundamental distinction that should be used when attempting to determine the extent of sovereign space should be what exists on either side of the border, between the identity of the "inner" from that of the "outer." What is seen as "outer," neighboring, whether benign or malignant, will directly, pivotally impact how the identity of

---

[24] 大城不可以不完，郭周不可以外通，里域不可以橫通。間閭不可以毋闔。宮垣關閉，不可以不修。故大城不完，則亂賊之人謀。郭周外通，則姦遁踰越者作。里域橫通，則攘奪竊盜者不止。間閉無闔，外內交通，則男女無別。宮垣不備，關閉不固，雖有良貨，不能守也。故形勢不得為非，則姦邪之人愨愿。 *Guanzi*, "Ba guan" 八觀, *Guanzi jiaozhu*, 1:256; *Guanzi*, 228.

[25] On exile in ancient Greece, see Danielle Allen, *The World of Prometheus: The Politics of Punishing in Democratic Athens* (Princeton, NJ: Princeton University Press, 2000), 202ff.

the "inner" is represented.[26] This emphasis on distinguishing "inner" from "outer" aligns with the concentric organization of space in classical China mentioned above. In the "Levies of Yu" ("Yugong") chapter of the *Shangshu*, as Dora Verafeeva-Lichtmann expounds, the description of the five zones "includes the distance between the border of the zone and that of the preceding one, its name, and the specification of its duties, functions or main characteristics. The zones have sub-divisions which are also featured from the point of view of the distance between their border and that of the preceding zone or sub-division of a zone."[27] This system, however, presupposes a sense of unified polity, with filial responsibilities weakening with the distance from the center. In much of the Warring States era, a period in which the idealizing and wistful "Levies of Yu" was ostensibly composed,[28] this notion would not have been realistically applicable, for the sense of any veritable "center" had by then dissolved into a medley of competing polities – thus the Levies' yearning for a "return" to an ideal that never really was. The pre-Qin era's discordant and fractious, uncentered sensibility is captured in a number of texts, of which the "Eight Observations" ("Ba guan" 八觀) chapter in the *Guanzi* may be treated as somewhat representative. Other texts, such as the *Zhanguoce* and the *Zuozhuan*, offer additional confirmatory evidence of this fractious sensibility and the effects it has on the formation of the consciousness of spatial disposition.

[26] Enno Giele illustrates this distinction with his study of the appearance of terms in excavated strips from the frontiers for non-Chinese persons. These terms are cast in belligerent language, but some, as with Xiongnu ("fearsome slaves"), seemed to have been "used exclusively for whomever the Chinese encountered on the other side of the great divide that was the Northern Border," while others, such as *hu* 胡 ("barbarians"), appeared to include non-Chinese "on both sides," demarcating differences in both threat and possibly even allegiance. See Enno Giele, "Evidence for the Xiongnu in Chinese Wooden Documents from the Han Period," in *Xiongnu Archaeology: Multidisciplinary Perspectives of the First Steppe Empire in Inner Asia*, ed. Ursula Brosseder and Bryan Kristopher Miller (Bonn: Friedrich-Wilhelms-Universität Bonn, 2011), 75.

[27] Dorofeeva-Lichtmann, "Conception of Terrestrial Organization in the *Shan hai jing*," 65. In a footnote, Dorofeeva-Lichtmann mentions that variations on this system are found in the *Guoyu*, the "Zhou ben yi" chapter of the *Shiji*, and the "Zhi fang shi" 職方氏 and "Da si ma" 大司馬 chapters of the *Zhouli*. See *Zhouli zhushu*, (Beijing) 2:759 and 869. This system, in some degree, accords with what Lori Khatchadourian labels the "satrapal condition," the "nested relations of sovereignty," "the double bind that draws subjects into the everyday logics of political reproduction as a requirement for the reproduction of their own situated authority." Adam T. Smith, *The Political Machine: Assembling Sovereignty in the Bronze Age Caucasus* (Princeton, NJ: Princeton University Press, 2015), 71.

[28] Michael Nylan groups this chapter along with the "Canon of Yao" and the "Counsels of Gao Yao" among those that were actually composed at a very late date, not much earlier than the Qin unification in 221 BC, perhaps even postdating unification. See Michael Nylan, *The Five "Confucian" Classics* (New Haven, CT: Yale University Press, 2001), 134.

Regardless of any relative fractiousness or calm, concern about that which lies "outside" (*wai*) is endemic in both the pre-Qin, pre-imperial period and post-Qin, post-imperial period. The difference is found in that which lies "outside," and thus how the inside defines itself. In the pre-imperial period, the concern with the "outside" consisted primarily with the other "Chinese" states; in the post-imperial, once the Chinese polity was unified, the "outside" was definitive of that which was non-Chinese. This shift can be seen not only in the literati or philosophical texts but also in the historiographical (or quasi-historiographical, as in the case of the *Zhanguoce*). When the "outside" was deemed not culturally approximate or recognizable, even when it was descriptive of another of the "Central States," the characterization was xenophobic and demonizing, casting the "outsider" in subhuman terms, as in this *Zhanguoce* passage describing Qin: "the men of the Horizontal Coalition (alternatively, 'wicked men') plot for the King to establish diplomatic relations with the mighty tiger-wolf, Qin, to assist it in taking over All-Under-Heaven."[29] Yuri Pines and others have demonstrated that this caricature is intentional, an offensive characterization to minimize the perception of the Qin's influence and stature, a diminution and depreciation common to the portrayal of representationally noncore cultures, whether Chinese or otherwise.[30] (This offensive characterization also included, not paradoxically, a begrudging respect.) The point remains that "outsiders" deemed not belonging to the traditional Central States cultural region were often described and perceived somewhat differently from those who were. The question is – how much did these differing perceptions play out in administratively efficacious ritual behaviors?

Separating "Inner" from "Outer" 外内不通

The distinction between "internal" and "external" was a common, efficacious, and valorized political distinction. The activities of the state were divided between them. With both idealized and realistic notions of sovereignty, whether in pre-imperial or early imperial China, belonging to the interior or exterior was gradual and perspectival, and identities could be fluid, open to reassessment.[31] Designations of "internal" and "external"

---

[29] 然横人謀王，外交強虎狼之秦，以侵天下. He Jianzhang, *Zhanguoce zhushi*, 2:819; Olberding, *Dubious Facts*, 79.

[30] Yuri Pines, "Beasts or Humans: Pre-Imperial Origins of the 'Sino-Barbarian' Dichotomy," in *Mongols, Turks, and Others: Eurasian Nomads and the Sedentary World*, ed. Reuven Amitai and Michal Biran (Boston, MA: Brill, 2005), 89–90.

[31] In the *Gongyang zhuan*, as Gentz observes, even the Central States could change status into new *Yidi* 夷狄: The *Gongyang zhuan* "takes a strongly relativist attitude toward

were not so much militarily defined as oriented to political allegiance. These designations were thus vague and mutable. Gradation and mutability of status did not, however, signify the terms had no stable meaning. The early texts reveal that with a change in status came a shift in administrative and ritualized treatment. In the *Gongyang zhuan*, for instance, those who were deemed *yidi* 夷狄 were not permitted to act within the Zhou ritual code.[32] Those who were deemed as "barbarians" were not treated as equal members in the Chinese ritual order, a denigration that could have administrative consequences. This denigration was irrespective of any demonstration of proper ritual conduct, as the histories were wont to report, ironically or not. According to the histories, "barbarians" could demonstrate more proper ritual conduct, and show a deeper understanding of ritual codes, than their "Chinese" peers. Whether these demonstrations were recorded as ironic jibes or actual fact is not discernable. Regardless, often those who were deemed "barbaric," as Qin or Chu were, displayed a keen comprehension of and appreciation for Zhou ritual norms. These "external" polities could, akin to relationships in the body, be appropriated into the "internal" or treated as hostile, depending on the current political circumstances.

When neighbors are perceived as being culturally commensurate with the internal cultural domain, loosely denotable as the "Chinese" domain, diplomatic disagreements and discussions of military engagements are repeatedly colored and directed by references to the cultural, ritualized obligations one owes these neighbors, whether in the late Zhou period, as represented by the *Zuozhuan*, or in the *Zhanguoce*, representative of a Warring States diplomatic sensibility. Even within Su Qin's appeal to the king of Wei, with the above-quoted hostile reference to its obligation to the duties it owes the "tiger-wolf, Qin," cultural presumptions are embedded, whether in its building imperial palaces for Qin, accepting Qin's titled cap and sash, or presenting offerings for Qin's annual sacrifices.[33] "Pledging its troth" to Qin would require Wei to apportion off land, to redefine itself and thus its borders, a definitive exchange that

---

notions of interior (*nei* 內) and exterior (*wai* 外) or to differences between Central States (Zhongguo 中國) and Yi-Di 夷狄 barbarians … The envisioned unity is not the unity of the Han state, which defends and expands its borders against non-Han people. It is rather the vision of an empire without political borders that is defined on cultural grounds." There thus was a process of cultural estrangement and rejection that could affect how previously included "insiders" could be effectively shunned and turned into outsiders. See Gentz, "Long Live the King!" 77–78. For an instance of this in the *Gongyangzhuan*, see the commentary for Duke Cheng, 15th year, *Chunqiu gongyangzhuan zhushu*, 400–401.

[32] Gentz, "Long Live the King!" 79.

[33] He Jianzhang, *Zhanguoce zhushi*, 2:819; Olberding, *Dubious Facts*, 79.

requires the presence of two established, settled state formations, for apportioning off the land of borderless regions without established populations would mean nothing, no shift in the shape of an established state, of its "form." This erasure of its territorial form corresponds to the erasure of its political sovereignty, with the king of Wei at risk of being persuaded by "criminal courtiers" to serve as Qin's "vassal" (chen 臣). Such would constitute a culturally unacceptable or even unrecognizable political submission in negotiations with non-Chinese polities, for non-Chinese polities, being primarily "unbounded" and thus "stateless" (except in the polities that attempt to mimic Chinese formations, such as the Xiongnu empire under Maodun), do not aim for vassalage as much as for tribute and submission. In the Chinese historical representation, for the non-Chinese, it's not territory itself but the extraction of the territory's resources that are aspired to.[34] There is little ambition to govern or serve as sovereigns to the territory; rather, the governance seems to be generally left to the Chinese (though perhaps not as much as the Chinese records wish to suggest). This has an effect on any thorough-going threat to the state's spatial disposition.

As I've underscored, population, and its settlement, is in some substantive measure definitive of borders in early China. Indeed, with state land defined as belonging to a "communal household," the state itself – and its boundaries – constitutes a settled, familially associative domain. As the celebrated Warring States persuader Su Qin maintained, any courtier recommending apportioning off land to curry favor with another adjacent polity and thereby create his own "household" is acting treasonously.[35] The only way for a king to avoid these treasonous betrayals is to tie his fate with that of his other neighbors, to have his boundaries become associated, in a "fraternal" (qin 親) manner, with theirs. Another Warring States persuader, Chen Zhen, instructs the king of Qin regarding his attacks on the neighboring state of Hann 韓 that the spatial disposition of the state is contingent on one's relationships to rival states: "If the spatial disposition

---

[34] This is insinuated in Emperor Wen's insistence on maintaining sovereignty over lands south of the Great Wall to allow the denizens of these lands to pursue agriculture (the economic engine of the state), on maintaining sociopolitical order, and not wishing to pursue violent activities that would upset this. SJ 110.2903; Sima Qian, Records of the Grand Historian: Han Dynasty, 146.

[35] "Any courtier who would apportion off his lord's lands in order to pursue diplomatic relations, snatching a day's success without giving thought to the consequences, destroying the communal household (i.e., the state) in order to build his own gate, outwardly relying on the strength of powerful Qin to steal from his lord, to urge him to apportion off land, I, Your servant, would wish that the Great King would carefully investigate him" 夫為人臣，割其主之地以求外交，偷取一旦之功而不顧其後，破公家而成私門，外挾彊秦之勢以內劫其主以求割地，願大王之熟察之也. He Jianzhang, Zhanguoce zhushi, 2:819; Olberding, Dubious Facts, 80.

of a state is not suitable [for defense], one retreats; if [diplomatic] relationships are not fraternal, one's lands will be cut away."[36] Whether there
is a spatial disposition, or "form," to one's lands has an effect not only on
one's own survival but the spatial disposition of one's neighbors' lands.[37]
Cultural and territorial relationships are thus intimately intertwined.

Yet cultural, ritualized relationships obviously do not in themselves
preserve territorial boundaries. As Zhang Yi in a response to the king of
Wei underscores, boundaries are vulnerable, highly porous and easily
trangressed:

in all directions Your land is level and open to the other feudal lords. Straight
roads converge on it as do the spokes of a wheel upon its hub. Not a single
[named] mountain nor great river lies athwart them. From Zheng, the capital of
Han, to Liang, the capital of Wei, is but a hundred leagues; from Chen, the capital
of Chu, to Liang, slightly more than two hundred. A horse might gallop or a man
run the distance and not feel weary on arrival in Liang. To the south of Liang are
the borders of Chu; to the west are the borders of Han; to the north are the borders
of Zhao; and to the east are the borders of Qi.[38]

Zhang Yi thus destabilizes the positive cultural potentials of the shared
boundary underscoring how unreliable fraternity and communal ties are,
how shared notions of culture are unsustainable in the face of persistent,
or overwhelming, threats to the sovereignty of one's state, and thus, in
politico-geographical terms, the fixity of one's borders. Even brothers
with the same father and mother, the biologically closest of siblings, he
remarks, "quarrel over property."[39]

In Zhang Yi's analysis, not only would these neighboring states pose
direct challenges, they would also abandon Wei, immediately betray any
fraternal bond, were Wei faced with Qin's onslaught. Qin would annex
neighboring states, such as Han, that border both Wei and Qin, would
dissolve their spatial dispositions, their "forms," swallow them whole, and
transform a neutral or fraternal border into a hostile one. All that Qin
fears, Zhang Yi imputes, is Wei's border with Chu. It is Wei's borders
with Chu that serve its own strategic position, that transform its spatial
disposition from one of vulnerability to strength, were it to employ its
border shared with Chu to Qin's, and thus also Wei's, advantage. Chu's

---

[36] 陳軫謂秦王曰：「國形不便故馳，交不親故割。」 He Jianzhang, *Zhanguoce zhushi*,
3:981.

[37] 建信君輕韓熙，趙敖為謂建信侯曰：「國形有之而存，無之而亡者，魏也。」 He
Jianzhang, *Zhanguoce zhushi*, 3:1077.

[38] 地四平，諸侯四通，條達輻湊，無有名山大川之阻。從鄭至梁，不過百里；從陳至梁，
二百餘里。馬馳人趨，不待倦而至梁。南與楚境，西與韓境，北與趙境，東與齊境. He
Jianzhang, *Zhanguoce zhushi*, 2:823; Olberding, *Dubious Facts*, 82.

[39] He Jianzhang, *Zhanguoce zhushi*, 2:824; Olberding, *Dubious Facts*, 83.

geography, like its reputation, is hollow, empty, because its geography, being poorly defended, is easily overtaken, conquered. In statist terms, an undefended, or indefensible, spatial disposition is really no substantial disposition, no "true" disposition at all. Though Chu's troops "are legion, they are quick to flee and easy to force into retreat. They do not have the mettle to put up a strong fight." Were the king of Wei to muster all of his people – the foundation to the strength of his state, of his borders, and thus of his spatial disposition – Wei would "certainly overcome Chu." Zhang Yi suggests that Wei preserve a quasi-marital relationship with Qin. Qin, ostensibly as husband, protecting the borders of Wei, would leave Wei somewhat intact, as a sovereign presence. Agreeing with Su Qin, Zhang Yi insists that courtiers persuading otherwise are simply aiming to set up their own states, to "ride off in one of the king's chariots." At the end of Zhang Yi's address, the king of Wei offers his kingdom as a vassalage, to annex itself politically, and show physical and ceremonial deference, through building palaces for Qin on Wei lands, receiving Qin's cap and sash, making annual sacrifices on Qin's behalf, and even ceding geographic space, with all attendant resources and benefits, military, topographical, economic, or otherwise.[40]

Wei's temptation to annex itself to Qin reflects the dangers involved in even a reluctantly permitted confusing of sovereignties, in muddling the difference between "inside" and "outside" sovereign boundaries. When "inside" and "outside" become confused in definition, and thus in prioritization, the prospect for treasonous behavior that debilitates, even destroys, the notion of a sovereign realm, both politically and geographically, is high. A passage in the *Hanshu* expounds:

When those inside the realm embrace cruelty and malevolence, they [then] desire to control the court's government. Those who press for fraternal relations and approach government clerks [wish to] control government documents and expose its affairs in order to act as the secretariat, to blind those above and block those below. Inside the realm, they create barriers on the roads to court; outside they form relationships with the buffer vassals. They are overbearing and avaricious to usurp the power of the above, ravaging and disordering regulations and measures.[41]

When those inside the court, those ostensibly committed to preserving the integrity and survival of the sovereign realm – including the monarch himself – are driven by selfish motives for self-preservation, aggrandizement and enrichment, they simultaneously undermine internal

---

[40] He Jianzhang, *Zhanguoce zhushi*, 2:824; Olberding, *Dubious Facts*, 84.
[41] 内懷姦邪，欲筦朝政，推親近吏主簿張業以為尚書，蔽上壅下，內塞王路，外交藩臣，驕奢僭上，壞亂制度. *HS* 98.4028.

governance and pursue external relationships that deeply imperil the longevity of the state. These attractions of self-preservation and potential enrichment are that against which Su Qin had cautioned the king of Wei. In some cases, however, sovereignty was preserved through external associations, as is evident in the following passage from the *Zuozhuan*, in which Zijia Yibo 子家懿伯, an adviser to Lord Zhao 昭公 of Lu, declines to join a covenant with the lord's followers, a covenant that forbade any "association between insiders and outsiders" 無通外內. In his rejection of the covenant, Zijia Yibo raises the prospect that any hope of a singular purpose in which there is a strict, clean divide between insiders and outsiders is a pleasant fiction.[42]

However, this obscuration of a clean divide should not be equated with ignorance of a need for any separation of internal from external. In a passage just prior to the one above, Zijia Yibo also advised against Lord Zhao accepting a pared off land grant from the prince of Qi, because it distracts him from his task of reclaiming the sovereignty of his home state, Lu 魯.[43] The depredations brought on by private, selfish, self-segregating ambitions, ambitions that oppose the self against the needs of the public realm, have very concrete geographic consequences, as evidenced in the prevalence of strategic negotiations in which lands are "severed off" from the sovereign realm. Early Chinese texts repeatedly adjure rulers not to pursue geographic acquisitions that would contradict their responsibilities to the broader ritually tied community. Zijia Yibo is counseling Lord Zhao not only against his selfish – and yet politically self-destructive – ambitions, he speaks also against Lord Zhao's rupturing of ritual obligations between Qi and Lu to the Zhou ruler: Lord Zhao's land was an allotment granted originally to the duke of Zhou by the Zhou king, as was Qi's land to the Qi rulers. To accept Qi's (relatively remote) land grant would be to go against his ritual duty to the Zhou king to preserve

---

[42] *Zuozhuan*, Zhao 25.6g; *Zuo Tradition (Zuozhuan)*, 3:1648–1649. In the Roman context, Emperor Claudius attributed an aspect of the failure of Greek culture to survive and flourish to their inability to integrate non-Greeks: "In a speech to the Senate in 48, the Emperor Claudius attributed some Greek problems to failure to assimilate those they conquered. 'Was there any cause for the ruin of the Lacedaemonians and the Athenians, though they were flourishing in arms, but the fact that they rejected the vanquished as aliens?'" Hamilton and Langhorne, *Practice of Diplomacy*, 13. Modified for our Chinese context, this speaks to the question of by what process average non-Chinese foreign commoners, meaning those who are not treated as culturally integrated, achieve a culturally inclusive status, being transformed from *di* 敵 (or any of the other denigrating terms for those not culturally integrated, such as *hu* 胡 or *lu* 虜) to *min* 民. How much a role do these foreign commoners have in modifying their own status? Integration into a tax structure may have been a necessary condition but it was certainly not sufficient.

[43] *Zuozhuan*, Zhao 25.6f; Yang Bojun, *Chunqiu zuozhuan zhu*, 4:1465; *Zuo Tradition (Zuozhuan)*, 3:1646–1647.

sovereignty over his ritually allotted Lu lands, to put personal self-preservation over the obligation to his public, ritual duty to protect Lu. It was enough for the duke of Zhou to have held to Lu – why wouldn't Duke Zhao feel similar obligations? As Zijia Yibo at the end of his dissent poignantly queries Lord Zhao, "If, having lost Lu, you hold a thousand [*she*-altars, equivalent to 25,000 families] as vassal of another ruler, who will join with you to reestablish you as ruler [of Lu]?"[44]

Territorial dispensations that were part of a strategic calculus to prevent further aggression or curry favor were regular occurrences, sometimes referred to as the "paring off" of land, *xuedi* 削地, important not so much for the actual territory but for the resources and people occupying it. Between recognizable administrative and cultural formations, such a paring off presumably could be somewhat quickly managed, with one set of statist rules and regulations relating to economic and legal relationships being quickly traded for another. Was a paring off, with its potentially ritualized aspect, also regularly practiced with nonstatist entities, with non-Chinese adversaries? Such a question directly bears upon the boundaries of the state, for if such boundaries were administratively moved or replaced most often largely between culturally recognizable formations, this will speak to their efficacy and the need for the existence of a similarly structured competitor to give state boundaries much expressive value.

Enemies vs. Friends

With the preservation of the state at issue, attention to the external other in the early Chinese records was often accorded when the other was an antagonist. Indeed, as Thongchai Winichakul has perceived with regard to modern Thailand, this attention was sometimes as much manufactured as in response to an actual threat. Without the enemy, the state's maintenance and extension of coercive force would be unwarranted: the state and its security apparatus often survive exactly because of the existence, manufactured or not, of a rival – whether internal or external. The enemy, he insightfully concludes, "is always projected – if not overtly *desired*." To confirm a state's identity is, in some measure, to confirm the identity, and thus the existence, of the enemy, however abstract. For a state to have a sense of itself, it, in some significant, identifiable measure, must have its enemies.[45]

---

[44] 失魯而以千社為臣，誰與之立? Yang Bojun, *Chunqiu zuozhuan zhu*, 4:1465; *Zuo Tradition (Zuozhuan)*, 3:1646–1647.

[45] "The creation of otherness, the enemy in particular, is necessary to justify the existing political and social control against rivals from without as well as from within. Without this

This definitory import of the external enemy is borne out in the records, for while antagonistic neighbors are repeatedly marked with the moniker of "adversarial" or "enemy" states (*diguo* 敵國), friendly neighbors have no true correspondingly underscored antonymic conceptual term.[46] Such a lacuna is evident in various texts, whether the *Guanzi*[47] or the address by Chao Cuo to Emperor Wen,[48] in the latter of which, as noted previously, there is noticeable, perhaps intentional, overlap with the analysis of various state "dispositions" in the *Guanzi*. In both, the state's spatial dispositions presume an identifiable state structure, even if such were not truly exigent. For the *Guanzi*, the state is analyzed in terms of its size or power, its being identifiable as one of the "central" states, its status as an enemy, and its idealization as a "kingly" state. Chao Cuo, advising Emperor Wen on how to manage the Xiongnu menace, qualifies state identities more reductively in terms of small size, adversarial status, or belonging to the "central" states, that is, being part, even if only weakly or somewhat symbolically, of the Han political sphere.

If the reference in Chao Cuo's address is actually to this portion of the received *Guanzi* text, or an identical or similar text, Chao Cuo is intentionally deleting the denotation of the "powerful" and the "kingly" states but both, in their definition of the spatial disposition of the Central States, insinuate using distant, or noncentral populations ("states bordering the four seas," meaning states on the border of the familiar world, in the *Guanzi* passage; "foreign tribes" (the "Manyi" tribes) in Chao Cuo's

---

discursive enemy, all the varieties of coercive force, from a paramilitary organization on every border of Thailand to the professional army, would be redundant. In contrast to the general belief, the state and its security apparatus survive because of the enemy. Discursively, if not actually, what actively creates the enemy and produces most threats to a country if not the state's security mechanism? The enemy must be presented, produced, or implicated and then discursively sustained. It is always projected – if not overtly *desired*." "To confirm Thainess, it does not matter if the enemy is relatively abstract or ill defined. The enemy must always be present." Winichakul, *Siam Mapped*, 167–168.

[46] There are terms, such as *fan* 藩 "buffer," *yuan* 援 "supporter," or *bin* 賓 "guest," that could possibly serve as approximates of "ally," but these are not terms that carry the same conceptual heft, or attract the same argumentative focus, naturally, as "adversary." Occasionally, the foreign tribes, such as the Xiongnu or "Hundred Man," would declare themselves as "allies" or "guests," though, of course, these allegiances or signs of submission were utterly transient and unreliable. (See, for an instance of these tribes declaring themselves "buffers" or "guests", *HS* 24A.1143: 王莽因漢承平之業，匈奴稱藩，百蠻賓服.) Liu An complains of the unreliability of these allegiances: "The name given to the Yue people was 'Border Servants' yet they ship no harvest or sacrificial tribute to the Great Interior, nor is one solider offered up for service" 越人名為藩臣，貢酎之奉，不輸大內，一卒之用不給上事. *HS* 64A.2778; Olberding, *Dubious Facts*, 193.

[47] See *Guanzi*, "Ba yan"; *Guanzi jiaozhu*, 1:479.

[48] Ibid.; *HS* 49.2281, Olberding, *Dubious Facts*, 186–188.

address). Notions of alliance are consistently put in terms of the prospects of close, fraternal association but the disposition of a fraternal association is never scrutinized or even included in these two analyses, a potentially important omission, for the omission demonstrates that such an association was not considered structurally fundamental to the perception of other states, not as fundamental as another state's power, size, or rivalry. In these two texts, the circumstance of being "fraternal," or just "neighborly," does not appear to be a central analysand in strategic positioning. By contrast, being an enemy, a rival, was.

I contend that this lacuna points to a larger pattern. As discussed, fraternity (*qin*), unlike rivalry, was a transient, fickle state, dependent on fleeting goodwill, strategic agreement, and trust. Rivalry was the more permanent state of contestation, as permanent as size and power.[49] The most curious, intriguing aspect of the *Guanzi* and Chao Cuo analyses is their characterization of "Central States." In both analyses, the term "Central States" noticeably carries no fraternal association, nothing about friendship or cultural bonds or strategic allegiance. Instead, it is cast in terms of the employment of distant peoples, distant both in space and culture, for strategic ends: "Pitting foreign tribe against foreign tribe is the disposition of the Central States."[50] The Central States are thus defined explicitly against a cultural other.

Inclusion into the fraternity of the Central States demanded a solemn, ritualized fealty. Those states, such the grotesquely caricatured Qin, that did not ostensibly value and protect those polities with which they shared this cultural, ritualized kinship were deemed animalistic, "wild beasts," those toward which the Central States owe little allegiance.[51] In Zou Yang's 鄒陽 early Han address to Liu Pi 劉濞, the king of Wu 吳, Qin's demise was squarely placed on the lack of a fraternal allegiance, a trusting bond, whether between the "various commanderies" or the "ten-thousand households."[52] By contrast, as is explicit in Liu An's address to Emperor Wu, it is exactly when those within one's purview ("those

---

[49] Pertaining to the Xiongnu, it is significant that the border officials who composed reports about them referred to the Xiongnu mostly as the "captives" 虜 or "barbarians" 胡 (sometimes as "horsemen" 騎). Thus, the concept of the enemy deeply impacted the identification and relation with the Xiongnu. Even more significant is that the reference to them as *lu* 虜 and not *di* 敵 signifies how their enemy status was not of an equal, or, even possibly, that it was of a "betrayer" as much as an opponent. See Giele, "Evidence for the Xiongnu in Chinese Wooden Documents from the Han Period," 50ff.

[50] 以蠻夷攻蠻夷，中國之形也. *HS* 49.2281. In the *Guanzi*, the phrase is rendered as this: 以負海攻負海，中國之形也. *Guanzi jiaozhu*, 1:479.

[51] He Jianzhang, *Zhanguoce zhushi*, 2:907; Olberding, *Dubious Facts*, 158.

[52] "The various commanderies had no allegiance to each other and the ten thousand households did not come to each other's aid" 列郡不相親，萬室不相救也. *HS* 51.2338; Olberding, *Dubious Facts*, 189.

close by") feel attachment to the ruler that the state is deemed more secure, when its condition is more conducive to future prosperity.[53] This is, indeed, stated as a central feature of the civilized – in supposed contrast to the barbarians, cast as the Qin or other "foreign" tribes – that they "cherish their relatives,"[54] those with whom they have a stable, enduring fraternal bond. Nonetheless, this bond does not appear to have an enduring strategic function. A maintained bond was an aspiration, not a durable state, whether with other Central States or with foreign peoples, such as the Xiongnu. The expectation was that such bonds could not last for long.

Further diminishing the value of a cultural or ritualized fraternity, there was clearly collusion across (artificially) defined boundaries, obscuring any secure sense of a monolithic enemy.[55] From various excavated documents, from Juyan and elsewhere, it is clear that non-Chinese were more than occasionally involved or allied with the Chinese, not only martially and diplomatically, but territorially. They were included in military ventures, rewarded for their performance, even enfeoffed.[56] In the excavated documents, with respect to those who were actively opposed to the Chinese – "the captives" (lu 虜) or, more precisely, those who deserved to be captured, and killed, as one would hunting prey – the operative distinction was more performative than descriptive, more prescriptive than descriptive.

Yet the epithet, "captives," it bears noting, was never applied to those who could be counted as "Chinese" enemies. Indeed, it is possible to diachronically trace the translation, transfixing, and inclusion of those formerly debased as not worthy of sovereign inclusion by the terms with which they are named, whether they be the Yin–Shang, the Qin, or the Xiongnu. And it is furthermore plausible that once such populations are deemed effectively transformed, part of the "Chinese" cultural space, they eventually cease to be part of the "other," and are included among the numbers, and named, as part of the "Chinese" space. Thus, Xiongnu border opponents can not only become min 民, they can become

---

[53] 近者親附. HS 64A.2777; Olberding, Dubious Facts, 191–192.

[54] Of course, as the general Zhao Chongguo 趙充國 makes clear, these filial bonds are not singular to the Chinese. See HS 69.2987; Olberding, Dubious Facts, 202. My point is that this is what the Chinese flatteringly see as differentiating themselves from the less civilized.

[55] If nothing else, Sima Qian's punishment for being involved in frontier affairs, and his association with general Li Ling 李陵, should give an indication of how problematic such involvement was, or even insinuations that one was involved. See SJ 130.3300.

[56] Giele, "Evidence for the Xiongnu in Chinese Wooden Documents from the Han Period," 61.

enfeoffed, those who are accepted and whose lands are treated as sanctified, as part of the sanctified realm.

As with the territory itself, in their sanctification, the "captives" are appropriated by being renamed, literally with Chinese titles and ranks. The enemy is defined by its incursions, its prohibited transgressions into sanctified, sovereign space, its "betraying" and "breaking" of what is permitted – more its actions than its ethnic identities. Thus, the "captives" "violate" (*fan* 犯) the frontiers by "entering" (*ru* 入) them,[57] commit the offense of "betrayal" (*bei pan* 背畔),[58] and inevitably lie "outside" the frontier. This has typically been interpreted to signify a martial line,[59] but I would argue that their very oppositional status contributes, even defines the placing, the territorializing of any frontier. Once they are included, their lands automatically, immediately, tautologically lie within the frontier.

Another piece of evidence for this is the repeated, anxious concern about spies, informational betrayals.[60] It is quite sensible to think that, given the general porousness of borders and political identifications, unstable loyalties were common. Ethnic identities[61] were not sufficiently pronounced for people of any political allegiance not to be able to shed their clothes, as it were, and assume a new identity. Thus rewards are offered to low-level clerks and commoners in the Juyan documents for those who can capture alive "rebellious" Qiang who come from outside the frontier in order to spy on the activities of the Central States. These people are not being hired to go out and capture them, they are finding them in their midst and capturing them.[62] The problem is not so much in the capture but in the identification. And how would this be an issue if identity were not obscurable?

How does this affect the sense of "neighbor," and thus shared boundary and spatial disposition? Fraternity is the converse of antipathy, the absence of rivalry and the possibility or presence of affectionate bonds; thus the character of rivalry (敵) can be indicative of the possibility and character of fraternity (親), of "neighborliness," and, consequently, how

---

[57] Giele, "Evidence for the Xiongnu in Chinese Wooden Documents from the Han Period," 75.

[58] Ibid., 55–56.

[59] Giele translates *sai* 塞, a "barrier," abstractly as a "defense line." Giele, "Evidence for the Xiongnu in Chinese Wooden Documents from the Han Period," 59–60.

[60] See Giele, "Evidence for the Xiongnu in Chinese Wooden Documents from the Han Period," 62–63.

[61] Giele, "Evidence for the Xiongnu in Chinese Wooden Documents from the Han Period," 75.

[62] Ibid., 64–65.

one perceives one's spatial boundaries, as well as how one's spatial boundaries and their influence are perceived by others. The effects of a state of fraternity can be most immediately felt at the border areas. The Xiongnu are praised for their acting in "fraternal" good faith toward those on the borders; when they plunder, the border areas are naturally those most affected.[63] It is the borders, the liminalities that are constantly in a state of insecure contestation. Their existential disposition is deeply impacted by the uncertainty of their security and the allegiances and affiliations of the people living in the region. It is they who are reformed into colonies, or asked to discontinue their regular activities to defend against external onslaughts, or to be used as bait to trap invaders.[64]

This semi-constant state of assault, this constant insecurity leads allegiances to waver and falter.[65] Pacifying the border areas needs be the primary aim of the state that wishes to have firm borders, to be established as a state. Borders are the delineation of the polis; without a strategic spatial disposition, there is, in essence, no security, and no sense of state. Those who, akin somewhat to diplomats, defend and manage the border are the frontline, and the most corruptible, as is evident from discussion of clerks and defending watchmen as figures who need monitoring.[66] By contrast, when the world is at peace, as explained in the *Hanshi waizhuan*, boundaries do not change and all is "regulated" (meaning, taxed and controlled) properly.[67] Indeed, Xun Yue in his *Records of the Former Han* (*Qian Han ji* 前漢紀) avers that, according to the *Spring and Autumn Annals* (*Chunqiu* 春秋), when the realm is governed peaceably by a king, there is no "outside," that the king aims for unity among All-Under-Heaven, including those who, like the Xiongnu, are not perceived as culturally aligned.[68]

With these mutually affective dispositions at work, producing rivalry or bond, the spatial disposition of the state is also dependent, active and reactive, with the external not only affecting internal dispositions but the internal having repercussions beyond itself. As a passage in the *Shuoyuan* states, "To those who spread advantage, good fortune will be their recompense; for those who extend resentment, misfortune will arrive. The

---

[63] *HS* 53.2398; Olberding, *Dubious Facts*, 114.

[64] *HS* 52.2401, 2403; Olberding, *Dubious Facts*, 119–120, 123–124.

[65] The fickleness of the "animalistic," barbarian other is portrayed in numerous passages. For several, see Olberding, *Dubious Facts*, 158.

[66] Liu An raises indirectly this concern when he asserts that the defending watchmen "are honest and cautious." Clearly, they may not be and may collude with the enemy. See *HS* 64A.2781; Olberding, *Dubious Facts*, 195.

[67] *Hanshi waizhuan*, 3.93.

[68] 荀悅曰。春秋之義，王者無外，欲一於天下也. *Qian Han ji*, "Xiao Xuan huangdi ji si" 孝武皇帝紀四; Xun Yue 荀悅, *Han ji* 漢紀 (Beijing: Zhonghua shuju, 2002), 20.356.

disposition of the inside affects repercussions on the outside. This cannot not be attended to."[69]

Uninvited Penetration

Haicheng Wang has pointed out in his study of early Zhou territory that inherent in the notion of territory is the possibility of its penetration, of transgression inside its limits. If the Western Zhou state, as Feng Li maintains, "did not exist as an integral geographic whole clearly demarcated by linear borders," then how could the Zhou king have had a sufficiently clear idea of his borders "when he says that Fu Zi attacked and occupied 'our land'"?[70] The crux then is not so much the linearity of the border as what would be deemed a hostile entrance, an invasion or penetration of a sovereign realm. How would such be distinguished from a more benign "visitation"? If linear borders did not exist, could there be exact spatial definientia or physical movements by which an "invasion" could be observed and reacted to? At issue is this: With borders in the ancient world being much more permeable, their crossing was not in itself a transgression. Those who lived on or around the border areas could regularly move from one sovereign space to another without knowing, or even caring, unless their movements were regulated strictly, for military or other reasons. Indeed, even foreign military troops would regularly pass through a sovereign area if they were given permission, a situation that would seem quite extraordinary in the modern spatially totalitarian nation-state, with military movement within borders strictly limited, in most cases, to the forces of that sovereign area.

Because of this permeability, the act of "entering" (ru 入) a sovereign area was politically ambiguous. Mention of entering a border, mention of the act itself, was significant, for it insinuated a heightened awareness of the limits and the vulnerability of a sovereign area. The question is – what physical transgression did this "entering" actually entail, with no clear borderline at issue? In other words, how does one "enter" a sovereign territory if there are no firm or clean boundaries or borders? Has one "entered" when passing nearby a mutually established natural, ritual, or military edifice? When passing human settlements? When one engages with the people of an area, or uses resources of an area? When one takes action against or on the peoples associated – whether of themselves or by the sovereign power – formally with a bounded territory, with less

---

[69] 利施者福報，怨往者禍來，形於內者應於外，不可不慎也. *Shuoyuan*, "Fu en" 復恩; *Shuoyuan jiao zheng*, 126.

[70] Feng Li, *Bureaucracy and the State in Early China*, 297. Cited in Haicheng Wang, "Western Zhou Despotism," 100.

attention paid to exactly where geographically this action was taken? Can the act of "entering" an area be correspondent with the act of "exiting" a territory (*chu di* 出地)? Is "exiting" the simple opposite of "entering"?

The records commonly reference meetings between officials or rulers at borders, or when sending off an official from the border. Though these official meetings or send-offs were of a different character than an invasion or military campaign into other regions, nonmilitary border activities also were not anodyne, for they naturally carried a risk to sovereignty, whether in the borderline interface between rival powers or in the trusting of an official not to betray their sovereign in interfaces abroad. As I will contend in the following chapter, these border activities also shared an analogic kinship with "border" contacts between humans and the spirits, that is, interface afforded between human representatives and spirit representatives through the priestly activities from which messages or signs from the spirit world were received. Indeed, I would argue that the choice of a specific area, such as a river, for the forging of a covenant was not unconnected to the spiritual powers associated with the area, and thus to the binding of human and spiritual powers together into the forging of cross-boundary political arrangements. Furthermore, as I will also argue, crossing a sovereign boundary may be more closely connected to ritually established boundaries than militarily defined ones. Crossing a mountain or a river, both associable with native natural powers that were arrogated by the ruler, may have been an indication of crossing a ritually established, sanctified sovereign boundary.

If we do not immediately conflate sovereign boundaries with military ones, as the barriers (*sai* 塞) are, we can more readily understand how military lines and boundaries can be moved without there necessarily being any immediate augmentation or reduction of the sovereign realm, as well as how movements beyond military boundaries may still be deemed "invasive" and a hostile threat. Furthermore, it can also explain how a *jie* 界-border can be moved "back" or "away from" a military line, a barrier. An indicative instance of this can be seen in the movement of a *jie*-border by the Xiongnu back to the "old frontier" during the chaotic period after Meng Tian's 蒙恬 execution and the beginning of anti-Qin uprisings. Such would point to the military barrier never having been the primary definition of a border but would also indicate that *jie*-borders were possibly at base economic, defining the limits of revenue extraction, a hypothesis I introduced in Chapter 1.[71]

The concern with entering or exiting barriers (入/出塞), and thus militarized boundaries, can be seen in excavated documents from Juyan

---

[71] 於是匈奴得寬，復稍度河南與中國界於故塞. *SJ* 110.2887–2888.

and elsewhere. In various instances, merely the act of "entering" or "exiting" is noted, with no elaboration. But in a number of others, the act is represented as hostile, an act that deserves an opposing response. What is also notable is that the activities of "entering" and "exiting" were not applied in numerous Warring States to Han excavated bamboo texts – at least when written continguously – to other words with (at least some-time) nonmilitary connections to boundary areas, words mentioned previously such as *jiang* 疆, *jie* 界, or *jing* 境 (which is actually best translated not as "border" but as "marches" or "frontier borderlands"). This is an indication that, in the excavated texts, the interest in the entering and exiting border areas was almost singularly with regard to military activities.[72]

Any movement into a sovereign area, including passing through it to reach another sovereign area, without the consent or permission of the ruler, is treating the territory as a possession and in effect annihilating the ruler's claims to that area. As is stated in the *Zuozhuan*, "To pass through our territory without seeking right of way is to treat us as the borderlands of Chu."[73] This not only bespeaks the importance of consent even when traveling – and thus the constant concern with unsurveilled transgression of sovereign boundaries – but also demonstrates the conception of soft sovereignty, that a particular sovereign territory can be treated as a subject, as an appendage of another, simply by the act of traveling through it without consent, and thus, state sovereignties can be combined, mixed, or layered. Indeed, one can thus state, as the *Hanshi waizhuan* stated, that even in a territorial sense, the notion of outside and inside are responsive to each other, that there is an active interplay between them, with tribute being a defining feature.[74] The question still remains – how does one determine transgression?

One might expect that military actions in themselves would automatically qualify as transgressions. Yet there are distinctions between sanctioned and unsanctioned military intrusions, seen in the contrast posed between "attacking" *fa* 伐 and "invading" *qin* 侵, a contrast explicitly made in the *Zuozhuan*. The contrast is couched in terms of a clear announcement of the military action with the use of bells and drums.

---

[72] See www.chant.org, 竹簡帛書1 database, accessed 9/19.

[73] 過我而不假道，鄙我也. *Zuozhuan*, Xuan 14.3; Yang Bojun, *Chunqiu zuozhuan zhu*, 2:755; *Zuo Tradition (Zuozhuan)*, 1:672–673.

[74] *Hanshi waizhuan*, 7.268. The *Guanzi* expresses the geopolitical sentiment more explicitly: "To have one's state in perfect order while those of one's neighbors fail to adhere to the Way is a major asset for becoming a lord protector or king. Now the survival of a state is affected by neighboring states" 國修而鄰國無道。霸王之資也。夫國之存也，鄰國有焉；國之亡也，鄰國有焉. *Guanzi*, "Ba yan"; *Guanzi jiaozhu*, 1:463–464; *Guanzi*, 358–359, translation modified.

To quote the *Zuozhuan*, "In all cases concerning military campaigns, when there are bells and drums, it is called 'an attack.' When there are none, it is called 'an invasion.'"[75] According to this contrast, with an attack one is accepting – and preliminarily announcing – in a ritualized manner one's responsibility for the intrusion and permitting one's opponent some measure of preparation; in an invasion, one is conducting a coarse, unannounced intrusion. An attack proffers one's opponent a ritualized mode of interaction in a way that an invasion does not. Whether or not these definitions hold in their uses in the text (and Yang Bojun offers examples in his commentary on this *Zuozhuan* passage in which they do not), the definitional contrast illustrates an undeniably transgressive aspect of *qin*, and that this transgressive aspect appears to involve some lack of ritualized conduct.

Qin as that which is in some way an unsanctioned or even somewhat criminally transgressive intrusion finds further employment in later records. In the early Han histories, both *qinru* 侵入 and *qindao* 侵盜 are applied most generally, if not unilaterally, to invasions by non-Chinese peoples. The term *qinru* 侵入 is only used twice in the early Han histories, in reference to the Xiongnu invading the frontier and then swiftly leaving.[76] If the pairing of *qin* with *dao* and its etymological association in the *Shuowen* with *fan* 犯 is any indication, its aggression is not only unexpected, it is seen as unwarranted, unjustified, criminal. With this negative connotation, the "paring off" of lands modified by *qin* is unwarranted. These invasive entries are "criminal" in that they (presumably) are for acquisitive purposes or are not sanctioned by the authorities.

In Han texts, *qindao* is frequently connected to non-Chinese raids or invasions, whether by the Xiongnu, the Nanyue, or others. The distinctive addition of *dao*, "thieving," for non-Chinese raids, may also suggest that the use of *qin* by itself in certain contexts can be specifically for those acts in which the acquisition and succeeding maintenance of administratively similar formations (or administratively formalizable areas) is the aim. In the pre-Han texts, *qindao* is never used. In texts such as the *Zhanguoce*, to designate an unsanctioned raid or invasion, the sources simply used *qin*. In these pre-Han cases there is no distinctive assignment between non-Chinese and Chinese. But there are indications that it is an affront, a transgression of sanctioned boundaries, rather than simply a neutral term for "invasion." In the *Xunzi*, for instance, the term is used to castigate those ministers who exceed their mandates, those who

---

[75] 凡師，有鐘鼓曰伐，無曰侵. *Zuozhuan*, Zhuang 29.2; *Zuo Tradition (Zuozhuan)*, 1:216–217, Yang Bojun, *Chunqiu zuozhuan zhu*, 1:244.

[76] *SJ* 110.2912, *HS* 94A.3775.

might "trespass upon [*qin*] and seize" what does not accord with their mandates.[77] A similar abstract usage of *qin* can be found in the *Liji*, in which it is specifically put in terms of the demands of ritual, its context illustrating that it demands one not going beyond what is permitted.[78]

Yet given its widest use, *qin* appears clearly to have had most broadly a politico-military employment, applied to territorial concerns, paired occasionally with terms denoting military aggression or attack, such as *gong* 攻 or *fa* 伐. With its territorial objectives, we see it not infrequently paired with *xue* 削, "pare off," and furthermore, sometimes see it used even in relation to attacks on non-Chinese areas, such as when the Qin general Meng Tian "trespasses" into Xiongnu lands.[79] Thus its basic meaning is definitive of antagonistic, aggressive, transgressive action, whatever the opposing party's ethnicity or affiliation. Though there are, at times, mentions of boundaries being established or moved upon the end of any such politico-military aggression, as when Meng Tian established the Yellow River area as a frontier after his aggressive invasion (以河為境), these boundaries were not plotted nor were they necessarily of primary military use. From a broad examination of the employment of *qinxue* 侵削, it is applied mostly with respect to administratively (and thus somewhat ritually) congruent entities, those that can take over, occupy, and manage the areas they "invade."[80] "Trespassive paring off" is pursued by those that aim to take over, occupy, and politically administer the areas they trespass, to extract revenue from them. Thus, it is an aggressive taking of a portion of another's settled lands, or lands with resources that can be harvested.

The "paring off" or "cutting off" of lands appears to be an activity limited to those polities that have demarcated spatial dispositions (*xing*), with areas that are administratively defined (though they do not, as the *Book of Lord Shang* makes clear, need to be ones devoted singularly to agriculture[81]). The "cutting off" of lands (*gedi* 割地) required a settleable space, but the bestowal of these pared or cut off lands was not absolutely

---

[77] 而不可使侵奪，是士大夫官師之材也. See *Xunzi*, "Jun dao" 君道; Wang Xianqian, *Xunzi jijie*, 1:245; *Xunzi: The Complete Text*, 132.

[78] *Liji*, "Quli shang"; *Liji jijie*, 1:6–7: "According to the rules of ritual propriety, one should not please others in a wanton manner, nor be wasteful in speech. According to the rules of ritual propriety, one does not exceed the measure, does not transgress (侵) and insult, is not eager to take liberties" 禮，不妄說人，不辭費。禮，不逾節，不侵侮，不好狎. Translation mine.

[79] 蒙恬為秦侵胡. *HS* 52.2401.

[80] Evidence for this can be seen in the fact that the territory of the "many lords" 諸侯 or the commoners 民 are most frequently stated as the explicit object of such trespassive parings off. For instance, see *HS* 35.1907, 42.2102, 49.2300; *Lüshi chunqiu jishi*, 1:219.

[81] *Shangjunshu*, "Nongzhan" 農戰: "That is why those, who govern the country well, wish the people to take to agriculture. If the country does not take to agriculture, then, in its

limited to culturally synonymous polities. For instance, in the *Zuozhuan* it is mentioned that Lord Hui of Jin bestowed (admittedly poor) agricultural lands on a Rong tribe.[82] And the *Hanshu* notes that the Xiongnu "transgressively pared off" (*qinxue*) territory from the Wusun 烏孫 tribe, but these examples of non-Chinese being given lands or "paring off" lands to them were the exception in the historical records. In short, at least in the Chinese representation, those who were not part of the Chinese administrative sphere were not regularly represented as being involved in "trangressive" territorial exchanges.

That of which they *were* represented as being part was the aggressive raiding and pillaging of Chinese settlements. Whether this was due to a form of ethnocentric condescension, with those non-Chinese tribes who had not been incorporated into the Chinese administrative sphere being treated as somehow unable to capture, hold, and maintain settled polities, or because such was actually the case is not clear in many instances. Certainly non-Chinese peoples could and did accept and take on Chinese administrative norms, with the Chinese state's soft sovereign power being thereby extended more formally into the frontierlands. (More broadly, soft sovereign power was regularly extended through any number of tribute or contract relationships. As with contemporary "soft" empires, sovereignty was frequently asserted through diplomatic or economic channels.) Such formal political acceptances of soft sovereign power demanded, at least rhetorically, a minimal acknowledgment of the value of the cultural norms of the sovereign sphere. As will be illustrated in the next chapter, those political entities seen as culturally non-peer who

---

quarrels over authority with the various feudal lords, it will not be able to maintain itself, because the strength of the multitude will not be sufficient. Therefore the feudal lords vex its weakness and [take advantage] of its state of [decay]; and if the [lands are] invaded and dismembered [*qinxue* 侵削], without the country being stirred to action, it will be past saving. A sage knows what is essential in administrating a country, and so he induces the people to devote their attention to agriculture" 故治國者欲民之農也。國不農，則與諸侯爭權不能自持也，則眾力不足也。故諸侯撓其弱，乘其衰，土地侵削而不振，則無及已。聖人知治國之要，故令民歸心於農. *Shangjunshu zhuizhi*, 24; *The Book of Lord Shang*, trans. J. J. L. Duyvendak (London: A. Probsthain, 1928), 192.

[82] *Zuozhuan*, Xiang 14.1b: "Lord Hui, making manifest his great virtue, said that we, the various Rong tribes, were the descendants of the chiefs of the Four Peaks, and that we were not to be cut off and abandoned. He bestowed on us the [agricultural] lands of Jin's southern marches" 惠公蠲其大德，謂我諸戎，是四嶽之裔胄也，毋是翦棄，賜我南鄙之田. Admittedly, these were not the best of what Lord Hui had to offer, for they were lands "where foxes and wild cats made their lairs, and where jackals and wolves howled" 狐狸所居，豺狼所嘷, and where brambles grew. Nevertheless, as the Rong leader declared, the Rong cleared and settled the lands, and "became subjects" of the Jin lord, presumably paying him some form of economic and/or military tribute, as subjects would. Of course, what is also noteworthy is how more in tune the Rong leader is with what "virtuous" conduct should look like, more in tune that the "Chinese" ruler of Jin. *Zuo Tradition (Zuozhuan)*, 2:1008; Yang Bojun, *Chunqiu zuozhuan zhu*, 3:1006.

visited the Chinese court in diplomatic fora were usually not treated with the same deference as peer powers. Concomitantly, to remove evidence of such soft power, to rhetorically distance those who are not or no longer part of the sovereign sphere is to separate them from the bounds of civilization. It is for this reason that those who are to become part of the sovereign sphere are described as being "embraced" (*huai* 懷) by the sovereign. For this reason also do those "Daoist" passages antagonistic to formal state apparatuses acclaim spaces that have lost their territorialization and thus devalorize assertions of spatio-cultural supremacy. As the *Huainanzi* states, "A standing wall is better once it topples; how much better if it had never been built."[83]

The gifting of territory was a means to bringing another formally into a ritually empowered administrative sphere. Territory would be "severed off" (*lie* 裂) to "enfeoff" (*feng* 封) the new member (裂地而封).[84] Such a process is recorded both in the received and the excavated record.[85] Vice versa, for one's polity to be carved up by another was disempowering, the treatment of oneself as a weak subordinate or rival. Indeed, the "paring off" (*xuedi*) of another's land was a punishment or penalty, a reduction of political status. The more one was "territorialized," the greater one's status. Attentive treatment to the political lord, and his associated altars, was a condition of the receipt and keeping of territory. As the "Royal Regulations" ("Wangzhi") chapter of the *Liji* states, "Where any of the spirits of the hills and rivers had been unattended to, it was held to be an act of irreverence, and the irreverent ruler was deprived of a part of his territory."[86]

Unsanctioned military (or even diplomatic) movements into another's territory were an abrogation of one's ritual duties, when one was part of a ritual order. This naturally was encouragement to forge ritual bonds between proximate territories or recently acquired "foreign" territories.

---

[83] 牆之立, 不若其偃也, 又況不為牆乎? *Huainanzi*, "Jing shen" 精神 7.13; Liu An, *The Huainanzi*, 256; Liu An, *Huainanzi jishi*, 2:547. It is, I suspect, for this reason that the "nomadic," unformed space (*wuxing* 無形) is that which is lauded at various places in "Daoist" texts.

[84] 君裂地而封之 "The ruler severs off a piece of land to enfeoff him." For instance, see *Yanzi chunqiu zhujie* 晏子春秋注解 (Jinan: Qi Lu shushe, 2009), 157; *SJ* 80.2431; *HS* 34.1888.

[85] In the excavated record, see, for instance, the Mawangdui *Laozi yiben*, "Guoci" 國次: 列 (裂) 其土地, 以封賢者 (http://www.chant.org/Jianbo1/Search.aspx, accessed 10/19).

[86] 山川神祇, 有不舉者, 為不敬; 不敬者, 君削以地. *Liji jijie*, 1:328–329. In a note, the Qing dynasty compiler, Kong Xidan 孔希旦, remarked that mountains and rivers are "external" spirits (*waishen* 外神) on the frontier marches (*jing* 境) of the state. They are at a liminal territorial point where they (and, one may assume, the territory lying within their ritually associated area) may be "pared off" by the overlord, if sacrifices to them were not performed adequately by the designated ruler of the polity to which they adhered.

However, assertion of a ritual bond with or sovereignty over another territory does not by itself translate into any efficacious sovereignty. To some degree, sovereignty must be acquiesced to before it holds any force. As Hsing I-tien notes, according to a documented complaint in the Shuihudi texts, Chu peoples had not acquiesced fully to Qin's authority even fifty years after conquest.[87] Yet, such resistance also does not mean sovereignty is not asserted and hegemonic.

In short, as the above discussions highlight, assertions and exercises of sovereignty, particularly in the border areas, were commonly incomplete and difficult to maintain. Multiple overlapping power structures, on various levels, were continually in contestation.[88] What would seem to be included in an area of hard sovereignty could, gradually or suddenly, shift into an area of soft sovereignty, in which the territory shifted to a "contracted" (*mengguo* 盟國) or "subsidiary" (*shuguo* 屬國) arrangement – or, vice versa, soft into somewhat hard. Administrative and fiscal formations in the borderlands were multifarious and fluid. This of course meant that diplomatic arrangements were often at the core of any negotiation over sovereign dispositions, even when territory, as it was in the case between Qin and Chu cited above, was formally already "conquered."[89] In other words, sovereignty far from the immediate influence of the central court was eminently malleable and thus corruptible. Through the study of diplomatic interface, we can see how transgressions, conflicts in sites of multiple power layers affect the arbitration and execution of central command structures.

Chapter Summary

The incursions of external competitors provides a further essential element in the definition of sovereign space. How the state's boundaries were regarded spatially shifted in relation to the modes of their contestation:

---

[87] Hsing I-tien 邢义田, "Zhongguo huangdi zhidu de jianli yu fazhan" 中国皇帝制度的建立 与发展, in *Tianxia yijia* 天下一家 (Beijing: Zhonghua shuju, 2011), 4.

[88] Alexis Lycas highlights this in a recent study on arrangements with the Man 蠻 peoples in southern China during the Han. A household register from Liye "shows that not every Man had to pay taxes and, furthermore, that the payment of taxes probably depended on both the discretionary power of the local official in charge and on the status of the Man in question." Alexis Lycas, "The Southern Man People as a Political and Fiscal Problem in Han Times," *Monumenta Serica* 67, no. 1 (2019), 150.

[89] There are numerous instances in the histories of shifting politico-administrative arrangements. For an examination of another instance of such shifting "soft" sovereignty within the Wusun and Han relationship, which changed from neighboring states to contract (*mengguo*) states to tributary/subsidiary (*shuguo*) states, see Hao Shusheng 郝樹聲 and Zhang Defang 張德芳, *Xuanquan Hanjian yanjiu* 懸泉漢簡研究 (Lanzhou: Gansu wenhua chubanshe, 2009), 16.

Perceptions of a state's boundaries and territorializations were distinct depending on the apprehended cultural, and thus spatial, commensurability of the competitor, a distinction that is rendered visible in the noticeable shift in attention toward non-peer neighbors from the Warring States period to the Han dynasty. The spatial disposition (*xing*) of peer entities was distinguishable by a comparably ritualized administrative state structure. This influenced both the "paring off" of territory (*xuedi*) and, as will be discussed in the final chapter, diplomatic treatment. The early Chinese state disparaged areas outside of its spatio-cultural purview as the "wilds," but, in keeping with the zonal conception of space, the distinction between internal and external was gradual. The possibility of a ritualized fraternity impacted the character of a rivalry, and the spatial commensurability of rival polities. Because borders were fungible, crossing them was not itself a transgression; sovereignty was not equatable with a military line. Invasion (*qin*) was the penetration of a ritually sanctified space without permission.

6   Transgressions: Rupturing the Boundaries Between Sovereignties

The Transgressive Potential of the Diplomat

At base, diplomacy is driven by the aim for a nonmilitaristic negotiation of frequently competing interests, a negotiation that ideally should reinforce the definition of each party's sovereign realm and palliate any conflict between them. But this negotiation is also, by the very act of transacting across political and cultural boundaries, a kind of transgression, and thus a danger to the integrity of the state polity. In diplomacy, the interests of the state can be not only unsuccessfully negotiated but intentionally undermined, just as, in military campaigns, the interests of the state can be subverted, and betrayed, by false or careless action, or even intentional inaction, as is so often depicted in the early Chinese narrative histories.[1] Indeed, the very reason for Sima Qian's brutal castration is his support of a general, Li Ling, who "treasonously" capitulated to the Xiongnu after a failed engagement.[2] As Carl von Clausewitz's by now clichéd equation so aptly insinuates, military and diplomatic engagement are aspirationally congruent: War is the continuation of politics "by other means."[3]

---

[1] Anne McClintock analogously asserts that sailors and explorers, as members of the liminal condition also were "dangerous": "There on the margins between known and unknown, the male conquistadors, explorers and sailors became creatures of transition and threshold ... the dangers represented by liminal people are managed by rituals that separate the marginal ones from their old status, segregating them for a time and then publicly declaring their entry into their new status. Colonial discourse repeatedly rehearses this pattern – dangerous marginality, segregation, reintegration." Anne McClintock, *Imperial Leather: Race, Gender and Sexuality in the Colonial Contest* (New York: Routledge, 1995), 24–25.

[2] For the most detailed *Shiji* accounts of the Li Ling failure, see *SJ* 110.2918 and *SJ* 109.2877–2878. For lengthier accounts, one must peruse the *Hanshu*. See *HS* 54.2451–2457 and 62.2730.

[3] Carl von Clausewitz, *On War* (New York: Penguin Books, 1982), 119: "We see therefore, that War is not merely a political act, but also a real political instrument, a continuation of political commerce, a carrying out of the same by other means. All beyond this which is strictly peculiar to War relates merely to the peculiar nature of the means which it uses." This congruence is evident in various ministerial addresses and debates represented as part of the Warring States and Han eras. For my close, detailed analysis of these addresses and debates, see Olberding, *Dubious Facts*, chapters 6 and 8.

For diplomatic interface, transgression resides not only in the possibility of betrayal and rearrangement or distortion of alliances, and thus in the possibility of state action, but also in the actual rhetorical reframing of one's diplomatic mission or of the representation of the current state of affairs.[4] I argue that understanding the transgressive activity of the diplomat requires a nuanced understanding of a ritualized conceptualization of early Chinese diplomacy, which we can acquire through the examination of formal restrictions on ambassadorial exchange, obligations to and from guests, and the idea of the "alien" or "monstrous." To gain greater depth in these examinations, I hazard that an analogous diplomatic transgression of boundaries is that pursued by the *wu* 巫, "spirit mediums" (employed by the state as "invocators," *zhu* 祝) who act as diplomatic intermediaries between the physical and supernatural, their sacrifices cognate with monarchial tribute, their prayers with diplomatic pleadings.[5] Using an invocator was to conduct diplomacy with the spirits. Indeed, rulers very clearly relied on assistance from the spiritual realms for not only maintenance of their realms, but also their expansion.[6] According to Michael Puett, in the Shang the ritual of the "guest" (*bin* 賓), in use for the "entertainment" of spiritual powers, was to both

---

[4] As expressed by the figure of Confucius in the *Zhuangzi*, the conveying of messages between rival sovereign parties is very difficult and dangerous: "Whenever we are dealing with neighbours we have to rub along with each other on a basis of trust; but with people more distant we have to show our good faith in words, and the words must have some messenger. To pass on the words of parties both of whom are pleased or both of whom are angry with each other is the most difficult thing in the world. In the one case there are sure to be a lot of exaggerated compliments, in the other a lot of exaggerated abuse. Every sort of exaggeration is irresponsible, and if language is irresponsible trust in it fails, and the consequence of that is that the messenger is a doomed man. Therefore the book of rules says: 'If you report the straightforward facts and omit the exaggerated language, you will be safe enough'" 凡交近則必相靡以信，遠則必忠之以言，言必或傳之。夫傳兩喜兩怒之言，天下之難者也。夫兩喜必多溢美之言，兩怒必多溢惡之言。凡溢之類妄，妄則其信之也莫，莫則傳言者殃。故法言曰：「傳其常情，無傳其溢言，則幾乎全。」 *Zhuangzi*, "Renjian shi" 人間世 ("Worldly business among men"); *Chuang-tzŭ: The Inner Chapters*, trans. A. C. Graham (Indianapolis, IN: Hackett Publishing, 2001), 70; *Zhuangzi zhushu* 莊子注疏 (Beijing: Zhonghua shuju, 2011), 86–87. *Analects* 14.25 also has Confucius ostensibly ruing the impolitic critique by an envoy of his lord.

[5] One could say that among the most famous of Christian quotations is the request by Jesus of Nazareth who asks, in the position of the diplomat, for the monarch God not to punish those who are mistreating God's missionary representative, himself: "Forgive them, Father, for they know not what they do." Luke 23:34. One could go even further to suggest that Jesus's performance of healing miracles is as one who transgresses the divide between the human and spirit world and that his actions are seen, in some way, as transgressions of the natural order, as its deformation, and thus, dangerous to it.

[6] As the First Emperor of Qin stated in an edict: "Insignificant person that I am, I have called up troops to punish violence and rebellion. Thanks to the help of the ancestral spirits, these six kings have all acknowledged their guilt and the world is in profound order" 「寡人以眇眇之身，興兵誅暴亂，賴宗廟之靈，六王咸服其辜，天下大定。」 *SJ* 6.236; Sima Qian, *Records of the Grand Historian: Qin Dynasty*, 42.

maintain a hierarchy and to bring alien deities, such as Di, into the ancestral pantheon.[7] The spirits "descend" (*jiang* 降) into the world and involve themselves in its affairs through a spirit medium, a vertical journey that the monarch or his representatives replicate through ascent on natural or constructed elevations.[8] But these deities, Puett maintains, could not be depended upon for any assistance and in point of fact, at least in the Shang, "the assumption seemed to be that spirits were capricious and quite possibly malicious."[9] Whether the relationship between the spirit and human worlds was later ever fully harmonized, there was necessarily a rift, and potential conflict, between the two, requiring the diplomatic intervention of spiritual mediators, however unreliable their own allegiances were.

The profession of the diplomat or envoy – either within the human world or analogously as priests or spirit mediums toward the spirit world – involved manifold tasks that could conceivably, and very easily, compromise the sovereignty of and the territorial extent governed by the monarch. Succeeding is a partial list of the envoy's commonly sanctioned activities: Pass messages; obtain information directly and indirectly, as the sovereign's official informant; act as the monarch's representative in ritual, political, and military fora; and, most invidiously, speak on the monarch's behalf. It is not clear what plenipotentiary powers the envoys of the sovereign were afforded; one would suspect it would depend on the envoy's politico-military status and the task at hand. Regardless, in their activities, they could covertly exceed their prerogatives, impinging on or brazenly usurping the monarch's prerogative. In this, envoys were somewhat similar to the generals acting as the monarch's representatives on the battlefield. Whatever their official charge, their powers abroad were potentially destabilizing, bringing "disorder" (*luan* 亂).[10] Most flagrantly, they would upend the monarch's sovereignty, intentionally eroding or abrogating his position in their negotiations with other powers. Such opportunities for misdeeds were certainly a reason for the monarch to secure "*immutable mobiles*" such as visual representations of distant areas, "representations which can be detached from the place (or object) which

---

[7] Puett, *To Become a God*, 52.   [8] Lewis, *Construction of Space in Early China*, 300.
[9] Puett, *To Become a God*, 53.
[10] "I, Your servant, have heard that when the high ancient kings dispatched generals, they kneeled and pushed the axle [to the generals' carts], saying, 'Within the city gates, I, the solitary person, make regulations, outside the city gates the generals make regulations. The degrees of merit, orders of honor, and material rewards to be awarded to members of the army are all determined abroad. Only when you return do you present them.' This is not an empty saying" 臣聞上古王者遣將也，跪而推轂，曰：『閫以內寡人制之，閫以外將軍制之；軍功爵賞，皆決於外，歸而奏之。』此非空言也. See *HS* 50.2314; Olberding, *Dubious Facts*, 64.

they represent," by which the monarch could, in Bruno Latour's phrase, "act at a distance."[11]

But indirect undermining was more the rule: Envoys could have supposed "enemies" of the monarch dispatched, when these "enemies" were really those of the envoy or his associates; they could make self-serving political and economic pacts; they could embezzle, and thereby betray the economic order, or miscarry politico-legal justice, for instance, by punishing without warrant. Even more frequent was their habit to distort messages to and from the monarch or to collude with the enemy in their presenting of sensitive information, as Jing Ke was to do in presenting what was taken to be a strategically valuable map of Yan 燕 territory to the first Qin emperor. It is furthermore plausible that, with the interaction with the spirits perceived as having manifest effect on the affairs of the human world, the envoy could use his role as representative in ritual sacrifices[12] to attempt to "negotiate" with the spirits against the interests of the sovereign.

In short, like a passage in the *Hanshi waizhuan* asserts, envoys were the pivots of the state's survival, the crux of any gain or loss.[13] It should therefore be unsurprising that a classicist Warring States text devoted to expounding on proper governance, the *Xunzi*, dedicates a lengthy passage to the prescribed and proscribed behavior of official representatives. The official representative is not to deviate from his charge, not "to add or subtract." He is to have no inclination but to serve his lord properly. These officials must be trustworthy enough to be "employed in far away places to make clear [the lord's] intentions and resolve

---

[11] Ola Söderström, "Paper Cities: Visual Thinking in Urban Planning," *Ecumene* 3, no. 3 (1996), 253.

[12] See, e.g., in *HHS* 3.14: 使使者祠唐堯於成陽靈臺; or *HHS* 3.144: 遣使者祠太上皇於萬年，以中牢祠蕭何、霍光. David Schaberg has associated the position of the envoy, or *shi* 使, with that of the *shi* 史, the professional ancestor of which conceivably was the spiritual medium or "shaman" (*wu* 巫). He notes that none of the typical terms for "envoy" – *shi* 使, *shizhe* 使者, or *xingren* 行人 – appeared "as such" in sources portraying the Western Zhou, whether the bronze inscriptions or received texts. In the *Zuozhuan*, Schaberg states, the most common duties of the *shi* 史 were "the duties relating to sacrifices, especially to natural spirits or in response to natural disasters. The *shi* 史 are responsible for identifying and responding appropriately to unknown spirits and for conducting sacrifices at such sites as the Luo river ... Perhaps due to this responsibility for sacrifices to natural powers, they also serve frequently as interpreters of divinations (usually by milfoil), omens, and dreams and more generally as prophets of good and ill fortune." See David Schaberg, "Functionary Speech: On the Work of *Shi* 使 and *Shi* 史," in *Facing the Monarch: Modes of Advice in the Early Chinese Court*, ed. Garret Olberding (Cambridge, MA: Harvard Asia Center Publications, 2013), esp. 21, 23, and 27–28.

[13] "Thus those advisors and assistants who serve as envoys, they are the crux of survival or demise, the essential point of gain or loss. This must not be ignored!" 故輔弼左右所任使者、有存亡之機，得失之要也，可無慎乎! See Han Ying 韓嬰, *Han shi wai zhuan ji shi* 韓詩外傳集釋 (Beijing: Zhonghua shuju, 2009), j. 5, *zhang* 18, 186.

uncertainties."[14] While they cannot abrogate the responsibilities associated with polite, formal interaction, they also must defend the state and the monarch against insults, as well as maintain the state's and the monarch's claims to sovereignty. Deference was to be shown to the monarch's representative, as would be shown to the monarch himself.[15] Without such reliable representatives, the state, according to the *Xunzi*, will fall.[16] But this faithful rhetorical adherence to monarch's prerogative was irregular. As David Schaberg acknowledges, representatives frequently spoke irreverently and impoliticly.[17] If advisers could be acidly condescending toward their rulers while at court, when acting as envoys, they could easily be so. Even more dangerously, their transmission of the ruler's intentions, and relevant information, was also suspect.

[14] *Xunzi*, "Jun dao" 君道 (The way to be a lord); *Xunzi: The Complete Text*, 131–132; Wang Xianqian, *Xunzi jijie*, 1:244–245.

[15] "When a message from the ruler comes (to a minister), the latter should go out and bow (to the bearer), in acknowledgment of the honour of it. When the messenger is about to return, (the other) must bow to him (again), and escort him to the gate. If (a minister) send[s] a message to his ruler, he must wear his court robes when he communicates it to the bearer; and on his return, he must descend from the hall, to receive (the ruler's) commands" 君言至，則主人出拜君言之辱；使者歸，則必拜送于門外。若使人於君所，則必朝服而命之；使者反，則必下堂而受命. *Liji*, "Quli" A 曲禮上; *Li Chi: Book of Rites*, 1:86. In this aspect, the early Chinese envoy was akin to a medieval European *nuncius*: "Dealing with a *nuncius* was, for legal and practical purposes, the same as dealing with the principal ... How complete the identification was between *nuncius* and principal can be further gauged from the fact that a *nuncius* could receive and make oaths that ought to be performed in the presence of the principal. It was also clear that the status of the *nuncius* was reflected in the immunity from harm which he was expected to be given. All diplomatic messengers from the earliest times had been accorded some kind of security for their persons, usually on religious grounds, and the special status of ambassadors was clearly understood. In the case of *nuncii*, there was a special sense that harming a *nuncius* was the same as harming his principal, as there was that a *nuncius* should be received with the ceremony that would be due to his principal." Hamilton and Langhorne, *Practice of Diplomacy*, 24–25.

[16] "And so, the ruler of men must have people who will suffice for being employed in far away places to make clear his intentions and resolve uncertainties, and only then are they acceptable. Their demonstrations and persuasions must suffice to dissolve worries. Their wisdom and deliberations must suffice to resolve uncertainties. Their swiftness and decisiveness must suffice to ward off disasters. They must not circumvent protocols or act confrontationally toward other lords, but nevertheless their response to derogatory treatment and their defense against troubles must suffice to uphold the state's altars of soil and grain" 故人主將有足使喻志決疑於遠方者，然後可。其辯說足以解煩，其知慮足以決疑，其齊斷足以距難，不還秩，不反君，然而應薄扞患，足以持社稷。 *Xunzi*, "Jun dao" (The way to be a lord); *Xunzi: The Complete Text*, 131; Wang Xianqian, *Xunzi jijie*, 1:244–245.

[17] David Schaberg, "Playing at Critique: Indirect Remonstrance and the Formation of *Shi* Identity," in *Text and Ritual in Early China*, ed. Martin Kern (Seattle: University of Washington Press, 2005).

This is likely a significant reason for the widespread regulatory controls pertaining to the preservation and recording of diplomatic missives, and their carriers, detailed in both received and excavated sources. Information in general was insecure and comparatively difficult to verify in the ancient world;[18] this would be ever more the case when the information could be used to personal advantage. Jidong Yang has observed in the Xuanquan manuscripts that foreign envoys were under strict supervision, at all times accompanied by a Chinese official and required to carry a passport:

The original passport had to be carried by the foreign envoys at all times when traveling within the Han empire. On arriving at a postal station or a local government mansion, the envoy would show the travel document to the officials in charge in order to receive accommodation; the officials offering the service would furthermore make a copy of the passport for their own records.[19]

These diplomatic precautions are easily comprehensible for, as Yang mentions, most designated envoys (shizhe 使者) from Central Asia acted as merchants who rarely moved far beyond the empire's perimeter, interacting and socializing with the officials of these border areas. These interactions were monitored carefully, with the duration of the stay, the departing direction and time of departure, and the number of meals offered recorded,[20] conceivably to inhibit collusion between border officials and foreign powers, just as the fastidious recording of each article of mail passing through the Xuanquan station[21] probably also in part aimed to do. Envoys were to act as spies for their lords,[22] but, as mentioned above, they also acted as informants for the lord's rivals.

The envoy's moving into a nonstate space, without the protections, such as they were, of state protocols and laws, was in itself dangerous. Indeed, a passage in the *Liji* advises rulers be cautioned about leaving the state with the admonishing query, "Why are you leaving the altars of the spirits of the land and grain?" suggesting not only a danger to the state but

---

[18] Olberding, *Dubious Facts*, 61.

[19] Jidong Yang, "Transportation, Boarding, Lodging and Trade Along the Early Silk Road: A Preliminary Study of the Xuanquan Manuscripts," *Journal of the American Oriental Society* 135, no. 3 (2015), 428.

[20] Yang, "Transportation, Boarding, Lodging and Trade Along the Early Silk Road," 428–429.

[21] Ibid., 426.

[22] "Upon arriving at Jinyang, [Liu Bang, the future Han emperor] heard that Han Xin together with the Xiongnu together wished to attack the Han armies. Liu Bang was very angry and sent an envoy to the Xiongnu. The Xiongnu hid their strong soldiers and fat cows and horses, only revealing the old and weak and the young herd animals. The envoy came ten times and always said the Xiongnu could be attacked" 至晉陽, 聞信與匈奴欲共擊漢, 上大怒, 使人使匈奴。匈奴匿其壯士肥牛馬, 但見老弱及羸畜。使者十輩來, 皆言匈奴可擊. *SJ* 99.2718.

also to the ruler himself.[23] To be exiled, to be sent abroad without state protections' was for this reason a punishment, for it could very readily mean death or serious injury. Nonstate territory was *defined* by this very lack of administrative oversight, and was a place where societal cast-offs, where the socially "dead" could be sent.[24] This area of the unknown and unprotected was the place of the symbolically monstrous and the effaced. Indeed, as Martin Kern has noted, the sovereign space was measured by "the terminal points to which all crime is relegated." According to Han commentators of the "Canon of Shun" ("Shundian" 舜典), in the "Canon of Yao" ("Yaodian" 堯典) the "four criminals" and "their places of exile or execution were associated with the barbarian areas of the four directions: Dark Province in the north, Exalted Mountain in the south, Threefold Precipice in the West, and Feathered Mountain in the East."[25] For those not being punished, being sent into the wilds, as Shun himself was by Yao,[26] was a perilous trial, of one's person and one's loyalties.

Ritual Obligations Involved in Travel Abroad

Oddly enough, comparatively little has been written on the general form of premodern diplomacy, whether in China or even in Europe, apart from broader concerns of foreign relations. At base, diplomacy assumes a secure source of political power that can actually be represented, for which negotiations can be made and agreements secured. If there is no secure source of power, if power is too fragmentary, diplomats naturally have no one stable subject or entity to represent. Between diplomatically symmetrical entities, that is, between those polities that are treated as of reciprocally recognizable structure, diplomats are treated as representational metonyms of their supporting polities; between asymmetrical entities, the "superior" polity condescends to demand for tribute or obeisance but will not offer corresponding duties to the "inferior." Thus when the Han opposed the Xiongnu state polity organized under the *shanyu*, they engaged in high-level diplomatic exchanges and negotiations, with both sides treating the diplomatic representatives according to protocols. According to the *Shiji*, the Xiongnu's protocols for

---

[23] *Liji*, "Quli" B 曲禮下: "When the ruler of a state (is proposing to) leave the state, they should (try to) stop him, saying, 'Why are you leaving the altars of the spirits of the land and grain?'" 國君去其國，止之曰：「奈何去社稷也！」 *Li Chi: Book of Rites*, 1:107; *Liji jijie*, 1:125.

[24] According to Danielle Allen, casting out the dead from the city, from the acculturated center, was practiced very literally by the ancient Greeks. A return to civilized space, to the city, was a return to the world of the living. See Allen, *World of Prometheus*, 207.

[25] Kern, "Language and the Ideology of Kingship in the 'Canon of Yao,'" 140.

[26] Ibid., 135.

interacting with diplomats depended on the diplomat's status. Early idealizing literature such as the *Zhouli*, *Liji*, and *Yili* 儀禮 (*Book of Ceremony and Rites*) preserves ritualized protocols for diplomatic interface but whether any approximation of such was properly and fully applied to foreign, non-Chinese adversaries cannot be certain. As will be discussed later, if the debate of 51 BCE about the status of a Xiongnu *shanyu* in relation to the Han aristocrats is any indication, full application was probably the exception. What *is* clear, from the Zhangjiashan legal texts, is that there were strict regulations about who could travel abroad, and with what objects they could travel. Metal tools, for instance, were tightly regulated, presumably because of the danger of their being transformed into weaponry. Even coffins were inspected for illegal items, though this was ruled improper.[27] When there were disagreements, each side would hold the other's emissaries hostage.[28]

Ritual obligations impinged heavily on travel abroad for those with official status. When travel was not properly sanctioned, the itinerant could face severe consequences, a loss of title, or worse, a loss of identity, becoming essentially stateless. As Haicheng Wang notes, travelers were expected to pass forts located at "strategic points such as ferries and mountain passes."[29] The Han ordinances on fords and passes discovered at Zhangjiashan detail punishments for commoners who cross frontiers without permission, including tattooing, building walls for men, pounding grain for women, and amputation of the left foot.[30] For county officials, fines were assessed.

Especially for representatives of the sovereign state, such as diplomats, crossing boundaries without permission was in effect the nullifying of one's position, one's subjecthood.[31] In the *Zuozhuan*, for instance, were a nobleman to flee, "as long as he had not crossed the border, the ruler could stop him and request his return, and presumably his status would be unaffected."[32] Were a nobleman to flee his home state, the news would be formally passed to other regional rulers:

In any case of a nobleman of the regional lords departing, it was reported to the regional lords, saying, "The lineage head, So-and-so of Such-and-such a clan, has

---

[27] Osamu Oba, "The Ordinance on Fords and Passes Excavated from Han Tomb #247, Zhangjiashan," *Asia Major* 14, no. 2 (2001), 124.

[28] *SJ* 110.2911.   [29] Wang, *Writing and the Ancient State*, 204.

[30] In Wang, *Writing and the Ancient State*, 207. See also Oba, "Ordinance on Fords and Passes Excavated from Han Tomb #247, Zhangjiashan," 122–123n1.

[31] In a reversal of this power, as Paul J. Kosmin details, in the Seleucid Empire, borders could also be the point at which one's status was augmented; for instance, from prince into king. See Kosmin, *Land of the Elephant Kings*, 131–134.

[32] Newell Ann van Auken, "What If Zhào Dùn Had Fled? Border Crossing and Flight into Exile in Early China," *Journal of the American Oriental Society* 139, no. 3 (2019), 581.

failed to keep watch over the ancestral temple. We dare report it." (Zuǒ, Xuān 10, 706) 凡諸侯之大夫違，告於諸侯曰：「某氏之守臣某，失守宗廟。敢告。」 [33]

Crossing a state boundary without proper sanction, Newell Ann van Auken has noted, was equal to the "abandonment of state altars, that is, with abdication of religious responsibilities as head of state."[34] Indeed, according to a passage in the *Zuozhuan*, ritual invocators were not permitted to cross a frontier march (*jing* 竟), "if the domain's altars do not move."[35] Van Auken observes that "Similar language was used in reference to nobility, but instead of abandoning the state altars, a nobleman was said to have 'failed to keep watch over the ancestral temple' 失守宗廟."[36] Those eastern Zhou officials or aristocrats who left their states without sanction relinquished their noble status by leaving the state, becoming a threat – or just officially "dead" – to the state.[37] As van Auken suggests, this transgression was not simply one toward the living but also toward the spiritual world.[38]

Van Auken has also mentioned that in the *Zuozhuan*, before any official interstate travel a ruler had to give sanction (*ming* 命), with specific religious ceremonies held and reports (*gao* 告) rendered to the ancestors, presumably in the temple, before departure.[39] This requirement, van Auken observes, is reflected in the "Pin li" 聘禮 ("Rites for Peer Visitation") chapter of the *Yili*,[40] as well as in the "Zengzi wen" 曾子問 ("Inquiries of Zengzi") chapter of the *Liji*. For my analysis, the passage in

---

[33] Van Auken, "What If Zhào Dùn Had Fled?" 581.   [34] Ibid., 580.

[35] "The rules for officials stipulate that an invocator does not cross the [frontier march] if the domain's altars do not move. When the ruler travels with the army, he performs a purification sacrifice at the altar of earth, and he anoints the drums with blood; the invocators accompany him to attend to their duties, and in this way the group crosses the borders" 社稷不動，祝不出竟，官之制也。君以軍行，祓社、釁鼓，祝奉以從，於是乎出竟. See *Zuozhuan*, Ding 4.1b; *Zuo Tradition (Zuozhuan)*, 3:1746–1747; Yang Bojun, *Chunqiu zuozhuan zhu*, 4:1535.

[36] Van Auken, "What If Zhào Dùn Had Fled?" 580. Yuri Pines notes a similar tension in his study of Qin almanacs, in the making of offerings before travel, with the area beyond state boundary walls becoming a dangerous space: "A special exorcist ritual had to be performed upon leaving the state, similar to the ritual performed upon leaving one's native settlement." Yuri Pines, "The Question of Interpretation: Qin History in Light of New Epigraphic Sources," *Early China* 29 (2004), 41.

[37] Van Auken, "What If Zhào Dùn Had Fled?" 583.   [38] Ibid., 584.

[39] These religious ceremonies announcing the departure of a potentially politically destabilizing force, the diplomat, are somewhat similar to those held by military officials before embarking on a campaign or engaging in battle: "[A]ccording to a passage in the *Zuo zhuan* 左傳, the army commander received his orders in the ancestral temple (miao 廟)." See Albert Galvany, "Signs, Clues, and Traces: Anticipation in Ancient Chinese Political and Military Texts," *Early China* (2015), 4.

[40] *Yili zhushu* 儀禮注疏 (Beijing: Beijing daxue chubanshe, 1999), 356–375.

the *Liji* bears particular notice. It speaks of the regional lord, when setting out to pay court to the son of Heaven or another regional ruler, making reports not only to his father's shrine but to the altars of grain and soil and to the spirits of mountains and rivers.[41] Ritual activities furthermore surrounded arrivals in another state as well as returns to one's home state.[42]

If we can adopt the official travels abroad of those who were deemed *shi* 使 – commonly translated as "emissary" or "diplomat" – in the early histories as being somewhat representative of diplomatic engagement, we can get a sense of the range of the duties of early Chinese diplomats. Schaberg provides the following list:

Besides their ritually scheduled visits and occasional trips for wedding preparations, funerals, and the recognition of newly acceding rulers, there were also journeys to meetings (*hui* 會), whether for covenants or for joint military action. Battlefield confrontations with enemies also brought states together and required sensitive communication through intermediaries. Prisoners taken in battle and hostages – sometimes envoys detained in the course of their missions – were yet another part of the web, as were noble brides and the retinues accompanying them to their new home.[43]

Schaberg also acknowledges the connection between the religious and nonreligious duties of the *shi* 使, captured in their cognate relationship to the *shi* 史 (commonly translated as "scribe"), but he phrases this connection in terms of a mastery of "specialized speech" and their exercising "some discretion in determining the appropriate speech to use on specific occasions."[44] There is a further cognate association: that of acting as intermediaries across boundaries, whether secular or sacred, with the

---

[41] Van Auken, "What If Zhào Dùn Had Fled?" 579; *Liji*, "Zengzi wen" 曾子問: "Confucius said, 'When princes of states are about to go to the (court of the) son of Heaven, they must announce (their departure) before (the shrine of) their grandfather, and lay their offerings in that of their father. They then put on the court cap, and go forth to hold their own court. (At this) they charge [the liturgist or invocator] and the recorder to announce (their departure) to the (spirits of the) land and grain, in the ancestral temple, and at the (altars of the) [mountains] and rivers" 孔子曰：「諸侯適天子，必告于祖，奠于禰，冕而出視朝。命祝、史告於社稷、宗廟、山川…」 *Liji jijie*, 2:510–511. When state princes visit one another, they too are obliged to inform (and presumably ask permission of) the spirits, both at home before they leave, through an invocator, and while enroute, to the spirits of the hills and rivers they pass: "[T]hey charge the [liturgist or invocator] and the recorder to announce (their departure) at the five shrines in the ancestral temple, and at the altars of the hills and rivers which they will pass" 命祝、史告于五廟、所過山川. *Liji jijie*, 2:511. In both of the above instances, travelers are also to present sacrifices to the spirits of the roads. For the above translations, see *Li Chi: Book of Rites*, 1:314–315.

[42] Van Auken, "What If Zhào Dùn Had Fled?" 579. As she mentions, "For a description of the rites involved when a *pìn* mission crossed the border into another state, see *Yí lǐ*, 'Pìn lǐ,' *SSJZS*, 19.9ab (230)." Van Auken, "What If Zhào Dùn Had Fled?" 579n36.

[43] Schaberg, "Functionary Speech," 32.   [44] Schaberg, "Functionary Speech," 39.

leadership of other states, or the spiritual powers, particularly, as Schaberg notes, natural spirits, that have a hand in matters of state.[45] These transactional interfaces across boundaries, political and spiritual, were within the purview of the envoy.

The Ritual Status of the Guest

The envoy being received, his status and treatment was that due to a "guest," *bin* 賓 or *binke* 賓客.[46] Thus the ceremonial protocols due the guest give a sense to what was ceremonially due an envoy while abroad. With the offices they undertook religiously sanctified, the diplomat himself was sacralized. As Hugo Grotius (1583–1615 CE) states in "On the Right of Legation" relating to Roman norms, "Pomponius says: 'If any one has struck the ambassador of an enemy, it is thought that a crime has been committed against the law of nations, because ambassadors are considered sacred.' Tacitus calls this right which we are treating 'the right of enemies and sanctity of embassy and divine law of nations'."[47] Like the spirit medium, who interceded on behalf of others with the spiritual powers, or military generals paying tribute at the altar before starting battle,[48] the diplomat's secular office was to pay tribute and intercede on behalf of others with earthly powers. The attention directed to the conduct between host and guest in the *Liji* suggests their relationship is almost as significant as the mourning rites, or any number of other basic social relationships, such as between father and son, or husband and wife. In the twilight of one's life, release from duties to guests comes late, at seventy, with only mourning responsibilities left to endure, according to the "Royal Regulations" ("Wangzhi"). All other duties requiring any physical exertion had by that age been abrogated.

For the *Liji*, embedded within the duties between hosts and guests were the norms of *yi* 義, often translated thickly as "righteousness," but which more conservatively could be simply and broadly translated as "social propriety," the moral attitude that shapes proper social interaction, especially in formal contexts. Duties between foreign guests of noble peerage and their hosts were articulated in the "Pin yi" 聘義 chapter, this chapter title mostly explicitly rendered as "social propriety with regard to visiting

---

[45] Schaberg, "Functionary Speech," 27–28, 30.

[46] This equation is sometimes explicitly rendered, as in this passage from the *Shiji*: 諸侯賓客使者相望於道 *SJ* 85.2513.

[47] G. R. Berridge, ed. *Diplomatic Classics: Selected Texts from Commynes to Vattel* (New York: Palgrave Macmillan, 2004), 107.

[48] Tamara Chin draws this analogy between the general and the diplomat. Chin, *Savage Exchange*, 173.

dignitaries of noble peerage." But non-peerage foreign visitors were also treated as "guests," as numerous texts, such as the *Bamboo Annals* (*Zhushu jinian* 竹書紀年) reveal. In the *Bamboo Annals*, many foreign tribes "come to court as guests," *lai bin* 來賓.

We may find further insight into the character of "guests" by the territories prescribed to them. The duties prescribed for those whose territory, and thus political association, is described as being in the "guest realm" *binfu* 賓服, are distinct from those in more associationally distant realms, such as the *yaofu* 要服 or the *huangfu* 荒服. The *binfu* is the second distant from the central monarchial *dianfu* 甸服, following after the *houfu* 侯服, the realm of the aristocrats or lords. The *binfu* is substituted in two early texts, the *Shangshu*'s "Levies of Yu" ("Yugong") and the *Shiji*'s "Annals of the Xia" ("Xia benji" 夏本紀), replaced by the *suifu* 綏服, the "security" or "pacification" realm. In the *Xunzi*, the *Guoyu* 國語, and the *Shiji*'s "Annals of the Zhou" ("Zhou benji" 周本紀), the *binfu* is the third realm from the center. Each of these realms is denoted by their relation to the central court, in what manner their "submission" (*fu* 服) can be characterized.

"Guests" are those who are submissive. They are associationally considered somewhat reliable but are at the liminal edge of the perimeters of loyalty. As the *Shangshu* states about its security/pacification realm, its denizens were enjoined to cultivate the "virtues" (*de*) or prepare military defenses[49] – two activities meant to protect against internal disloyalty and external incursions. Beyond the guest realm lie the realms regularly associated with non-Chinese tribes whose loyalties were unreliable and suspect. According to the *Xunzi*, the Man 蠻 and Yi, southern tribespeople collectively,[50] lay in the fourth *yao* 要 realm (the "guard" realm, not infrequently the zone of somewhat allied non-Chinese); the Rong and Di, northern tribespeople, in the last, distant *huangfu* 荒服, the realm of the "wilds."[51]

---

[49] 五百里綏服：三百里揆文教，二百里奮武衛. Li Xueqin, *Shangshu zhengyi*, "Yu gong," 168–169). Kong Yingda's (574–648 CE) commentary interprets the activities of those in this zone to be aimed at pacifying and keeping at bay those hostile elements in the adjacent "guard" zone: 要服去京已遠，王者以文教要束使服.

[50] Erica Brindley notes that the southern Yue were employed historiographically as foils of the Chinese self, "but instead of being a lesser or odious 'other' (aka 'barbarian'), they often served in varying roles as an exaggerated reflection of the self or instantiation of human existence at the remote corners of both the world and individual psyche. Especially in contexts that do not provide a strong articulation of the notion of Hua-xia cultures and polities, the Yue other appears to be a foil used to critique or shed light on the nature of the localized self." The Yue were associated with "the extremity of common ideals." Erica Brindley, *Ancient China and the Yue* (New York: Cambridge University Press, 2015), 121–122.

[51] This outermost region within this "wild" zone was that to which convicts were to be sent. One might hazard that the locating of particular tribespeople in the zones may reveal how

It was in the *huangfu* in which the Xiongnu would later be located in the *Shiji* chapter devoted to them, the "Account of the Xiongnu."

The symbolism of these realms naturally does not exclude the extension of the term "guest" to those visiting from beyond any guest realm. And yet the treatment of guests most certainly depended on their politicocultural associations. Guests who were perceived to be from within accepted cultural groups were handled – or at least were *expected* to be handled – differently from those who weren't. Arguably the status distinctions across peers or apparent supporters and sympathizers in their treatment as guests remained in some manner even between those considered foes – in other words, status distinctions were more important than loyalty. Evidence for this is vividly present in the debate of 51 BCE surrounding the ritual obligations, including the awarding of gifts and bestowing of a title, to the visiting Xiongnu *shanyu*. The status of those who felt themselves internal and integral to the sovereign realm of Han was impugned, threatened by the inclusion and elevation of the *shanyu*. In the 51 BCE debate, two high-level officials, Imperial Counselor Huang Ba 黃霸 and Chancellor Yu Dingguo 于定國 contended that because of his cultural exteriority, the political standing of the *shanyu* needed to be below that of the Liu family kings, a position they justified using the above realm divisions. Arguing the adverse, Xiao Wangzhi 蕭望之 nevertheless situates his contention to place the *shanyu* in a position superior to the Liu kings in the very ritualized exteriority Huang Ba and Yu Dingguo utilized to demote him.[52]

According to protocol manuals such as the *Zhouli*, guests, such as envoys, were to receive strictly ritualized treatment. Guests also were spoken about in relation to other ritual activities discussed in these protocol manuals. In the *Liji*, for instance, the rendering of sacrifices (*jisi* 祭祀) and the receiving of guests (*binke* 賓客) are frequently paired. Powerful and potentially destabilizing social relationships, such as host and guest, father and son, husband and wife, or the spiritual relationship between the living and dead, itself mirroring live social relationships, were treasured and monitored because of their potential to enhance or damage sociopolitical structures. The lack of due deference could signal or effect drastic changes impacting the welfare of the state. Without ritualized social interactions between host and guest, and prescriptions on the guest's speech and behavior, restrictions imposed both by the host and

much of an issue their associated area might be at the time of that particular text's composition.

[52] *HS* 78.3282 For a discussion of this debate, see Luke Habberstad, "How and Why Do We Praise the Emperor? Debating and Depicting a Late Western Han Court Audience," *Journal of the Economic and Social History of the Orient* 60, no. 5 (2017).

the official delegating the guest abroad, envoys would free themselves uninhibitedly from codes that preserved the privileges and responsibilities of group membership. Andrea Nightingale quotes an observation by C. A. Morgan about ancient Greek official trips abroad to religious festivals: "For the individual as citizen of a state, going 'beyond the bounds' was a dangerous move, since community boundaries mark the extent of the security and status conferred by group membership. Yet for the individual, it allowed the freedom to act in whatever way he might deem to be in his own interest." As Nightingale quotes further in a footnote, "the sanctuaries and institutionalized cults within [community boundaries] served (to some extent) to 'limit the actions of individuals to those acceptable to the city'."[53] Intrinsically, the guest was also an intruder, the bringer of the "monstrous" foreign unknown, dangerous outside, even when integrated into known norms.

Of course, in early China, ritual prescriptions for behavior toward guests was not limited to the Chinese, nor were the concerns about envoys' pernicious influence. According to the *Shiji*, the Xiongnu had protocols for managing the potential manipulations and conniving of arriving Chinese diplomats. They were keenly aware of the kinds of speech to expect from different types and statuses of Chinese guests – palace eunuchs versus classicists, young strivers versus seasoned elders.[54] One can presume that concerns about visiting envoys and the need to keep any nefarious influence in check governed such Xiongnu protocol responses as deeply as they governed Chinese ones.

The duties to one's guests, and the guests' acknowledgment of and respect for these duties are all symbols of soft sovereign power, of the power to regulate action and attitude across the various lines of power – economic, political, and otherwise. The diplomatic jostling between sovereign entities – encapsulated in letters between the Han emperor and the *shanyu* – reveals unadulteratedly how the powers of state, and their territorial boundaries, required careful, intricate negotiation. In contrast to the negotiations of diplomat-persuaders whose allegiances to the state are ever dim and

---

[53] From Andrea Wilson Nightingale, "The Philosopher at the Festival: Plato's Transformation of Traditional Theōria," in *Pilgrimage in Graeco-Roman and Early Christian Antiquity: Seeing the Gods*, ed. Ján Elsner and Ian Rutherford (New York: Oxford University Press, 2005), 161, quoting Catherine A. Morgan, "The Origins of Pan-Hellenism," in *Greek Sanctuaries: New Approaches*, ed. Nanno Marinatos and Robin Hägg (London: Routledge, 1993), 31.

[54] In Enno Giele's (modified) translation: "It is a Hsiung-nu habit that, when they receive a Han envoy and he is not a palace eunuch, but a Confucian scholar, they assume that he wants to [persuade] and [skew] his [distinctions]; when he is a youth, they assume he wants to [make his words] sting and [skew the substance of what he is saying]" 匈奴俗，見漢使非中貴人，其儒先，以為欲說，折其辯；其少年，以為欲刺，折其氣. *SJ* 110.2913; Ssu-ma Ch'ien, "Xiongnu," 294–295.

uncertain, in the negotiations between heads of state, in the persons of the state *themselves*, we can lay bare the possible transgressions of diplomatic boundaries, and thus the boundaries of state power itself. In these direct interactions, traded insults, sarcasm, borrowed marks of tradition, and purposeful omissions themselves are the actual diminution of the other's sovereignty. A potent instance of this is found in the diplomatic exchanges between Emperor Wen and the Xiongnu *shanyu*.

According to the *Shiji*, in 179 BCE, the first year of the reign of Emperor Wen of Han, the Xiongnu and the Han attempted to reclaim a peaceable, diplomatic relationship. Two years earlier, in 181 BCE, a Xiongnu king, the Worthy King of the Right, invaded and occupied the region south of the Yellow River, marauded and robbed non-Chinese people (*Manyi*) at the Bao Barrier 葆塞, murdering and kidnapping them. Thereupon Emperor Wen issued an edict to the chancellor Guan Ying 灌 嬰 to send out 85,000 units of chariots and cavalry to travel to the Gaonu 高奴 district and attack the Worthy King of the Right. The Worthy King of the Right fled beyond a military barrier. Because of revolts elsewhere, these attacks were broken off. The next year, the *shanyu* sent the Han emperor a letter, which was followed by a response by the emperor craftily excerpting from the *shanyu*'s missive. The underlined passages are those quoted by the Han emperor in his later reply:

The great Xiongnu *shanyu*, established by Heaven, respectfully inquires whether the August Thearch is free from worry. In past the August Thearch spoke of the matter of peaceful negotiations (*heqin*), promoting the notions of the [agreement] document. [In this we are in] friendly accord. The Han frontier officials invaded the area of and insulted the Worthy King of the Right. The Worthy King of the Right, not requesting [permission], listened to the plans of [the Xiongnu general] Yilu Hounanzhi, among others, to repulse the Han officials, abrogate the agreement of the two leaders (i.e., the Han emperor and Xiongnu *shanyu*), and cool the close relationship between older and younger brother. The August Thearch's chastising letters [related to this issue] repeatedly arrived, and [We] dispatched envoys to deliver letters in reply, but they did not return, nor did Han envoys come. If because of this the Han is not in harmony [with Us], other neighboring states will not support [the Han]. Now, though [Your] petty officials are the reason for our agreement being ruined, [We] have punished the Worthy King of the Right and dispatched him to the west to request [territory from] the Yuezhi and to attack them. Having Heavenly fortune, good officials and infantry, and strong horses, [the Worthy King of the Right] used [Our] barbarians to crush the Yuezhi tribes, completely cutting them down, killing or subjugating them. He subdued the Loulan, Wusun, Hujie, and their bordering twenty-six states, all of whom became Xiongnu. [Because of his success,] all of the bow-drawing common people have now joined together into one household. With the northern regions being subdued, [We] wish to allow the troops to rest, to release the officers and infantry and pasture the horses, to have done with the earlier matter [involving the King of the Right] and return to our old agreement, in order to give peace to the common people on the frontier and to accord with the [state of] earliest antiquity, to allow the young to reach their maturity and the elderly to live peacefully in their domiciles, generation upon generation tranquil and happy. Not having received the August Thearch's envisioned intentions, [We] are sending Palace Attendant Xiyu Qian to present a letter requesting [a response], offering one camel, two cavalry horses, and two outfitted chariots. If the August Thearch does not desire the Xiongnu to approach the barriers, He should immediately issue an edict commanding the officials and common people to reside more distantly [from the barriers]. After the envoy has arrived [to deliver this message], immediately dispatch him [with a reply].

「天所立匈奴大單于敬問皇帝無恙 。前時皇帝言和親事，稱書意，合歡。漢邊吏侵侮右賢王，右賢王不請，聽後義盧侯難氏等計，與漢吏相距，絕二主之約，離兄弟之親。皇帝讓書再至，發使以書報，不來，漢使不至，漢以其故不和，鄰國不附。今以小吏之敗約故，罰右賢王，使之西求月氏擊之。以天之福，吏卒良，馬彊力，以夷滅月氏，盡斬殺降下之。定樓蘭、烏孫、呼揭及其旁二十六國，皆以為匈奴。諸引弓之民，并為一家。北州已定，願寢兵休士卒養馬，除前事，復故約，以安邊民，以應始古，使少者得成其長，老者安其處，世世平樂。未得皇帝之志也，故使郎中系零淺奉書請，獻橐他一匹，騎馬二匹，駕二駟。皇帝即不欲匈奴近塞，則且詔吏民遠舍。使者至，即遣之。」 [55]

The Han emperor's excerpts underscore a perception of Xiongnu self-interested disingenuousness in their confrontation with the Yuezhi. The emperor's letter also removes references to traditional Chinese religio-moral standards, whether to "Heaven" or to "ancient" precedents, to any "accord with the origins of antiquity" (應始古). Indeed, as if to stress how little Chinese religio-moral norms pertain to their inter-action, no mention is made to Heaven in Emperor Wen's letter at all, an absence made all the more pregnant when placed in comparison to the manifold references to "Heaven" in communications to Chinese peers. When the early precedents of the sage rulers are referred to, it is done so patronizingly, in approving the *shanyu*'s appreciation of their wisdom. In his summary judgment, the Han emperor caustically, sarcastically indicts the *shanyu* for any abrogation of peaceful, "brotherly" relations:

The Han and the Xiongnu agreed to be as brothers; thus we have been very generous to the *shanyu*. Yet those who have repudiated the agreement and abandoned the close relation of brothers have frequently been among the Xiongnu. If the matter of the Worthy King of the Right occurred before the imperial amnesty, the *shanyu* should not condemn him too strongly. Were the *shanyu* to want to promote the [agreement] document's notions, he would

[55] *SJ* 110.2896.

openly instruct his many officials [to do so], directing [everyone] not to go back on the agreement, to faithfully [adhere to it], to respectfully [act] in accord with the *shanyu*'s [agreement] document. My envoy states that the *shanyu* himself led attacks against states [hostile to the Han] and was successful, and is deeply pained by military affairs [and thus would be reluctant to take them up against the Han].

漢與匈奴約為兄弟，所以遺單于甚厚。倍約離兄弟之親者，常在匈奴。然右賢王事已在赦前，單于勿深誅。單于若稱書意，明告諸吏，使無負約，有信，敬如單于書。使者言單于自將伐國有功，甚苦兵事。[56]

At the end of his missive, Emperor Wen lists various gifts his intermediaries are to present to the *shanyu*, in accord with the "meaning" of the station of the *zhongdafu* 中大夫, to which, in the emperor's eyes, the *shanyu* belongs. Thus the list of gifts themselves are symbolic insults, gifts for a station far below that of a formidable leader.

   This exchange distorts, makes mockery of a more respectful diplomacy. Within the exchange there is little mutual feeling or understanding, the alienated distance expressed pointedly through the ease in which negotiations were abrogated, with only the pretense of ritual civility on display. Indeed, the emperor's ignoring the *shanyu*'s (possibly sarcastic) use of traditional religio-moral references in his response clearly denies the assertion of any ritual connection, whether genuine or not, by the *shanyu*. The disingenuously offered list of gifts, a common feature in ritualized negotiations, similarly signaled such a denial. The assertion or denial of ritual norms is a sign for or against the acceptance of diplomatic parity. For the Xiongnu side, when Han diplomats did not accede to Xiongnu diplomatic norms, such as tattooing his face with ink (the tattooing of the face in the Chinese realm being the mark of a criminal and thus starkly transgressive), the envoy would not be allowed to enter the Xiongnu yurts and treated with diplomatic parity.[57] Each side attempts, through barbed remarks and gestures, to reduce the other's claims to sovereign action and status, to treat the other as foreign, unworthy of ritual propriety. On the Chinese side, this informs the sense of the wilds, the areas of the strange and the monstrous.

The Alien

Among the earliest passages about the perils of venturing into the wilds, the world beyond civilized space, is that in the *Zuozhuan* about the casting of depictions of various beings into the nine bronze tripods:

[56] *SJ* 110.2897.   [57] *SJ* 50.2913.

In the past, just when Xia possessed virtue, men from afar depicted [or "mapped"?] various creatures, and the nine superintendents submitted metal, so that cauldrons were cast with images of various creatures. The hundred things[58] were therewith completely set forth, and the people thus knew the spirits and the evil things. That was why when the people entered rivers, marshes, mountains, and forests, they would not meet what could harm them, and the sprites of the hills [i.e., trees and rocks][59] and waters could not get at them. Thus, they were able to harmonize with those above and below them and to receive Heaven's blessings.[60]

昔夏之方有德也，遠方圖物，貢金九牧，鑄鼎象物，百物而為之備，使民知神姦，故民入川澤山林，不逢不若，螭魅罔兩，莫能逢之，用能協于上下，以承天休。

The attribution to the Xia fits with the common flood narratives regarding Yu's labors to distinguish the human from the animal world.[61] In these diagrammatic definitions, Yu's labels not only distinguish but also demonize, casting the world of the spirits, of sprites and other "evil things," as perils to be avoided. Concomitantly, the bronze tripods themselves, as avatars of the civilized world, stand stalwartly and stolidly against the unknown multifariousness of the natural world – the world in which monsters roam untrammeled – as patriarchal, monarchial protectors of the basis of sovereign power, the common people. Robert F. Campany argues that the many strange, "evil" things are represented on the cauldrons "to neutralize their danger, allowing safe passage for 'civilizers' from the center and thus securing Heaven's favor for the people of these liminal zones."[62] From the identifying and locating of strange beings we can see where boundaries are uncertain: "the presence of monsters not only marks boundaries, but also indicates where lines or demarcation are problematic, with weird hybrid bodies the signs of

---

[58] Robert F. Campany notes that the traditional interpretation of the "many things," propounded by the likes of Du Yu 杜預 (222–284 CE) and Wang Chong 王充 (27–100 CE), is that they are strange; Campany, *Strange Writing*, 103n3. Certainly this accords with several references to this passage in the *Lüshi chunqiu*, such as those in the "Xianshi lan pian" 先識覽篇 and the "Shiwei pian" 適威篇. *Lüshi chunqiu jishi*, 2:398, 532; *Annals of Lü Buwei*, 376, 496.

[59] Donald J. Harper, "A Chinese Demonography of the Third Century BC," *Harvard Journal of Asiatic Studies* 45, no. 2 (1985), 481. *Wangliang* is a tree and rock sprite.

[60] *Zuozhuan*, Xuan 3; *Zuo Tradition (Zuozhuan)*, 1:600–603; Yang Bojun, *Chunqiu zuozhuan zhu*, 2:669–671.

[61] Yu is explicitly named as their creator in the *Shuowen*'s entry for the character, *ding* 鼎: 昔禹收九牧之金，鑄鼎荊山之下，入山林川澤者，螭魅蝄蜽，莫能逢之，以協承天休。
Xu Shen, *Shuowen jiezi zhu*, 319a. For Lewis's observations about these labors, see Mark Edward Lewis, *The Flood Myths of Early China* (Albany: State University of New York Press, 2006), 71.

[62] Campany, *Strange Writing*, 104.

a breech or a crossing, or of some other uncommon connection between worlds."[63]

Clearly, as evident in the designs of excavated Shang and Zhou bronzes, which often include depictions of natural and "strange" beings, there is a connection to and concern with the natural world, a connection that perhaps suggests a concern with managing or controlling its powers. However, nowhere in early Chinese texts mentioning the nine bronze tripods is there any insinuation that the common people are wanting or needing broad, apotropaic protection from central powers in defense against the natural world, that they are frightened of or imperiled by it, and covetous of their leaders' protection. Just as likely, the dangers are fabricated, or the fictions reinforced, to dissuade commoners from straying too far from the civilized, settled areas, and their economic duties to these areas. This connection between natural forces and the strange is also demonstrated in sacrifices and portents. In the *Liji* essay, "The Method of Sacrifices," natural places – mountains, forests, streams, valleys, hills, and mounds – at which one might perform sacrifices, would manifest their powers in the production of climatic events, such as clouds, wind, and rain, but also in the appearance of "strange things," *guaiwu* 怪物. As mentioned previously, only to those natural powers *within their realms* were the many lords to perform sacrifices.[64]

The *Zuozhuan* passage I just cited spatializes the notion of *de*, identifying it with the area of sanctioned sovereign control. By passing beyond the frontiers, the traveler, or exile, was penetrating into the fearsome unknown, into the "disordered" (*luan*) "wilds" (*ye* 野). The wilds are where the monarch attempts to broaden his influence, through sacrifices and enforced cultural integration.[65] Those areas that are defined as wild are those that to some extent remain imperfectly attached or integrated. The farther away from the "central" regions, the more unpredictable, uncertain, and unstable. This sentiment is captured most picturesquely and frighteningly in those texts portraying mysterious, monstrous phenomena, including spiritual phenomena. Until the spirits themselves were included ritually by official processes into the central order, they remained dangerous and malevolent *toward* that order.

---

[63] Karin Myhre, "Monsters Lift the Veil: Chinese Animal Hybrids and Processes of Transformation," in *The Ashgate Research Companion to Monsters and the Monstrous*, ed. Asa Simon Mittman and Peter Dendle (Burlington, VT: Ashgate, 2012), 222.

[64] *Liji jijie*, 3:1194–1196.

[65] For a recent analysis of the integration of southern non-Chinese peoples in the early Han dynasty, see Alexis Lycas, "Représenter l'espace dans les textes du haut moyen âge chinois: Géographie politique, humaine et culturelle de la région du Jingzhou" (PhD diss., École Pratique des Hautes Études, Paris, 2015).

The most conspicuous example texts of monstrosities would be those detailing the strange and unnatural, whether the *Shanhaijing* or chapters from a large number of other books, such as the *Lunheng* 論衡, *Fengsu tongyi*, or *Baopuzi* 抱朴子.[66] But there also exist any number of passages from a host of texts – historical, philosophical, and literary – that speak of animalia in terms that suggest the references are actually, or associationally, to "bestial" human cultures, the most widely referenced being the analogizing of Qin with predatory animals.[67] Conversion into or being affected by "bestial," uncivilized peoples was to be converted into the unrecognizable, the monstrous, the fearsome. Such was the risk for the envoys and other representatives of the state, military or not, who passed over into the "beyond," the distant wilds, just as would possession or being affected by unknown or unintegrated spirits. Being possessed or simply affected by the beyond, as both spirit mediums and earthly diplomats were, was to become in a sense strange and monstrous. Possession by external powers was not just a loss of the representative but was the possibility of bringing the infection of chaos, both literally and figuratively, into the state.

Across cultures, the wild power of nature, of feral creation, and the monstrous are intimately intertwined. The roots of misogyny, particularly of the male fear of female fecundity and thus her sexual attractions, pass through much of world literature. As with other wildnesses – disease, foreign cultures – the female symbolizes a savagery that can contaminate and destroy the order prepared and cultivated by patriarchies. According to C. R. Whittaker, in relation to ancient Greece and Rome, "The boundary was a magico-religious line between the sacred and the profane, between the outside and the inside, and it was often signaled by sexual landmarks, such as the phallus, Hermes or Priapus. Such symbols possessed power to mediate the act of crossing the threshold, but also to penetrate or pierce the feminized, often dangerous unknown."[68] Many Greek monstrosities – harpies, gorgons, medusas – are either described as female or have aspects that are symbolically associated with female

---

[66] For a sampling list of texts on anomalous occurrences, see Campany, *Strange Writing*, 32–99.

[67] Myhre observes this associational phenomenon in her discussion of the generations of commentaries attempting to identify the referent of *yu* 蜮: "The identification of the word *yu* as a place, a people, a creature, *and* a food recalls images of the shifting and illusionistic *taotie* as well as presaging critical thinking about 'others': those beings definitively distinct which simultaneously express most perfectly the essential nature or values of the group from which they are circumscribed." Myhre, "Monsters Lift the Veil," 223. Similar associational identifications were made between humans and animals in Warring States and Han writings, "according to natural criteria such as geography, climate, and biotype." Sterckx, *The Animal and the Daemon in Early China*, 93.

[68] Whittaker, *Rome and Its Frontiers*, 127.

physicality. For instance, according to Debbie Felton, in early Mediterranean societies, serpents are associated with chthonic forces, Greek harpies ooze fluids in ways that suggest menstruation, and medusas have serpentine hair and lower bodies, and freeze their male combatants by their (gendered) gaze.[69] But it is also the case that Greek monsters are often representing or are located in wild areas, not infrequently near mountains and rivers.[70] Similarly, in early China, as Mark Lewis points out, mountains were the "homes and the topographic equivalents for the hybrid creatures who blended elements of the human and the unearthly, and who moved as omens and messengers between the world of spirits and that of men."[71] It is no coincidence that the taming of waters and appropriation of the products and spiritual powers of mountains is a repeated theme in the civilizing of the world by male sages, whether Moses, Jesus of Nazareth (whose walking on water and pacifying winds and waters demonstrates his control over these natural powers), or the Chinese sage-king Yu.

The conquering or subjection of wild forces, whether in prehistory or history, in nature, of female forces, or of "bestial" peoples, is represented as a triumph of civilization. Indeed, as Lewis observes, the very founders of civilization "appear as progenitors of the most distant peoples ... and as actors at the remote periphery."[72] One of the four reasons Lewis cites for the sages' appearance as such is their aim to separate humans from animals. In primordial time, humans lived in common with animals, physically and morally intertwined. The Chinese sages "created the tools and introduced the moral and ritual practices that rescued people from their animal condition and created distinctions where none had existed before."[73] Non-Chinese peoples, from the enforced central perspective, can be defined by their closer association with animality, with the wearing of animal skins, furs, and feathers, with their animal morals and practices, and their animistic religions.

To reiterate, occasionally when early texts speak of animals, it is not certain whether they are literally speaking about nonhuman animals, or more figuratively about those peoples who are perceived as being

---

[69] In a footnote, C. R. Whittaker refers to A. McClintock's list of how many gendered boundary phenomena there are: sirens, mermaids, female ship figureheads, etc. See Whittaker, *Rome and Its Frontiers*, 140n50. McClintock states: "the feminizing of terra incognita was, from the outset, a strategy of violent containment." McClintock, *Imperial Leather*, 24.

[70] Felton, "Rejecting and Embracing the Monstrous in Ancient Greece and Rome," 105.

[71] Mark E. Lewis, "The Feng and Shan Sacrifices of Emperor Wu of Han," in *State and Court Ritual in China*, ed. Joseph P. McDermott (New York: Cambridge University Press, 1999), 56.

[72] Lewis, *Flood Myths of Early China*, 70.   [73] Lewis, *Flood Myths of Early China*, 71.

animalistic or bestial.[74] In the three instances in which the term, *qinshou* 禽獸, appears in the *Zuozhuan*, it is employed analogously, for the "bestial" non-Chinese people who are not sufficiently civilized. In the first instance, in the chapter for Duke Xiang's 襄公 third year, the Rong are simply defined as "animals," or, more precisely, animals of feather and fur (*Rong qinshou ye* 戎禽獸也). The second and third, in the entries for Duke Xiang's twenty-first and twenty-eighth year, insult various people by comparing them to animals, the speakers declaring that they would eat them and sleep on their skins.[75] One might argue this is only analogy, but in other texts, the analogy seems to suggest that there are peoples who are in the same class as animals, so far removed from what is civilized that they can be categorized simply as animals of "feather and fur." Indeed, the defining feature of most animals in texts such as the *Mengzi* and the *Xunzi* is their lack of civilizing, ritual habits.

If this is broadly the case, then the distinction is not only of species but of civilized versus noncivilized, of those close, integrated, settled peoples who are under the influence of Chinese ritual culture and those distant, non-Chinese peoples who are not. This distinction is the definitional constant both in classicist, "Confucian" literature and in Daoist literature. To have a heart of a beast is just identifiable with not having the requisite ritual and social habits to be considered fully "human." But beasts can be redeemed and educated, as Roel Sterckx explains.[76] Are we to believe that this education was meant literally, or simply, for animals, or also, and more especially, for those who are analogous with animals, those who are not sufficiently enculturated? I would suggest that the

---

[74] Indeed, Lewis mentions, "As noted in Roel Sterckx's discussion of the early Chinese discourse on animals, local custom and animal character formed a single complex tied to their places of origin. The extreme form of this discourse was accounts of barbarians in distant lands who took on the attributes of the animals with whom they lived." Lewis, *Construction of Space in Early China*, 235. Sterckx writes, "Numerous sources portray barbarians who shared the habitats of the exotic bestiaries in the periphery of the Chinese cultural epicenter as having the inner disposition of animals. The bodily function and behavioral features of foreign tribes and exogenous peoples were said to have undesirable animal associations. Their temperaments and desires were equated with those of animals." Sterckx, *The Animal and the Daemon in Early China*, 159. Additional support for the identification of the barbarian Other with animals can be found in Roderick Campbell's *Violence, Kinship, and the Early Chinese State*, when he argues that the word *qiang* 羌 in Shang sacrificial inscriptions, instantiates "a process of 'pseudo speciation' rendering captives available for ancestral consumption along with cattle, sheep, pigs and dogs." See Roderick Campbell, *Violence, Kinship and the Early Chinese State* (New York: Cambridge University Press, 2018), 206–210. I am grateful to an anonymous reader for recommending this source.

[75] Xiang 21: 「臣為隸新，然二子者，譬於禽獸，臣食其肉而寢處其皮矣。」 Xiang 28: 盧蒲嫳曰: 「譬之如禽獸，吾寢處之矣。」 Yang Bojun, *Chunqiu zuozhuan zhu*, 3:1063–1064, 1146.

[76] Sterckx, *The Animal and the Daemon in Early China*, 137–147.

insufficiently civilized peoples are perhaps the truer referent of these attempts at enculturation, and thus of the "civilizing," normalizing aspirations of the Chinese court, pursued through their diplomatic representatives.

Chapter Summary

Diplomacy is an essentially transgressive activity, inhering the potential to subvert state interests in its very rhetorical phrasing of affairs. Ritual codes, or their intentional absence, played a vital role in these exchanges. Like the transgressions of spirit invocators, state ambassadorial transgressions across boundaries were religious, with secular administrative effects. This might in part explain the widespread regulations pertaining to diplomatic activities. Indeed, the very movement of the ambassador beyond the sanctified state space, without its protections, was perilous. Nonstate territory was equated with the criminal, the socially dead, the monstrous. Overcoming the "bestial" peoples of such "criminal," "monstrous" external realms was perceived as a triumph of civilization. Received guests (*bin*) from these areas were naturally affected by entailed condescensions. Rhetorical jostlings about ritual obligations between rulers, prominent in the exchange between Emperor Wen of Han and the Xiongnu *shanyu*, were intentionally meant to have an effect on the soft sovereign power of the interlocutor.

Conclusion

Charles S. Maier, in his *Once Within Borders*, has distinguished empires from states in how carefully state boundaries are delineated, and how stable their frontier areas are: More "cohesive" than the space of empires, the state space "aspires to frontiers stabilized by treaty – often as well by the so-called natural barriers of rivers and mountains – and to a more direct, uniform, and pervasive administration at home." Empires, by contrast, "have tolerated enclaves of local autonomy and relatively loose frameworks for adherence of tributary communities." The Russian tsars and Ottomans, for instance, "developed ideas of a coherent territory only relatively late and thought primarily in terms of tribal overlordship."[1] Though Maier does not immediately elaborate on exactly what lends a state greater "coherence," in a footnote, he cites Weber's celebrated definition of the state as that which claims a monopoly of legitimate physical power. But, as he later admits, "there is no simple progression from zonal borderland to delineated frontier, nor from authority over groups to territorial sovereignty: the two forms of boundary can coexist."[2]

Upon this admission, any firm distinction between empire and state appears to evaporate. Pre-totalitarian states absent rigidly surveyed and patrolled borders become as loose a formation as Maier defines empire. Particularly in pre-totalitarian formations, local autonomy, of whatever degree, remains a recalcitrant feature of most (if not all) states, particularly those locales that lie physically far from nodes of central authority. But even in totalitarian formations, with the state's power promising unmediated and complete application, the inherent variations in its local administration inevitably result in inconsistencies. Power formations thus, even in totalitarian state apparatuses, as yet do not sustain even application forever.

Over the course of this current investigation, I have contended that the state's power in ancient China functions less evenly than the majority of

---

[1] Maier, *Once Within Borders*, 15.   [2] Maier, *Once Within Borders*, 300–301n4.

previous studies have insisted, either explicitly or implicitly. The state's power, as illustrated by a presumption of a border, was neither fully hegemonic nor even fully assumed. There was never a total monopoly of legitimate physical power, particularly at the areas, especially in larger states, far from central government apparatuses. Instead, what existed, as Clifford Geertz observed as existing in Bali, was a medley, an overlapping, intertwining, sometimes conflicting hodgepodge of authorities. The most conspicuous physical demarcations of power, military barriers, were themselves not extensive with the political power of the state. Sometimes they extended beyond, sometimes within those political boundaries. Instead, political power in the early Chinese state was more aptly captured in zonal notions. These zones were based firmly both in ritual allegiance and in administrative oversight.

With ritual allegiances a definitive factor in boundary formation, penetration or crossing of these zones was marked by the danger of the abrogation of ritual bonds, and thus the abrogation of the state's ritual "coherence," the ritual allegiances that lent an internal coherence as well as connection with other ritually synonymous polities. It is this ritual synonymity, however imperfectly enforced, that provided, to borrow Benedict Anderson's now clichéd phrase, an "imagined community" across a Chinese empire of incredible diversity. It is these ritual allegiances, I have argued, more than any wall or other military barrier, that prompted a sense of state, of the state's threat of physical force.

If so, then threats to state sovereignty are as much, if not more, from diplomatic interactions as from military confrontations. The above observations and analyses about the power of diplomacy highlight the dangers to the sovereignty of the state of the adventures of the diplomat beyond the bounds of the state, bounds whose ritual force is symbolic of devotion to its cultural norms and political structures. In his very occupation, the diplomat is in the exceptional position to ignore and even undermine such norms and structures, whether through nefarious revelation and rhetorical reframing, or simply inept representation. The more stark the ritual divide, the more unable the parties to see each other as peers, the more "monstrous" the opposing side can appear to be, and the more perilous to one's state of contact. The "Chinese," however defined, were not alone in their diplomatic and sovereign vulnerabilities; their non-Chinese counterparts felt them as well.

It is in the diplomat's transgressive negotiations that one can view the liminal aspect of state sovereignty and the dangers of being even in contact with the foreign. Thus through analysis of diplomatic exchanges, we can perceive yet another definitional and also very much spatialized aspect of the parameters of political sovereignty, an aspect that can affect immediately the maintenance of past, and establishment of additional, areas of sovereignty. These diplomatic exchanges are not just with terrestrial others but with spiritual powers. Diplomacy's transgressive aspect generates an uncertain effect, the uncertainty of a multiplicity of outcomes. It is a discourse that intimately involves not only possible future action but ritualized systems of knowledge and their negotiations, producing movements of territorialization and de-territorialization, with realities being not "a matter of the absolute eyewitness, but a matter of the future."[3]

Extensions

To speak to this study's broader application, I have argued that walls, and military structures in general, should not necessarily be identified with the early Chinese state's discrete sovereign borders, an equation that continues to affect how Chinese state space is defined and discussed. Were such a contention plausible, scholars might need to reexamine their assumptions about the extent of the exercise of state power in the borderlands. But there are various additional analytical ramifications that proceed from the above findings, some of which I offer here.

First and foremost, scholars of early China need to resist the temptation to thoroughly secularize state power, to dismiss or reduce ritual or moral considerations to simply a dramatic artifice, cynically ignoring it as mere theater. This is not to say that ritual or moral concepts or exercises were not used cynically, as a superficial justificatory veneer for pragmatic needs, as they frequently can be. Whatever the genuineness of any subscription, ritual power was a force that had numerous real applications, with serious, deep administrative and legal effects. To some degree, I maintain, ritual prescriptions in early China, as in other ancient societies, had something akin to the force of law.

Relatedly, the application of state force, and its contestation, needs more fine-grained spatialized contextualization, which receives valuable input from archaeological work but which also needs more detailed, careful interpretive work done with received texts. Administrative regulation and military action did not in itself demonstrate the smooth, unruptured coverage of state power. Assertions in the classical texts of the universal reach of the monarch's power were rhetorical displays, more aspirational than actual. In the borderlands, the cultural and ethnic distinctions between local peoples, and thus the distinctions on the

---

[3] Jean-François Lyotard, *The Differend: Phrases in Dispute* (Minneapolis: University of Minnesota Press, 1988), 53.

grander scale between the state-reinforced self and the nonstate other, were not mutually opposed but maintained artificially. These state versus nonstate identificatory artifices themselves were pliant, and sometimes overlooked or ignored. In short, we need to have a greater spatialization of the self and a greater awareness of the limitations of any state-sponsored artifices related to an assertion of a common identity – ethnic, cultural, ritual, or otherwise.

Graphic reflections of state power, pictorial or textually described, therefore need to be analyzed in terms of action and ritual significance as much as, if not more than, any surveyed measurement, for a comprehension of their true expression of state power and its contestations. We would be well advised to discontinue the insistence of the simply linear, clearly defined divisions between state and nonstate, "Chinese" and other, across the graphically described space. Lines, as with walls, themselves only gestured toward boundaries; they were not the exact definition of boundaries. Thus, the lines on the map are something of a distortion. No map is truly lived or experienced as represented; they cannot be viewed as the exact graphic representations of travel reports. Some facts of lived experience on the map are rendered somewhat visible while others are not. Early Chinese maps should most fundamentally be treated as the graphic representation of *possibilities for action*. Thus scholars would be well advised to focus on vectors of action and perception, and the aims behind these vectors, before they may fully comprehend why certain features of the terrain are mentioned. Were such to be considered properly, in an analysis of maps, we must consider whether various geographic features were falsely inserted or inserted for largely symbolic or prescriptive ends, especially when the actions or intentions informing the map's composition were in tension or in conflict. In other words, we may need to ask if certain geographic features were a part of something akin to a ritual or symbolic "thought-scape."

Finally, most broadly, there needs to be a much greater acknowledgment of the role of the local in the situation and application of the state superstructure, not simply from analyses of the local administrative documents but from analyses of state responses to local concerns. Herein, however, lies an obstruction: it seems that microstructures were intentionally made invisible (including spiritualist microstructures) in the insistence on an imagined seamless macrostructure. In accord with an almost universalizable pattern, the early Chinese state attempted to eviscerate, to efface or mute local structures. A truer sense of place comes into view not only in local activities and music but also in the administrative responses (whether legal or even those bound up in naming) that the state superstructure employed to eradicate the "corruptions" to the sense of efficient state power at the microlevel. All of this recommends a greater appreciation for active definitions – changeable, lived, and thus more difficult to define carefully over time – rather than static definitional regimes.

Bibliography

Primary Chinese Sources

Baihutong shuzheng 白虎通疏證. Beijing: Zhonghua shuju, 1994.

Ban Gu 班固. *Hanshu* 漢書. Beijing: Zhonghua shuju, 1962.

Cai Yong 蔡邕. *Duduan* 獨斷. In *Sibu congkan* 四部叢刊, 子部, 卷上, 9.

Chen Shou 陳壽. *Sanguozhi* 三國志. Beijing: Zhonghua shuju, 1982.

Chunqiu gongyangzhuan zhushu 春秋公羊傳注疏. Beijing: Beijing daxue chu-banshe, 1999.

Fan Ye 汜曄. *Houhanshu* 後漢書. Beijing: Zhonghua shuju, 1965.

Fang Xuanling, et al. 房玄齡等. *Jinshu* 晉書. Beijing: Zhonghua shuju, 1974.

Guanzi jiaozhu 管子校注. Compiled by Li Xiangfeng 黎翔鳳. 2 vols. Beijing: Zhonghua shuju, 2004.

Han Ying 韓嬰. *Han shi wai zhuan ji shi* 韓詩外傳集釋. Beijing: Zhonghua shuju, 2009.

Hanfeizi jijie 韓非子集解. Beijing: Zhonghua shuju, 1998.

Hanshi waizhuan 韓詩外傳. Beijing: Zhonghua shuju, 2009.

He Jianzhang 何建章, ed. *Zhanguoce zhushi* 戰國策注釋. 3 vols. Beijing: Zhonghua shuju, 1990.

Jia Yi 賈誼. *Xinshu jiaozhu* 新書校注. Beijing: Zhonghua shuju, 2000.

Liang Han ji 兩漢紀. Beijing: Zhonghua shuju, 2002.

Li Bujia 李步嘉, ed. *Yuejueshu jiaoshi* 越絕書校釋. Beijing: Zhonghua shuju, 2013.

Li Fang 李昉. *Taiping yulan* 太平御覽. Beijing: Zhonghua shuju, 1960.

Liji jijie 禮記集解. 3 vols. Beijing: Zhonghua shuju, 2010.

Li Xueqin 李学勤, ed. *Qinghua daxue cang zhanguo zhujian* 清华大学藏战国竹简. Shanghai: Shanghai zhongxi, 2010.

——— ed. *Shangshu zhengyi* 尚書正義. Beijing: Beijing daxue chubanshe, 1999.

Liu An 劉安. *Huainanzi jishi* 淮南子集釋. 2 vols. Beijing: Zhonghua shuju, 1998.

Liu Xiang 劉向. *Zhanguoce jianzheng* 戰國策箋證. 2 vols. Shanghai: Shanghai guji chubanshe, 2008.

Liye Qin jian 里耶秦簡. Beijing: Wenwu chubanshe, 2012.

Lunyu jijie 論語集解. 3 vols. Beijing: Zhonghua shuju, 2010.

Lüshi chunqiu jishi 呂氏春秋集釋. 2 vols. Beijing: Zhonghua shuju, 2011.

Maoshi zhengyi 毛詩正義. Beijing: Beijing daxue chubanshe, 1999.

Mengzi zhengyi 孟子正義. 2 vols. Beijing: Zhonghua shuju, 2009.

Mo Di 墨翟. *Mozi xiangu* 墨子閒詁. Beijing: Zhonghua shuju, 2001.

"Rongchengshi 容成氏." In *Shanghai bowuguan cang Zhanguo Chu zhushu* 上海博物館藏戰國楚竹書, edited by Ma Chengyuan 馬承源, 249–293. Shanghai: Shanghai guji chubanshe, 2001.

Shangjunshu zhuizhi 商君書錐指. Beijing: Zhonghua shuju, 1986.

Shanhaijing 山海经. Translated by Fang Tao 方韜. Beijing: Zhonghua shuju, 2011.

Shenzi jijiao jizhu 慎子集校集注. Beijing: Zhonghua shuju, 2013.

Shuihudi Qinmu zhujian 睡虎地秦墓竹簡. Beijing: Wenwu chubanshe, 1978.

Shuoyuan jiao zheng 說苑校證. Beijing: Zhonghua shuju, 1987.

Sima Qian 司馬遷. *Shiji* 史記. Beijing: Zhonghua shuju, 1959.

Song ben li dai di li zhi zhang tu 宋本歷代地理指掌圖. Shanghai: Shanghai guji chubanshe, 1989.

Song shi 宋史. Beijing: Zhonghua shuju, 2007.

Sunzi yizhu 孫子译注. Shanghai: Shanghai guji chubanshe, 1984.

Tanglü shuyi 唐律疏議. Nanjing: Nanjing shifan daxue chubanshe, 2007.

Wang Chong 王充. *Lunheng jiaojian* 論衡校箋. 2 vols. Shijiazhuang: Hebei jiaoyu chubanshe, 1999.

Wang Fu 王符. *Qianfulun jianjiao zheng* 潛夫論箋校正. Beijing: Zhonghua shuju, 1985.

Wang Xianqian 王先謙, ed. *Hanshu buzhu* 漢書補注. Beijing: Shumu wenxian chubanshe, 1995.

    ed. *Xunzi jijie* 荀子集解. 2 vols. Beijing: Zhonghua shuju, 1997.

Wei Zheng 魏徵. *Suishu* 隋書. Beijing: Zhonghua shuju, 1973

Xu Shen 許慎. *Shuowen jiezi zhu* 說文解字注. Shanghai: Shanghai guji chubanshe, 1988.

Xun Yue 荀悅. *Han ji* 漢紀. Beijing: Zhonghua shuju, 2002.

Yang Bojun 楊伯峻, ed. *Chunqiu zuozhuan zhu* 春秋左傳注. 4 vols. Beijing: Zhonghua shuju, 1981.

Yanzi chunqiu zhujie 晏子春秋注解. Jinan: Qi Lu shushe, 2009.

Yili zhushu 儀禮注疏. Beijing: Beijing daxue chubanshe, 1999.

Ying Shao 應劭. *Fengsu tongyi jiaozhu* 風俗通義校注. Taipei: Hanjing wenhua shiye, 2003.

Yinque shan Han mu zhu jian 銀雀山漢墓竹簡. Beijing: Wenwu chubanshe, 1985.

Zhang Cang 張蒼 (漢). *Jiuzhang suanshu* 九章算數. Chongqing: Chongqing daxue chubanshe, 2006.

Zhouyi zhengyi 周易正義. *Shisanjing zhushu* 十三經注疏. Beijing: Beijing daxue chubanshe, 1999.

Zhouli zhushu 周禮注疏. 2 vols. Beijing: Beijing daxue chubanshe, 1999.

Zhouli zhushu 周禮注疏. Shanghai: Shanghai guji chubanshe, 2011.

Zhuangzi zhushu 庄子注疏. Beijing: Zhonghua shuju, 2011.

Secondary Sources in Chinese

Cang Xiuliang 倉修良, ed. *Hanshu cidian* 漢書辭典. Shandong: Shandong jiaoyu chubanshe, 1996.

Cao Wanru 曹婉如. *Zhongguo gudai ditu ji: Zhanguo – Yuan* 中國古代地圖集, 戰國—元 (An Atlas of Ancient Maps in China: From the Warring States to the Yuan Dynasty 476 B.C.–A.D. 1368). Beijing: Wenwu chubanshe, 1990.

Hao Shusheng 郝樹聲 and Zhang Defang 張德芳. *Xuanquan Hanjian yanjiu* 懸泉漢簡研究. Lanzhou: Gansu wenhua chubanshe, 2009.

Hsing I-tien 邢義田. "Cong chutu ziliao kan Qin–Han juluo xingtai he xiangli xingzheng" 從出土資料看秦漢聚落形態和鄉里行政 [Examining Qin and Han settlement patterns and adminstration of the xiang and li using archaeological materials]. In *Zhiguo anbang* 治國安邦, 249–355. Beijing: Zhonghua shuju, 2011.

"Cong gudai tianxia guankan Qin–Han changcheng de xiangzheng yiyi" 從古代天下觀看秦漢長城的象徵意義. In *Tianxia yijia* 天下一家, 84–135. Beijing: Zhonghua shuju, 2011.

"Zhongguo huangdi zhidu de jianli yu fazhan" 中國皇帝制度的建立与發展. In *Tianxia yijia* 天下一家, 1–49. Beijing: Zhonghua shuju, 2011.

Li Xueqin 李學勤. "Xi Zhou jinwen zhong de tudi zhuanrang 西周金文中的土地转让." In *Xin chu qingtongqi yanjiu* 新出青铜器研究, 106–109. Beijing: Wenwu chubanshe, 1990.

Na Zhiliang 那志良. *Liangjian zhuming de guobao* 兩件著名的國寶. Taipei: Guangwen shuju, 1964.

Sun Zhongming 孫仲明. "Zhanguo Zhongshan wangmu Zhaoyutu ji qi biaoshi fangfa de yanjiu" 戰國中山王墓兆域圖及其表示方法的研究. In *Zhongguo gudai ditu ji: Zhanguo – Yuan* 中國古代地图集：战国—元 *(An Atlas of Ancient Maps in China: From the Warring States to the Yuan Dynasty 476 B. C.– A.D. 1368)*, edited by Cao Wanru 曹婉如, 1–3. Beijing: Wenwu chubanshe, 1990.

Tan Qixiang 谭其骧, ed. *Zhongguo lishi ditu ji* 中國歷史地圖集. Beijing: Zhongguo ditu chubanshe chuban, 1982.

Wan Fang 万方. "Zhongguo gudi tu – Fangmatan yihao Qinmu" 中国故地图–放馬灘一号秦墓出土地图. *Shuwu* 书屋 (2006).

Wang Jing 王晶. "Sanshipan mingwen jishi ji Xi Zhou shiqi tudi peichang anjian shenli chengdu kuitan" 散氏盘铭文集释及西周时期土地赔偿案件审理程度窥探. *Changchun gongye daxue xuebao* 長春工业大学学报 24, no. 1 (2012): 47–53.

Yang Shuda 楊樹達. *Ji wei ju jin wen shuo* 積微居金文說. Beijing: Kexue chubanshe, 1959.

Yang Xinhe 杨新河. "Zhongguo faxian shijie zuizao de ditu" 中国发现世界最早的地图. *Keji chao* 科技潮 1 (1998): 5.

Zhang Guiguang 張桂光, ed. *Shang Zhou jinwen moshi zongji* 商周金文摹釋總集. 2 vols. Beijing: Zhonghua shuju, 2010.

Sources in English and Other Languages

Aineias the Tactician. *How to Survive Under Siege*. Translated by David Whitehead. New York: Oxford University Press, 1990.

Albu, Emily. "Imperial Geography and the Medieval Peutinger Map." *Imago Mundi* 57, no. 2 (2005): 136–148.

Alconini, Sonia. "The Dynamics of Military and Cultural Frontiers on the Southeastern Edge of the Inka Empire." In *Untaming the Frontier in*

Anthropology, Archaeology, and History, edited by Bradley J. Parker and Lars Rodseth, 115–146. Tucson: University of Arizona Press, 2005.

Allan, Sarah. *Buried Ideas: Legends of Abdication and Ideal Government in Early Chinese Bamboo-Slip Manuscripts.* Albany: State University of New York Press, 2015.

Allen, Danielle. *Why Plato Wrote.* Chichester, UK: Wiley-Blackwell, 2013.

The World of Prometheus: The Politics of Punishing in Democratic Athens. Princeton, NJ: Princeton University Press, 2000.

Alpers, Svetlana. *The Art of Describing: Dutch Art in the Seventeenth Century.* Chicago: University of Chicago Press, 1983.

Ames, Roger. *Sun-Tzu: The Art of Warfare.* New York: Ballantine Books, 1993.

The Analects of Confucius: A Philosophical Translation. Translated by Roger T. Ames and Henry Rosemont Jr. New York: Ballantine Books, 1998.

Anderson, Benedict. *Imagined Communities.* London: Verso, 1991.

Ando, Clifford. *Imperial Ideology and Provincial Loyalty in the Roman Empire.* Berkeley: University of California Press, 2000.

Annals of Lü Buwei. Translated by Jeffrey Riegel and John Knoblock. Stanford, CA: Stanford University Press, 2000.

Baines, John. "Civilizations and Empires: A Perspective on Erligang from Early Egypt." In *Art and Archaeology of the Erligang Civilization,* edited by Kyle Steinke, 99–119. Princeton, NJ: Princeton University Press, 2014.

Barbieri-Low, Anthony J., and Robin D. S. Yates. *Law, State and Society in Early Imperial China: A Study with Critical Edition and Translation of the Legal Texts from Zhangjiashan Tomb no. 247.* Leiden: Brill, 2015.

Baudrillard, Jean. *Simulations.* Translated by Paul Foss, Paul Patton, and Philip Beitchman. New York: Semiotext(e), 1983.

Behr, Wolfgang. "Placed into the Right Position: Etymological Notes on '*tú*' and Congeners." In *Graphics and Text in the Production of Technical Knowledge in China,* edited by Francesca Bray, Vera Dorofeeva-Lichtmann, and Georges Métailié, 109–134. Leiden: Brill, 2007.

Berridge, G. R., ed. *Diplomatic Classics: Selected Texts from Commynes to Vattel.* New York: Palgrave Macmillan, 2004.

Bertin, Jacques. *Semiology of Graphics.* Translated by William J. Berg. Madison: University of Wisconsin Press, 1983.

Bielenstein, Hans. "Notes on the *Shuijing.*" *Bulletin of the Museum of Far Eastern Antiquities* 65 (1993): 257–283.

Boileau, Gilles. *Politique et rituel dans la Chine ancienne.* Paris: Institut des hautes études chinoises, 2013.

The Book of Lord Shang. Translated by J. J. L. Duyvendak. London: A. Probsthain, 1928.

Brindley, Erica. *Ancient China and the Yue.* New York: Cambridge University Press, 2015.

Calanca, Paola, and François Wildt. "Les frontières: Quelques termes-clés." *Extrême-Orient-Extrême-Occident* 28 (2006): 17–56.

Campany, Robert. *Strange Writing: Anomaly Accounts in Early Medieval China.* Albany: State University of New York Press, 1996.

Campbell, Roderick. *Violence, Kinship and the Early Chinese State*. New York: Cambridge University Press, 2018.

Cao Wei, Yuanqing Liu, Katheryn M. Linduff, and Yan Sun. "The Rise of States and the Formation of Group Identities in the Western Regions of the Inner Asian Frontier (c. 1500 to the Eighth Century BCE)." In *Ancient China and Its Eurasian Neighbors*, edited by Katheryn M. Linduff, Yan Sun, Wei Cao, and Yuanqing Liu, 146–214. New York: Cambridge University Press, 2018.

Chan-Kuo Ts'e. Translated by James I. Crump. New York: Oxford University Press, 1970.

Chavannes, Édouard. "Les deux plus anciens spécimens de la cartographie chinoise." *Bulletin de l'École française de l'Extrême-Orient* 3 (1903): 214–247.

Chin, Tamara. *Savage Exchange: Han Imperialism, Chinese Literary Style, and the Economic Imagination*. Cambridge, MA: Harvard University Asia Center, 2014.

The Chinese Classics: The She King. Translated by James Legge. Hong Kong: Hong Kong University Press, 1960.

Chuang-tzŭ: The Inner Chapters. Translated by A. C. Graham. Indianapolis, IN: Hackett Publishing, 2001.

The Classic of Mountains and Seas. Translated by Anne Birrell. London: Penguin Books, 1999.

Confucius Analects. Translated by Edward Slingerland. Indianapolis, IN: Hackett Publishing, 2003.

Corner, James. "The Agency of Mapping: Speculation, Critique and Invention." In *Mappings*, edited by Denis E. Cosgrove, 213–252. London: Reaktion Books, 1999.

Cosgrove, Denis. *Geography and Vision: Seeing, Imagining and Representing the World*. New York: I. B. Tauris, 2008.

De Certeau, Michel. "Practices of Space." In *On Signs*, edited by Marshall Blonsky, 122–145. Baltimore, MD: Johns Hopkins University Press, 1985.

De Weerdt, Hilde. "The Cultural Logics of Map Reading: Text, Time, and Space in the Printed Maps of the Song Empire." In *Knowledge and Text Production in an Age of Print: China, 900–1400*, edited by Lucille Chia and Hilde De Weerdt, 239–270. Leiden: Brill, 2011.

"Maps and Memory: Readings of Cartography in Twelfth- and Thirteenth-Century Song China." *Imago Mundi* 61, no. 2 (2009): 145–167.

Deleuze, Gilles, and Félix Guattari. *A Thousand Plateaus: Capitalism and Schizophrenia*. Minneapolis: University of Minnesota Press, 1987.

Di Cosmo, Nicola. *Ancient China and Its Enemies*. New York: Cambridge University Press, 2002.

Dorofeeva-Lichtmann, Vera V. "Conception of Terrestrial Organization in the *Shan hai jing*." *Bulletin de l'École française d'Extrême-Orient* 82 (1995): 57–110.

"Political Concept Behind an Interplay of Spatial 'Positions.'" *Extrême-Orient-Extrême-Occident* 18 (1996): 9–33.

"Ritual Practices for Constructing Terrestrial Space (Warring States–Early Han)." In *Early Chinese Religion, Part One: Shang Through Han (1250 BC–*

220 AD), edited by John Lagerway and Marc Kalinowski, 595–644. Leiden: Brill, 2009.

Evans, Michael. "The Geometry of the Mind." *Architectural Association Quarterly* 12 (1980): 32–55.

Felton, Debbie. "Rejecting and Embracing the Monstrous in Ancient Greece and Rome." In *The Ashgate Research Companion to Monsters and the Monstrous*, edited by Asa Simon Mittman and Peter Dendle, 103–131. Burlington, VT: Ashgate, 2012.

Feng, Linda Rui. "Negotiating Vertical Space, Vistas, and the Topographical Imagination." *T'ang Studies* 29 (2011): 27–44.

Foong, Ping. *The Efficacious Landscape: On the Authorities of Painting at the Northern Song Court*. Cambridge, MA: Harvard University Asia Center, 2015.

Foucault, Michel. *The Order of Things: An Archaeology of the Human Sciences*. New York: Pantheon Books, 1970.

"Questions on Geography." In *Power/Knowledge: Selected Interviews and Other Writings, 1972–1977*, edited by Colin Gordon, 63–77. New York: Pantheon Books, 1980.

Frankel, Hans. *The Flowering Plum and the Palace Lady: Interpretations of Chinese Poetry*. New Haven, CT: Yale University Press, 1976.

Galvany, Albert. "Signs, Clues, and Traces: Anticipation in Ancient Chinese Political and Military Texts." *Early China* (2015): 1–43.

Geertz, Clifford. *Negara: The Theatre State in Nineteenth-Century Bali*. Princeton, NJ: Princeton University Press, 1980.

Gentz, Joachim. "Long Live the King! The Ideology of Power Between Ritual and Morality in the *Gongyang zhuan*." In *Ideology of Power and Power of Ideology in Early China*, edited by Yuri Pines, Paul R. Goldin, and Martin Kern, 69–117. Leiden: Brill, 2015.

The Geography of Strabo. Translated by Horace Leonard Jones. Cambridge, MA: Harvard University Press, 1930.

Giddens, Anthony. *The Nation-State and Violence*, vol. 2 of *A Contemporary Critique of Historical Materialism*. Cambridge: Polity Press, 1985.

Giele, Enno. "Evidence for the Xiongnu in Chinese Wooden Documents from the Han Period." In *Xiongnu Archaeology: Multidisciplinary Perspectives of the First Steppe Empire in Inner Asia*, edited by Ursula Brosseder and Bryan Kristopher Miller, 49–75. Bonn: Friedrich-Wilhelms-Universität Bonn, 2011.

The Glory of Yue: An Annotated Translation of the Yuejue shu. Translated by Olivia Milburn. Leiden: Brill, 2010.

Goldin, Paul R. "Representations of Regional Diversity During the Eastern Zhou Dynasty." In *Ideology of Power and Power of Ideology in Early China*, edited by Yuri Pines, Paul R. Goldin, and Martin Kern, 31–48. Leiden: Brill, 2015.

Graham, A. C. *Later Mohist Logic, Ethics and Science*. Hong Kong: Chinese University of Hong Kong, 2003.

Guanzi. Translated by W. Allyn Rickett. Boston, MA: Cheng and Tsui, 2001.

Habberstad, Luke. "How and Why Do We Praise the Emperor? Debating and Depicting a Late Western Han Court Audience." *Journal of the Economic and Social History of the Orient* 60, no. 5 (2017): 683–714.

Hamilton, Keith, and Richard Langhorne. *The Practice of Diplomacy: Its Evolution, Theory and Administration*. New York: Routledge, 1995.

Harley, J. B., and David Woodward, eds. *The History of Cartography*, vol. 1, *Cartography in Prehistoric, Ancient, and Medieval Europe and the Mediterranean*. Chicago: University of Chicago Press, 1987.

Harper, Donald J. "A Chinese Demonography of the Third Century BC." *Harvard Journal of Asiatic Studies* 45, no. 2 (1985): 459–498.

"Communication by Design: Two Silk Manuscripts of Diagrams (*tu*) from Mawangdui Tomb Three." In *Graphics and Texts in the Production of Textual Knowledge in China: The Warp and the Weft*, edited by Francesca Bray and Vera Dorofeeva-Lichtmann. Leiden: Brill, 2007.

"The Han Cosmic Board (*Shih*)." *Early China* 4 (1978): 1–10.

Harrist, Robert, Jr. *Painting and Private Life in Eleventh-Century China: Mountain Villa by Li Gonglin*. Princeton, NJ: Princeton University Press, 1998.

Heller, Natasha. "Visualizing Pilgrimage and Mapping Experience: Mount Wutai on the Silk Road." In *The Journey of Maps and Images on the Silk Road*, edited by Phillipe Forêt and Andreas Kaplony, 29–50. Leiden: Brill, 2008.

Hsu, Hsin-mei Agnes, and Anne Martin-Montgomery. "An Emic Perspective on the Mapmaker's Art in Western Han China." *Journal of the Royal Asiatic Society* 17, no. 4 (2007): 443–457.

Hsu, Mei-Ling. "The Han Maps and Early Chinese Cartography." *Annals of the Association of American Geographers* 68, no. 1 (1978): 45–60.

"The Qin Maps: A Clue to Later Chinese Cartographic Development." *Imago Mundi* 45, no. 1 (1993): 90–100.

Hucker, Charles O. *A Dictionary of Official Titles in Imperial China*. Stanford, CA: Stanford University Press, 1985.

Irby-Massie, Georgia L., and Paul T. Keyser. *Greek Science of the Hellenistic Era*. New York: Routledge, 2002.

Jacob, Christian. "Mapping in the Mind." In *Mappings*, edited by Denis E. Cosgrove, 24–49. London: Reaktion Books, 1999.

The Sovereign Map: Theoretical Approaches to Cartography Throughout History. Translated by Tom Conley. Chicago: University of Chicago Press, 2006.

Jullien, François. *The Great Image Has No Form: On the Nonobject Through Painting*. Chicago: University of Chicago Press, 2003.

Karlgren, Bernhard. *Grammata Serica Recensa*. Stockholm: Museum of Far Eastern Antiquities, 1957.

Kern, Martin. "Early Chinese Divination and Its Rhetoric." In *Coping with the Future: Theories and Practices of Divination in East Asia*, edited by Michael Lackner, 255–288. Leiden: Brill, 2018.

"Language and the Ideology of Kingship in the 'Canon of Yao.'" In *Ideology of Power and Power of Ideology in Early China*, edited by Yuri Pines, Paul R. Goldin, and Martin Kern, 118–150. Leiden: Brill, 2015.

The Stele Inscriptions of Ch'in Shih-huang: Text and Ritual in Early Chinese Imperial Representation. New Haven, CT: American Oriental Society, 2000.

Kosmin, Paul J. *The Land of the Elephant Kings: Space, Territory, and Ideology in the Seleucid Empire*. Cambridge, MA: Harvard University Press, 2014.

Lackner, Michael. "Diagrams as an Architecture by Means of Words: The *Yanji tu*." In *Graphics and Text in the Production of Technical Knowledge in China*, edited by Francesca Bray, Vera Dorofeeva-Lichtmann, and Georges Métailié, 341–377. Leiden: Brill, 2007.

"Zur 'Verplanung' des Denkens am Beispiel der t'u." In *Lebenswelt und Weltanschauung im frühneuzeitlichen China*, edited by Helwig Schmidt-Glintzer, 133–157. Stuttgart: Steiner Verlag, 1990.

Lai, Guolong. "The Diagram of the Mourning System from Mawangdui." *Early China* 28 (2003): 43–99.

Lau, D. C., and Roger T. Ames. *Sun Pin: The Art of Warfare*. New York: Ballantine Books, 1996.

Leung, Vincent. *The Politics of the Past in Early China*. New York: Cambridge University Press, 2019.

Lewis, Mark E. *The Construction of Space in Early China*. Albany: State University of New York Press, 2006.

"The Feng and Shan Sacrifices of Emperor Wu of Han." In *State and Court Ritual in China*, edited by Joseph P. McDermott, 50–80. New York: Cambridge University Press, 1999.

The Flood Myths of Early China. Albany: State University of New York Press, 2006.

Writing and Authority in Early China. Albany: State University of New York Press, 1999.

Li Chi: Book of Rites. Translated by James Legge. 2 vols. New York: Oxford University Press, 1885.

Li, Feng. *Bureaucracy and the State in Early China: Governing the Western Zhou*. New York: Cambridge University Press, 2008.

Lin, Fan. "Cartographic Empire: Production and Circulation of Maps and Mapmaking Knowledge in the Song Dynasty (960–1279)." PhD diss., McGill University, 2014.

Liu, An. *The Huainanzi*. Translated by John S. Major, Sarah A. Queen, Andrew Seth Meyer, and Harold D. Roth. New York: Columbia University Press, 2010.

Luo, Xinhui. "Omens and Politics: The Zhou Concept of the Mandate of Heaven as Seen in the Chengwu 程寤 Manuscript." In *Ideology of Power and Power of Ideology in Early China*, edited by Yuri Pines, Paul R. Goldin, and Martin Kern, 49–68. Leiden: Brill, 2015.

Luo, Zewen, Wenbao Dai, Dick Wilson, Jean-Pierre Drège, Hubert Delahaye, and Emil Bührer. *The Great Wall*. New York: McGraw Hill, 1981.

Lycas, Alexis. "Réprésenter l'espace dans les textes du haut moyen âge chinois: Géographie politique, humaine et culturelle de la région du Jingzhou." PhD diss., École pratique des hautes études, 2015.

"The Southern Man People as a Political and Fiscal Problem in Han Times." *Monumenta Serica* 67, no. 1 (2019): 145–164.

Lyotard, Jean-François. *The Differend: Phrases in Dispute*. Minneapolis: University of Minnesota Press, 1988.

Maier, Charles S. *Once Within Borders: Territories of Power, Wealth, and Belonging since 1500*. Cambridge, MA: Harvard University Press, 2016.

Marsili, Filippo. *Heaven Is Empty: A Cross-Cultural Approach to "Religion" and Empire in Ancient China*. Albany: State University of New York Press, 2018.

Mathieu, Rémi. "Fonctions et moyens de la géographie dans la Chine ancienne." *Études Asiatiques: Revue de la Société Suisse d'Études Asiatiques* 36, no. 2 (1982): 125–152.

McClintock, Anne. *Imperial Leather: Race, Gender and Sexuality in the Colonial Contest*. New York: Routledge, 1995.

Mencius. Translated by Irene Bloom. New York: Columbia University Press, 2009.

Mencius. Translated by D. C. Lau. New York: Penguin Books, 1970.

Mengzi, with Selections from Traditional Commentaries. Translated by Bryan W. Van Norden. Indianapolis, IN: Hackett Publishing, 2008.

"Metaphysics." In *The Complete Works of Aristotle*, vol. 2, edited by Jonathan Barnes, 1552–1728. Princeton, NJ: Princeton University Press, 1984.

Meyer, Andrew Seth. *The Dao of the Military: Liu An's Art of War*. New York: Columbia University Press, 2012.

Mitchell, Timothy. "The Limits of the State: Beyond Statist Approaches and Their Critics." *American Political Science Review* 85, no. 1 (1991): 77–96.

Morgan, Catherine A. "The Origins of Pan-Hellenism." In *Greek Sanctuaries: New Approaches*, edited by Nanno Marinatos and Robin Hägg, 18–44. London: Routledge, 1993.

Mozi: Basic Writings. Translated by Burton Watson. New York: Columbia University Press, 2003.

Munro, Donald. *The Concept of Man in Early China*. Stanford, CA: Stanford University Press, 1969.

Myhre, Karin. "Monsters Lift the Veil: Chinese Animal Hybrids and Processes of Transformation." In *The Ashgate Research Companion to Monsters and the Monstrous*, edited by Asa Simon Mittman and Peter Dendle, 217–236. Burlington, VT: Ashgate, 2012.

Needham, Joseph. *Science and Civilisation in China*, vol. 4, *Physics and Physical Technology*, pt. 3, *Civil Engineering and Nautics*. New York: Cambridge University Press, 1971.

Needham, Joseph, and Ling Wang. *Science and Civilisation in China*, vol. 3, *Mathematics and the Sciences of the Heavens and the Earth*. New York: Cambridge University Press, 1959.

Needham, Joseph, and Robin D. S. Yates. *Science and Civilisation in China*, vol. 5, *Chemistry and Chemical Technology*, pt. 6, *Military Technology: Missiles and Sieges*. New York: Cambridge University Press, 1994.

Nightingale, Andrea Wilson. "The Philosopher at the Festival: Plato's Transformation of Traditional Theōria." In *Pilgrimage in Graeco-Roman and Early Christian Antiquity: Seeing the Gods*, edited by Ján Elsner and Ian Rutherford, 151–180. New York: Oxford University Press, 2005.

Nivison, David. *The Ways of Confucianism*. Chicago: Open Court, 1996.

Nuti, Lucia. "Mapping Places: Chorography and Vision in the Renaissance." In *Mappings*, edited by Denis E. Cosgrove, 90–108. London: Reaktion Books, 1999.

Nylan, Michael. "Beliefs about Social Seeing: Hiddenness (wei 微) and Visibility in Classical-era China." In *The Rhetoric of Hiddenness in Traditional Chinese Culture*, edited by Paula Varsano, 53–78. Albany: State University of New York Press, 2016.

The Five "Confucian" Classics. New Haven, CT: Yale University Press, 2001.

Oba, Osamu. "The Ordinance on Fords and Passes Excavated from Han Tomb #247, Zhangjiashan." *Asia Major* 14, no. 2 (2001): 119–141.

Olberding, Garret. *Dubious Facts: The Evidence of Early Chinese Historiography*. Albany: State University of New York Press, 2012.

Orlove, Benjamin. "The Ethnography of Maps: The Cultural and Social Contexts of Cartographic Representation in Peru." *Cartographica* 30, no. 1 (1993): 29–46.

Parker, Bradley J. "At the Edge of Empire: Conceptualizing Assyria's Anatolian Frontier ca. 700 BC." *Journal of Anthropological Archaeology* 21 (2002): 371–395.

Pickles, John. *A History of Spaces: Cartographic Reason, Mapping, and the Geo-Coded World*. New York: Routledge, 2004.

Pines, Yuri. "Beasts or Humans: Pre-Imperial Origins of the 'Sino-Barbarian' Dichotomy." In *Mongols, Turks, and Others: Eurasian Nomads and the Sedentary World*, edited by Reuven Amitai and Michal Biran, 59–102. Boston, MA: Brill, 2005.

"The Question of Interpretation: Qin History in Light of New Epigraphic Sources." *Early China* 29 (2004): 1–44.

Po Hu T'ung: The Comprehensive Discussions in the White Tiger Hall. Translated by Tjan Tjoe Som. Leiden: Brill, 1952.

Powers, Martin. "When Is a Landscape Like a Body?" In *Landscape, Culture, and Power in Chinese Society*, edited by Wen-hsin Yeh, 1–22. Berkeley: University of California Press, 1998.

Puett, Michael J. *To Become a God: Cosmology, Sacrifice, and Self-Divinization in Early China*. Cambridge, MA: Harvard Asia Center Publications, 2002.

Qiu, Xigui. *Chinese Writing*. Berkeley, CA: Institute of East Asian Studies, 2000.

Rees, Ronald. "Historical Links Between Cartography and Art." *Geographical Review* 70, no. 1 (1980): 60–78.

Reid, Julian. "Foucault on Clausewitz: Conceptualizing the Relationship Between War and Power." *Alternatives* 28 (2003): 1–28.

Reiter, Florian C. "Some Remarks on the Chinese Word *t'u* 'Chart, Plan, Design'." *Oriens* 32 (1990): 308–327.

Rhees, Ronald. "Historical Links Between Cartography and Art." *Geographical Review* 70, no. 1 (1980): 60–78.

Riggsby, Andrew M. "Space." In *The Cambridge Companion to the Roman Historians*, edited by Andrew Feldherr, 152–165. New York: Cambridge University Press, 2009.

Rundstrom, Robert. "Maps, Man, and Land in the Cultural Cartography of the Eskimo (Inuit)." PhD diss., University of Kansas, 1987.

Schaberg, David. "Functionary Speech: On the Work of *Shi* 使 and *Shi* 史." In *Facing the Monarch: Modes of Advice in the Early Chinese Court*, edited by

Garret Olberding, 19–41. Cambridge, MA: Harvard Asia Center Publications, 2013.

"Playing at Critique: Indirect Remonstrance and the Formation of *Shi* Identity." In *Text and Ritual in Early China*, edited by Martin Kern, 194–225. Seattle: University of Washington Press, 2005.

Schmidt-Glintzer, Helwig. "Diagram (*tu*) and Text (*wen*): Mapping the Chinese World." In *Conceiving the Empire: China and Rome Compared*, edited by Fritz-Heiner Mutschler and Achim Mittag, 169–194. New York: Oxford University Press, 2008.

Schmitt, Carl. *The Concept of the Political*. Translated by George Schwab. Chicago: University of Chicago Press, 2007.

Schuessler, Axel. *A Dictionary of Early Zhou Chinese*. Honolulu: University of Hawai'i Press, 1987.

Scott, James C. *Against the Grain: A Deep History of the Earliest States*. New Haven, CT: Yale University Press, 2017.

Seeing Like a State: How Certain Schemes to Improve the Human Condition Have Failed. New Haven, CT: Yale University Press, 1998.

Shang, Yang. *The Book of Lord Shang: Apologetics of State Power in Early China*. Translated by Yuri Pines. New York: Columbia University Press, 2017.

Shelach-Lavi, Gideon. *The Archaeology of Early China: From Prehistory to the Han Dynasty*. New York: Cambridge University Press, 2015.

Shi, Jie 施傑. "The Overseeing Mother: Revisiting the Frontal-Pose Lady in the Wu Family Shrines in Second-Century China." *Monumenta Serica* 63, no. 2 (2015): 263–293.

Sima Qian. *Records of the Grand Historian: Han Dynasty*. Translated by Burton Watson. New York: Columbia University Press, 1993.

Records of the Grand Historian: Qin Dynasty. Translated by Burton Watson. New York: Columbia University Press, 1993.

Sivin, Nathan, and Gari Ledyard. "Introduction to East Asian Cartography." In *The History of Cartography*, vol. 2, bk. 2, *Cartography in the Traditional East and Southeast Asian Societies*, edited by J. B. Harley and David Woodward, 23–31. Chicago: University of Chicago Press, 1994.

Smith, Adam T. *The Political Landscape: Constellations of Authority in Early Complex Polities*. Berkeley: University of California Press, 2003.

The Political Machine: Assembling Sovereignty in the Bronze Age Caucasus. Princeton, NJ: Princeton University Press, 2015.

Smith, Richard J. *Chinese Maps: Images of "All Under Heaven."* New York: Oxford University Press, 1996.

Smith, Stuart Tyson. "To the Supports of Heaven: Political and Ideological Conceptions of Frontiers in Ancient Egypt." In *Untaming the Frontier in Anthropology, Archaeology, and History*, edited by Bradley J. Parker and Lars Rodseth, 207–237. Tucson: University of Arizona Press, 2005.

Söderström, Ola. "Paper Cities: Visual Thinking in Urban Planning." *Ecumene* 3, no. 3 (1996): 249–281.

Ssu-ma, Ch'ien [Sima Qian]. "Xiongnu," In *The Grand Scribe's Records*, edited by William H. Nienhauser, Jr., 237–303. Indianapolis: Indiana University Press, 2011.

Standen, Naomi. *Unbounded Loyalty: Frontier Crossings in Liao China.* Honolulu: University of Hawai'i Press, 2007.

Sterckx, Roel. *The Animal and the Daemon in Early China.* Albany: State University of New York Press, 2002.

Suetonius. *Lives of the Caesars,* vol. 1, *Julius. Augustus. Tiberius. Gaius. Caligula.* Translated by J. C. Rolfe. Cambridge, MA: Harvard University Press, 1914.

Sullivan, Michael. *The Birth of Landscape Painting in China.* Berkeley: University of California Press, 1962.

Talbert, Richard. "Cartography and Taste in Peutinger's Roman Map." In *Space in the Roman World: Its Perception and Presentation,* edited by Richard J. A. Talbert and Kai Brodersen, 113–141. Münster: LIT Verlag, 2004.

"Peutinger's Roman Map: The Physical Landscape Framework." In *Wahrnehmung und Erfassung geographischer Räume in der Antike,* edited by Michael Rathmann, 221–230. Mainz: Philipp von Zabern, 2007.

The T'ang Code, vol. 2, *Specific Articles.* Translated by Wallace Johnson. Princeton, NJ: Princeton University Press, 1997.

Van Auken, Newell Ann. "The Etymonic Determinatives of *Wanq* (望, 朢)." *Journal of the American Oriental Society* 122, no. 3 (2002): 520–533.

"What If Zhào Dùn Had Fled? Border Crossing and Flight Into Exile in Early China." *Journal of the American Oriental Society* 139, no. 3 (2019): 569–590.

Von Clausewitz, Carl. *On War.* New York: Penguin Books, 1982.

Waldron, Arthur. *The Great Wall of China: From History to Myth.* New York: Cambridge University Press, 1990.

Wang, Haicheng. "Western Zhou Despotism." In *Ancient States and Infrastructural Power: Europe, Asia, and America,* edited by Clifford Ando and Seth Richardson, 91–113. Philadelphia: University of Pennsylvania Press, 2017.

Writing and the Ancient State: Early China in Comparative Perspective. New York: Cambridge University Press, 2014.

Whittaker, C. R. *Frontiers of the Roman Empire: A Social and Economic Study.* Baltimore, MD: Johns Hopkins University Press, 1994.

"Mental Maps: Seeing Like a Roman." In *Thinking Like a Lawyer: Essays on Legal History and General History for John Crook on His Eightieth Birthday,* edited by Paul McKechnie, 81–112. Leiden: Brill, 2002.

Rome and Its Frontiers: The Dynamics of Empire. New York: Routledge, 2004.

Winichakul, Thongchai. *Siam Mapped: A History of the Geo-Body of a Nation.* Honolulu: University of Hawai'i Press, 1994.

Woolf, Greg. *Tales of the Barbarians: Ethnography and Empire in the Roman West.* Malden, MA: Wiley-Blackwell, 2011.

Wu, Hung. *Monumentality in Early Chinese Art and Architecture.* Stanford, CA: Stanford University Press, 1995.

Xu, Yinong. *The Chinese City in Space and Time: The Development of Urban Form in Suzhou.* Honolulu: University of Hawai'i Press, 2000.

Xunzi: The Complete Text. Translated by Eric L. Hutton. Princeton, NJ: Princeton University Press, 2014.

Yang, Jidong. "Transportation, Boarding, Lodging and Trade Along the Early Silk Road: A Preliminary Study of the Xuanquan Manuscripts." *Journal of the American Oriental Society* 135, no. 3 (2015): 421–432.

Yao, Alice. *The Ancient Highlands of Southwest China*. New York: Oxford University Press, 2016.

Yates, Robin D. S. "Cosmos, Central Authority, and Communities in the Early Chinese Empire." In *Empires: Perspectives from Archaeology and History*, edited by Susan Alcock, Terence N. D'Altroy, Kathleen D. Morrison, and Carla M. Sinopoli, 351–368. New York: Cambridge University Press, 2001.

Yee, Cordell. "Cartography in China." In *The History of Cartography*, vol. 2, bk. 2, *Cartography in the Traditional East and Southeast Asian Societies*, edited by J. B. Harley and David Woodward, 35–231. Chicago: University of Chicago Press, 1995.

Yoon, Hong Key. "The Expression of Landforms in Chinese Geomantic Maps." *Cartographic Journal* 29 (1992): 12–15.

Zhouyi: The Book of Changes. Translated by Richard Rutt. New York: Curzon, 2002.

Zuo Tradition (Zuozhuan): Commentary on the Spring and Autumn Annals. Translated by Stephen Durrant, Wai-yee Li, and David Schaberg. 3 vols. Seattle: University of Washington Press, 2016.

Index

accuracy, metric
  and aesthetic norms, 40
  and early mathematical geography, 51
  and early mensuration, 54–60, 64–65, 67, 72–81
  and interpretive legibility, 41
  and religious maps, 46n21
  and the experience of space, 89–93
  confirming, 35n121
  of early Chinese maps, 17
  of the Peutinger map, 12–13
  of Warring States maps, 85n13
allies, 142n46
Alpers, Svetlana, 11, 40, 60
altars of soil, 94
  and management of local spiritual powers, 106, 122
  and political administration, 104–105
Analects
  and *de*, 118
  on appealing to spirits outside one's realm, 110, 111
ancient Greek
  import of city boundaries, 133
  ritual significance of boundaries, 175–176
  trips abroad, 169
  using maps, 75, 87
Anderson, Benedict, 97, 180
"animalistic" human cultures
  and cultural kinship, 143–144, 146n65
  and the monstrous wilds, 143–144, 175
  classified as animals, 176–178
Antonine Itinerary, 11

"barbarian culture"
  and resistance to the central state, 121, 123
  as cultural other, 134n26, 135, 140n42
barriers
  and reputation, 101–102
  and sanctified space, 103–104

  as preventing movement, 83, 85
barriers, European, 22
Baudrillard, Jean, 53n54
borderlands (frontiers)
  and soft sovereign power, 152–153, 154
  and the wilds, 174
  as culturally pliant, 181
  as defined administratively, 6
  diplomatic crossing of, 163
  entering/exiting, 149
  modern, 21
  premodern, 95–98
  Roman, 9–10
  trespassing, 145, 151
boundaries
  ancient Greek ritual significance of, 175–176
  ancient, definition of, 6, 9
  city, ancient Greek import of, 133

Caesar, Julius
  and two-dimensional thinking, 10
captives (*lu* 虜)
  and sovereign inclusion, 144–145
Chao Cuo 晁錯, 130, 142–143
chorography, 39, 58, 61–62, 67, 68, 87
Chuci, 32–33
"climbing heights" poetry subgenre, 32
Confucius, 46, 100, 111, 118–119

de 德 *See* "political charisma"
Deng Ai 鄧艾 (d. 264 CE), 57
Di Cosmo, Nicola
  and amoral politics, 99
  on the function of the early Chinese northern walls, 19–20
diplomats
  and spirit mediums, 157–158
  and transgressive rhetorical action, 157, 158–159
  medieval European, 160n15

CPSIA information can be obtained
at www.ICGtesting.com
Printed in the USA
BVHW091952071222
653680BV00008B/118